JUGGLING

The Cross-Cultural Memoir Series introduces original, significant memoirs from women whose compelling histories map the sources of our differences: generations, national boundaries, race, ethnicity, class, and sexual orientation. The series features stories of contemporary women's lives, providing a record of social transformation, growth in consciousness, and the passionate commitment of individuals who make far-reaching change possible.

THE CROSS-CULTURAL MEMOIR SERIES

To Connie
who knows about
Juggling

JUGGLING
A MEMOIR OF WORK, FAMILY, AND FEMINISM

JANE S. GOULD

Jane S. Gould

September 1997

THE FEMINIST PRESS
AT THE CITY UNIVERSITY OF NEW YORK

Published by The Feminist Press at The City University of New York
311 East 94th Street, New York, NY 10128

First edition, 1997

Unless otherwise noted, all photographs are courtesy of the author.

Cover illustrations: (left) Jane Gould, 1980, photo courtesy of the Barnard Center for Research on Women; (center) Jane Gould, 1947, holding her daughter Nancy; (right) the ERA march on Washington, 1978, for which the Barnard Women's Center chartered a bus, photo courtesy of the Barnard Center for Research on Women.

Ellen Willis's and Esther Newton's personal statements are reprinted, by permission of the authors, from *Diary of a Conference on Sexuality*.

Library of Congress Cataloging-in-Publication Data

Gould, Jane S., 1918–
     Juggling : a memoir of work, family, and feminism / Jane S. Gould
        p.   cm. —(The Cross-cultural memoir series)
     Includes bibliographic references and index.
     ISBN 1-55861-172-X (hbk. : alk. paper). — ISBN 1-55861-173-8 (pbk.: alk. paper)
     1. Gould, Jane S., 1918–.   2. Women—United States—Biography.   3. Feminists—United States—
     Biography.   4. Work and family—United States.   5. Dual-career families—United States.
     I. Title.   II. Series
HQ1413.G684   1997
305.42'092—dc21   97-8017
[B]   CIP

The Feminist Press is grateful to Phyllis Kriegel, Joanne Markell, and Genevieve Vaughan for their generosity in supporting this publication.

Text design and typesetting by Dayna Navaro

Printed on acid-free paper by Royal Book Manufacturing, Inc., Norwich, CT

Manufactured in the United States of America

03 02 01 00 99 98 97   5 4 3 2 1

jug•gle \'jəg-əl\ . . . ~ vt . . . **3**: to handle or deal with usu. several things (as obligations) at one time so as to satisfy often competing requirements <~the responsibilities of family life and full-time job—Jane S. Gould>

Webster's Ninth New Collegiate Dictionary

■ CONTENTS

CONTENTS

This book was conceived as a narrative of my many years helping women broaden their options. It is also the story of my life and that of a long, close relationship with Barnard College. Little did I know, when I transferred to Barnard in 1937 for my last two years of undergraduate study, that this was to be the beginning of a lifelong association.

Thirteen years after graduation, I returned to Barnard as an alumna seeking career help, which led to my active participation on an alumnae vocational committee that, among other things, designed and implemented a pioneer program for women who wanted to return to work. This was then followed by serving as a Barnard administrator for eighteen years, through the administrations of four different college presidents: Rosemary Park, Martha Peterson, Jacquelyn Mattfeld, and Ellen Futter. I was privileged to be part of a small group that created the Women's Center in 1970 and even more privileged to be its first permanent director. Throughout these years, in these different capacities, I experienced a wide range of emotions: from approval and pride to frustration and disappointment—on occasion, feeling like an irreverent outsider in a traditional organization. At times I was impatient, ambivalent, and worried over my inability to bring about change quickly, but, in the final analysis, this strong tie to Barnard was also like a long love affair. Looking back from the perspective of my seventy-eighth year, I can see that along with a deep sense of satisfaction and pride in working at Barnard, there were also moments of anger and frustration—a reflection, I think, of the intensity of the high expectations that I always held for an institution so dedicated to the education of women.

This, then, is the life experience of one white middle-class woman, and I am keenly aware that it does not include the experience of working-class and poor women. The return-to-work movement of the 1950s and 1960s and the reemergence of feminism in the mid-1960s did not directly address the concerns of these women, many of whom worked most of their lives out of economic necessity or lived below the subsistence level and had more immediate problems than some of the issues we were concerned with. I like to think, however, that most of the questions we addressed in the period from 1954, when I returned to work, to 1983, when I retired, touched the lives of all women. I like to think that I helped to break down some of the stereotypes about women's lives and expectations and to bring to public attention issues of discrimination, reproductive rights, and violence against women—all of these cutting across lines of class, race, and ethnicity.

This book would not have been written nor would it have taken its current shape without the prodding and support of Florence Howe, Dorothy Helly, and Elizabeth Minnich. Ever since I retired from Barnard, they kept reminding me that I had a story to tell. Florence Howe demonstrated her faith in me by publishing the book and serving as my editor. Through all the drafts, she kept pushing me to make the book more personal. Dorothy Helly and Judith Friedlander read the first draft and made valuable comments and suggestions. Elizabeth Minnich helped me conceptualize the book and then read chapter after chapter, offering support, encouragement, sharp questions, and insightful comments.

Several others made significant contributions. I was fortunate to have the experienced editorial eye of Mary Cunnane, a member of the Board of The Feminist Press, who thoughtfully read and commented on a near-final draft. My lifelong friend Natalie Meadow, a retired editor, lived through the whole process with me, reading all the drafts, commenting, and always being available for a telephone call when I was searching for a word or a phrase. Sara Cahill, an editor at The Feminist Press, shepherded the project through copyediting and production with patience and good humor. Abby Adams gave me encouragement and helped me explore aspects of my life that I found difficult. Others who read and made contributions were Lila Braine, Esther Davidson, Martin Fleisher, Martha Green, Marjorie Polon, Ruth Simon, and Amy Swerdlow. I am grateful to Barnard archivist Jane Lowenthal for graciously providing me with needed historical material; to Leslie Calman, director of the Barnard Center for Research on Women, for her kind assistance and the loan of several photographs; and to Bill McDonnell, who made my computer work possible.

I also express my appreciation to my husband, Jay, who sets so fine an example as a disciplined writer himself, and beyond that, was always there for me: to rescue me from an unexpected computer glitch, to read a rough paragraph, and to take over some of my normal housekeeping tasks.

And finally, to all my colleagues with whom I have worked over the years, my deep gratitude for their expressions of enthusiasm and anticipation.

EPIPHANY

It was a sparkling spring afternoon in New York City, and I found my favorite bench in the playground. I unloaded the stroller, unpacked the pails and shovels for the sandbox, and helped seven-year-old Nancy and three-and-a-half-year-old David find their friends and get started in their play, as I did every day. I then sat down to read, to watch, to chat with the other mothers. The year was 1953; my days were filled with normal domestic tasks that I had learned to do well and thought I enjoyed. I was thirty-five years old; I was the full-time wife of a doctor who was struggling to build a practice after having served four years in the army during World War II, and the equally full-time mother of two young children. It seemed as if I had everything.

Suddenly, on this beautiful clear day with the happy shouts of children filling the air, I had a sharp insight—an epiphany that was to change my life. I found myself thinking of my college years when everything seemed possible. It seemed to me that I had reached the high point in my life when I was nineteen and it had been downhill ever since. This was such a disturbing thought that I dared not speak of it. It was daring just to consider it.

At nineteen, I was a junior at Barnard College, full of aspirations, deeply involved in my academic studies while working more than twenty hours a week to pay for most of my expenses. I loved feeling independent and purposeful. I assumed this would continue. College was going to lead to a career—to graduate school and to a profession. But what had happened? I had done what most of the women of my class and generation had done: given up my career dreams, married, had children.

At Barnard I always held a certain contempt for classmates who flaunted engagement rings and who dropped out before completing their degrees. We used to say laughingly, "And then she got married and that was the end of her." At the time, I was sure that this wouldn't happen to me. I saw myself as different. I majored in sociology, and, for a brief period during my senior year, I contemplated going on to graduate school in this field. I sent for the catalog from the

University of Chicago and reviewed their offerings with excitement. I had come to love being a student and wanted this to continue, even without a clear professional goal. I guess I thought this would emerge as I went along. But without encouragement from mentors or family, without role models and assurance of financial help, I gave up the dream very quickly. And two years after graduation, I, too, married.

Years later I came upon a study of my generation that documented the choice I had made. While many women college graduates of the early 1940s had accepted their traditional futures as wives and mothers, thus subordinating their own ambitions, they often selected husbands who embodied their values, their hopes, and their dreams. They became extensions of their husbands, proud to make a social contribution through them. They felt privileged to be their husbands' helpmates.

I had become one of those women. I had married Bernard Schwartz, a brilliant young doctor, three years my senior, who shared my social and political values. He was concerned with providing affordable medical care to everyone. He also had many interests and an intellectual breadth that many doctors lacked. I considered myself lucky to find a man of his caliber with whom I could share a life.

By 1953 I was the mother of two and I had comfortably settled in with a group of other young mothers who met daily at the West Eighty-sixth Street playground. There must have been about a dozen of us. A few of us were friends outside of the playground and regularly arranged play dates for our children in each other's homes, and, from time to time, we saw each other socially as couples. Most of us had either never been employed or had only briefly held insignificant jobs before starting a family. We were, for the most part, college graduates or college dropouts who had changed direction upon getting married.

I didn't know everyone's name. I knew a few only as Abby's or Danny's mother, but sharing this daily experience made us notice each day who was there and who wasn't, and we could tell when one of us had a day or an afternoon off because we would see a baby-sitter or a grandma taking over. We all took a vicarious pleasure in knowing that the missing mother was either downtown shopping, taking care of some errand, or even being "frivolous" and meeting a friend for lunch or going to a museum. There was a quiet air of restlessness among us, an undercurrent of dissatisfaction, that we never acknowledged. We talked mostly about our children, and seldom about books, politics, or how we felt about our lives.

We occasionally spoke about two women doctors a few of us knew well:

Natalie and Bea. Natalie was a full-time practicing pediatrician, the wife of a close colleague of my husband's, and the mother of two children. A couple of years older than I, Natalie was a petite woman with short, closely cropped hair. When carrying her black doctor's bag, she almost looked like a child. Her mother, a Russian-trained doctor, emigrated from Russia to the United States, with one child and no husband, to practice medicine, which she did, continuously, until retirement. Natalie had grown up always knowing she would "be somebody." We often talked about her, with shades of both disapproval and envy. We marveled at how she managed, how she juggled the different aspects of her life: how she set aside time for her children, yet took off many Sunday afternoons to paint. She had boundless energy and clearly enjoyed her life. From what I could see, neither her children nor her husband seemed to be neglected. What's more, her husband, Danny, must have been unusual too; he married a woman who was his equal, yet seemed unthreatened by having a professional wife.

Life was quite different for Bea. A tall, slender woman with black hair worn in an old-fashioned bun, Bea met her husband in medical school; they both graduated from Yale, but Bea stopped working when she had her first child and stayed at home as a wife and mother until her two children went off to college. Simple mothering and housework were difficult for her. She seemed to dread the normal entertaining expected among professional families. She often appeared ill at ease, although I never heard her complain. I am quite sure that, if she had been asked, she would have said that this was what she wanted to do. Needless to say, when Bea eventually decided to work, she had to return to school first. She took a degree in public health and finally used her training in an administrative job at the Columbia University School of Public Health. We spoke less about Bea since her life seemed more like ours. I often wondered whether she would have been happier had she chosen to continue her professional life. I could see her conflict and understood that it would have been almost impossible at that time to be a part-time doctor. I wondered what choice I would have made had I been in her situation.

I had one other close friend who worked full time. Janet lived on the next block with her architect-husband and two young children. She ran a successful antique shop with her uncle, a job she had held since she was sixteen. By the time I met her, her uncle was close to retirement and the shop was essentially hers. On the surface it seemed as if she had everything. She was my age, attractive, and always looked stylish. Her husband appeared supportive of her working; she had a full-time housekeeper, and her children went to a fine private school in the neighborhood. But she sometimes told me that she felt anguished leaving her children each morning and envied those mothers who stayed home. Of course, when a parent was needed at home or at school, Janet covered, never her husband. She felt she was depriving her children and she tried to compensate for the time she was away from them by constantly bringing them presents and by acquiescing to their every wish or demand.

What happened to me on that bright spring afternoon had been brewing for a long time. I began to consider the pluses and minuses in my life. The pluses were obvious: I had achieved society's expectations. I was happily married and the proud mother of two healthy children. The minuses were less obvious, more difficult to express. I felt that I lacked a sense of personal identity and an opportunity to grow. Only one activity took me away from the family: twice a month, during my children's nap times, I served on a book review advisory committee for the Child Study Association, a highly respected national organization, which, at the time, was considered the authority on child development and parent education.

Once I recognized my discontent, I began to sense it in others. As we sat in the park, day after day, my friends and I gradually began to talk about what lay ahead. We all believed that rearing children was important, but we could see the beginning of an end to this daily routine, especially once the children started school. What then? The poet Maxine Kumin expressed it beautifully some thirty-eight years later, in her essay "The Care Givers": "I was fulfilling all the expectations of my generation, but it left me emotionally drained, flattened, even despairing. I was realistic enough not to expect ecstasy, but where was a sense of satisfaction? Where, shining in the distance, was there a goal?" (62).

My discontent simmered over the next several months, and I found myself wondering what I could do to change my life. My own brief work experience after college had been so disappointing that it provided no clues as to how I might proceed. I tried to think of women other than Natalie, Bea, and Janet that I knew or had heard about who worked. The few women I could think of worked mostly out of economic need, as teachers, social workers, or nurses. Most were a few years older than I and had gone to work during the Great Depression when their families needed extra income. Or they were married to men who had been blacklisted during the McCarthy red-baiting years. All of them seemed perfectly happy. One of them had three children. The others had either one or none. I also knew several women who worked as part-time receptionists, nurses, or technicians in their husbands' medical offices. I think they considered themselves to be "helping out," although some of them kept at it for years. I tried to think of women who worked in fields outside of those traditionally defined as women's fields. Only two came to mind: a musician who gave piano lessons when she wasn't concertizing and an actress who never stopped performing, even when her children were very young.

During the next few months, I found myself daydreaming at odd moments, putting myself in the shoes of these working women and, alternatively, putting myself in the shoes of other "women like me"—women who had chosen the proscribed roles of mother and wife. I finally came to the realization that what I wanted to do was to learn enough to help other women like myself prepare to return to work. I saw this as an enormous and exciting challenge. If this meant helping to create a whole new source of labor power, which it did, this did not discourage me. Part of this would involve changing attitudes about women and work, particularly those attitudes about middle-class women with children and husbands quite able to support them.

I didn't talk about this to any of my friends or even my husband, for it seemed, on the face of it, preposterous. I didn't know anything about the current labor market, fields of work, or specific jobs within work fields. I didn't know anything about vocational counseling. I just sensed a growing, aching, unfilled need that affected many women in my situation—a need that for many of us was not primarily economic, but which had to be understood as nevertheless pressing: a need to achieve a sense of identity outside the home. What made me think I could accomplish this? Was it arrogance? Or was it an extension and affirmation of the only life I knew, one which was acceptable for women—that of caretaker? Or was it that "helping others like me" assuaged my guilt in stepping out of my conforming role? Whatever it was, I was confronted with the challenge of how to learn what I needed to know.

■ 2
MY HERITAGE, MY FAMILY, MY CHILDHOOD

I was brought up the second child of four, some thirty miles from New York City in the village of Pleasantville, where my family had deep roots and where my mother had summered as a child. My mother and father both grew up in New York City, and, when they started a family, they decided to move to Pleasantville and to build a house on the three and a half acres my mother's parents had given them as a wedding present.

My father, Irvin Auerbach, born in 1886, was a first-generation American Jew. I know little about his forebears, only that his parents had emigrated from Germany in the mid-1800s. They came to New York City, where my grandfather became a successful necktie manufacturer, settled with his wife, Pauline, and raised two sons in a brownstone on East Eightieth Street. My father used to tell us that his mother was not only a fearful hypochondriac but also nervously protective, hovering over her sons from the window above as they played on the street below. She died before I was born.

Louis Auerbach, my paternal grandfather, was a domineering man who made it clear from the time my father and his younger brother, Howard, could understand that they were to join him in his business. From his early years, my father was expected to rise every morning at 5:00 A.M., on Sundays at 6:00 A.M., to ride horseback with his father in Central Park. My Prussian grandfather believed that such activity established discipline and good living habits. When, at twenty-two, my father fell off a horse and was unconscious for over twenty-four hours, this activity ceased. He had one of the early brain operations, which saved his life, though it left a noticeable indentation and a rather large scar on the right side of his forehead.

As young men, my father and my uncle were never given a choice about their work; they were taken into the family company and given executive salaries. Unfortunately, neither of them had the slightest interest in or aptitude for the business world. My father's younger brother soon left the company but my father stayed; he often told me that he felt he had no other options. At the time of his marriage to my mother, he was drawing a huge salary for a twenty-eight-year-old without experience, but he was little more than a flunky for his strong-willed father. Grandpa Louis died in 1916, two years before I was born, and my father found himself the chief executive—a job for which he was ill prepared and ill suited.

My father was a sweet, somewhat reticent man, lacking all the qualities usually associated with corporate success. He was certainly not aggressive, and he was something of a dreamer. He cared about people, he had an intellectual bent, and he read extensively, particularly history. One year he read nothing but French literature in French. I think he would have made a wonderful teacher.

My mother's family, on the paternal side, had an unusually colorful history. They were Sephardic Jews whose ancestors were driven out of Spain in 1492 during the Spanish Inquisition; they were then driven from Portugal in the late 1600s. They settled and prospered in Holland until the early 1700s, when the six sons of Michael Hays immigrated to America. According to family records, they came in their own ship with their own servants, cattle, and agricultural tools.

The family split up upon arrival; my maternal grandfather's forebears settled in Bedford, a small village in northern Westchester, about fifty miles from New York City. There they became farmers and storekeepers. During the American Revolution they were active patriots. David Hays, my great-great-grandfather, fought in the New York colony contingent at Braddocks Field. The family also successfully drove several herds of cattle through enemy lines. On a moonless night they blindfolded the cattle and—to muffle the sound—tied their jaws together with rope and wrapped their hoofs in heavy sacking. The Hays's family farm served as a storehouse for the Colonial army until the retaliating British drove them from their farm and burnt it to the ground.

After the war David Hays and his family moved to Pleasantville, then a tiny village, where they bought a 170-acre farm. Called Clark's Corner, the farm was part of an estate confiscated from Tory supporters by the victorious young government. In recognition of the Hays's services during the war, the farm was sold to David and his brother at a low price by agents of the fledgling State of New York. For many years the family farmed and ran a general store. They gradually turned their attention to civic responsibilities, both in Westchester County and New York City.

David Hays built the Homestead, a comfortable, unpretentious house, one of the earliest structures in Pleasantville. It housed six generations of his family. When I was a child, one of my mother's sisters and her family lived there. Members of the Hays family intermarried with other well-known Sephardic families. Among these were the Ettings, the Pexiottos, and the Seixases. One of my ancestors, Michael Hays, participated in the drafting of the Constitution of the State of New York. Another, Jacob Hays, was the first High Constable of New York City, serving from 1802 to 1849. And later, much later, my mother's cousin, Benjamin Cardozo, served illustriously on the United States Supreme Court.

My mother was raised in a town house in New York City, where her father practiced law. In the summers, the family stayed in Pleasantville, first at the Homestead and later in a large house built by my grandfather on his land, high on a hill, called Hillcrest.

Both my grandfather, Daniel Peixotto Hays, who died in 1923 when I was five, and my grandmother, Rachel Hershfield Hays, were leaders in Jewish and community affairs. My grandfather gave up his allegiance to the Orthodox Sephardic community to help create the Reform movement in American Judaism. He was instrumental in the establishment of one of the first Reform temples, Temple Israel, over which he presided for many years. He served on a number of boards and committees, including the Executive Committee of the Union of American Hebrew Congregations and the boards of the Jewish Theological Seminary and the YMHA (Young Men's Hebrew Association). His portrait hangs in the Jewish Theological Seminary. He was a well-known lawyer in New York City and, among other numerous public service commitments, he was the mayor of Pleasantville for many years. In honor of his many contributions the local fire department was named The Daniel P. Hays Hose Company, and a street in Pleasantville is named after him.

My grandmother was born in Utica, New York, to Polish Jewish parents. I don't know much about her family, the Hershfields, but she herself was an unusual person. She was a member of the first graduating class of Hunter College in 1874 and, during the course of her life, served on the New York City Board of Education, the Lenox Hill Neighborhood House Board, the Harlem Philharmonic Board, and the Board of the School for Crippled Children, to mention only a few of her affiliations. This vigorous, unusual couple had six children, not one of whom followed in their footsteps, either as a public figure or as a practicing Jew.

My mother, Helen Hays, was born in 1891, the baby of the family. From the little I heard about her childhood, it seemed to be a happy one. She adored her parents and loved the attention she got from her brother and her four older sisters. And she had glowing memories of the many parties at the big house in Pleasantville. She often talked about how she helped her busy mother: sitting at the big desk, going through the mail, and paying household bills. She started piano lessons at a young age and showed an aptitude that resulted in her acceptance at the Walter Damrosch School of Music. Her schooling, however, was interrupted when her parents took her out of school for a European trip. This trip put an end to her musical training.

My parents met in 1912, when my mother was twenty-one and my father was twenty-six. They became engaged ten days after they met. Their engagement picture, which hangs in my study, shows an unusually handsome young couple: my father, tall and good looking, wearing white flannels and a blazer, and my mother, small and attractive, with a pretty, girlish face, her long, black hair worn up, as was the fashion in those days. In the picture, she wears a long white skirt and blouse, a dark scarf, and a dark sweater-jacket.

After they married, they set up housekeeping in an apartment in Manhattan and started making plans for building a house in Pleasantville on land similar to and adjoining my grandparents' lovely home. Unlike my grandparents, who spent only the summer months in their house and the rest of the year in New York City, my parents decided to make Pleasantville their permanent residence. When completed, the house they built was by any standard a grand one; in fact, it was an estate that stood out in this small, homogeneous middle-class community, where most people lived close to their neighbors in comfortable, unimposing houses.

I find it hard to picture a young couple living as my parents did, either then or now. The house in which I lived until I was sixteen years old was a thirteen-room brick Colonial with five fireplaces, a heated sun porch, a sleeping porch, a finished playroom in the attic, and separate quarters with a back staircase for sleep-in help. There were also a large garage and barn, with an apartment over each for the chauffeur and the gardener. The barn included a dairy, housing several milking cows and many chickens.

My father, a romantic, fancied himself a gentleman farmer. Yet his only experiences with animals and the outdoors had been the horseback riding he had done regularly with his father and the breeding and showing of four pedigreed collies, a hobby that he had pursued successfully for several years before his marriage. He was very proud of the many trophies won by his beautiful, elegant dogs. His dream was to provide milk, eggs, chickens, and produce for the family. He managed until it was discovered that the cows were tubercular. That was the end of the cows.

In addition to spacious, beautifully landscaped lawns with lush flower beds, my parents had an enormous vegetable garden, including a grape arbor, which was a special interest of my father's. On summer evenings he would often prune his grapes, while we were busy pulling Japanese beetles from the roses and dropping them into a jar of kerosene. My father paid us a penny for each beetle. My mother worked with a landscaper to create the gardens, achieving some national recognition in horticulture magazines. Her pride and joy were a beautiful rose garden with a sundial in the middle, a rock garden, and a fishpond, which was stocked with goldfish. Beyond our property, we were surrounded by beautiful, untouched, thick woods with a few hard-to-find pathways here and there.

In those early years, we had a staff of five: a cook, a chambermaid, a butler/chauffeur, a governess, and a gardener. The cook and chambermaid were Irish women who had worked for my father's family since they had arrived in this country as "greenhorns," when they were young women. Mother used to say they were "part of the family." This always made me wince because I knew it wasn't true. They seemed ageless. Maggie, a rather nondescript-looking woman with gray, stringy hair, was a first-rate cook, but also rather imperious; she would order us out of the kitchen whenever it suited her—and if she caught us with our hands in the cookie jar without asking, that was quite reason enough. Brownie did housework and sometimes helped with the children. She was a kind woman with a large brown wig that resembled a bird's nest. I always wondered what was underneath and what would happen if the wig blew off. Of course, I never dared ask. I knew that her allegiance was to the grownups, so I never counted on her or went to her when I was in trouble.

Until I was nine or ten there always seemed to be a governess in the house, sharing a bedroom with one of the four of us, teaching us good manners, maintaining discipline, and taking complete charge of us when our parents were away. I remember having my mouth washed out with soap for saying "shut up" and being put in the closet for misbehaving. Worst of all, I will never forget one particular governess, whom we called "Fraulein," who used her power in a way that haunted me for years. When my parents were away, she accused me of stealing some of her possessions that she kept in a bureau drawer in the room we shared. I must have been about six at the time. I knew I hadn't taken anything and I denied it vehemently. She insisted and pointed to a small black book in which she was keeping a record of all my misdemeanors; she threatened to show this book to my parents when they returned. Finally, after hours of weeping and repeated denials, I was forced to confess to this terrible crime. Although I knew I was innocent, I was too small and too insecure to trust myself. One part of me, then and for years after, questioned whether perhaps I had actually done it and then pushed it from my consciousness. It made me wonder if I was crazy, but it also undermined my trust of grownups. To this day, when I am accused of something I know I didn't do, I may have a moment of discomfort and a fleeting feeling that maybe I did do it and just don't remember. This same governess used to tell me to look under my bed every night because once there had been a man under her bed with a knife. I think I looked under my bed until I went off to college. I was also afraid of a butler named Smith, a tall, formal man whose job included seeing that all the doors in the house were locked every night. For many years after he left, I took on this job, obsessively checking every door.

Despite many privileges and comforts, I was, in many ways, a miserable little girl. Not only was I afraid of almost all the adults in the house, but I also felt lonely and unloved. Even worse, I often felt as if I deserved to be unloved. I was always being called to task by my mother for some wrongdoing, often reported to her by one of the household staff. She made me feel like a bad girl, and I could never understand what I had done to warrant her scolding or the punishments that were sometimes meted out, such as eating supper in my room because I had spilled lunch on my clean dress. In truth, I felt singled out. It seemed to me that none of my siblings were punished or treated as I was. Although I never saw my mother hugging or kissing either of my brothers, she did seem different with them. She never called down Louis and, in fact, seemed somewhat fearful of him. She favored Bob, my younger brother, and I used to think that she spoiled him with attention. She laughed at things he said or did, and this made me very jealous. And whatever tenderness she had, she showed to my baby sister, who grew up in quite a different household.

With all of us, however, my mother was very strict. She repeatedly spoke of "maintaining high standards" and she set the tone for the rest of the staff. These high standards found expression in rigid rules of discipline. For instance, when I was very little, I was afraid of the dark, yet I was not allowed to keep a small light on in my room until I fell asleep. We all had to eat everything on our plate, whether we liked it or not. And because my mother knew that fresh air was good for children, even in winter, we had to stay outdoors and play until 5:00 P.M., no matter how cold and dark it was, and by 4:30 it really was dark. The winters seemed longer and colder then, and often I would come to the kitchen or back door, when my fingers and toes were freezing, to ask what time it was and to beg to be allowed to come in. It never worked.

My mother had a beautiful dressing room, and, as a special treat, I was occasionally allowed to take my afternoon nap in it or to spend a couple of hours there when I was sick. It was a small room, a few steps down from her bedroom, leading to the sleeping porch, with a very comfortable chaise lounge, three closets with mirrored doors, and a mirrored dressing table laden with cosmetics and perfumes, all very exotic to a little girl. I loved these rare occasions. I would tightly close the two doors and pretend I was a princess. I would look at her beautiful dresses, try on her high heels, and smell her perfume, all in front of the mirrors. One time I spilled a bottle of perfume and was so scared that I slipped out and filled up the bottle with water. Of course, it was discovered, and I was asked if I had done it. I lied and, once trapped, I couldn't figure a way out. In the end I was punished, and my mother never let me rest in her boudoir again.

I spent my childhood believing that my mother didn't love me, and for years I was sure I must have been adopted—although I never dared ask. I can't remember that she ever hugged or kissed me. I never felt she was glad to see me, and I don't remember that she ever praised me. She felt that praise would "turn a child's head," and she often said she hated to see spoiled children. Though she was at home full time, she was inaccessible. She spent most of her time meeting with the gardener, the cook, or other members of her staff, discussing landscaping, menus, and general household matters. Or she was resting. Throughout my childhood, I would come home and be shushed and told that my mother was lying down with one of her frequent migraines or a mysterious malady that was finally diagnosed as a kidney stone.

There were a few instances when I felt she cared about me. When I was sick, she would express concern, tuck me into bed, feel my forehead for fever, bring me special treats, and even read to me once in a while. I couldn't count on this to last; she had little patience with the long days of convalescence that accompanied chicken pox, measles, and the other childhood diseases that we all had. But during the first few days of an illness, I felt so important and cared for that I almost looked forward to being sick. Another treasured activity was acquiring new clothes. Looking nice was very important to my mother; when I was little, a dressmaker came to the house and made my dresses. I savored being the center of attention and being allowed to express my likes and dislikes about color, material, and style, even though my mother and the dressmaker made the final decisions. By the time I was nine, my mother had given up the dressmaker and took me shopping whenever I needed something new. I loved those outings; we would drive to White Plains, about a half an hour away, where we would visit one of the department stores—Best's or Altman's—that were full of beautiful things. For a few hours I had my mother all to myself, giving all her attention to how I looked and even to what I wanted.

My father was much more approachable and loving, but I learned early on that I couldn't count on him to help me if I got into trouble, as I often did, with

Mother or one of the other grownups. He would listen attentively to my tale of woe and nod that I was right, and Mother, Maggie, or the governess was wrong, but he did nothing more than say "poor pussy," smooth my forehead, and tell me not to scowl or I would have wrinkles on my forehead when I grew up. I knew he loved—even favored—me, but it didn't take me many years to notice that we were often in the same position and that he couldn't even stand up for himself when Mother was angry with him.

As far back as I can remember, my brother Louis was an enigma. He was only two and a half years older than I, yet he wouldn't ever play with me. He was very quiet and spent hours in his room with the door shut. The only interest he seemed to have as he grew older was playing the clarinet, and I loved hearing him practice. I would knock on his door, begging him to let me in so I could watch him, but it was to no avail. When he was about ten, my parents took him to a well-known psychologist and were told he was fine, but, by the time he was twenty, Louis was a full-blown schizophrenic and was institutionalized. He died at the age of thirty, after undergoing one of the early experimental lobotomies.

My younger brother, Bob, two and a half years my junior, developed a chronic infection with a low-grade fever at the age of five. It was finally diagnosed as a tubercular gland—no doubt from our infected cows—and the doctor prescribed a long period of bed rest until the fever abated. He spent a whole year in bed and, besides being my mother's pet, he received love and attention from everyone in the household. Every time I saw someone running upstairs to read to him, play a game with him, bring him ice cream or whatever else he asked for, I was jealous and felt even more isolated. It wasn't until I was seven and my baby sister was born that I had someone to love and be close to—a relationship that continued and deepened until she died of lymphoma at the age of thirty-seven.

At the time of my sister's birth, I was reading a book called *Wee Anne*, and I begged my parents to name my new sister Anne. To my delight, they did: a clear signal to me that she was very special. At first it was like having a live doll, except the governess who cared for her kept all of us at a distance. From the time she was big enough to sleep in a bed, when I must have been about ten, we shared a room. She was an adorable little girl, with curly hair, deep blue eyes, and a remarkably sweet disposition. She loved cuddly soft animals until she was almost a teenager, and she gave me the kind of unqualified love that I desperately needed.

My memories of early childhood evoke painful feelings of loneliness—memories that blot out all the formidable grownups and that place me all alone in the large, unfriendly house. I knew then that there was something missing, and I often wondered what other families were like. I sensed that there were adult secrets that I would never understand until I grew up, and so, at an early age, I became an eavesdropper. I used to creep down to the landing on the stairs whenever my mother and father were having a party, straining to hear what was being said. In the summer, when large dinner parties were given out of doors, I would sneak onto the sleeping porch, listening intently to small talk I didn't understand, and stay there until it got dark and the guests went inside. Eavesdropping became a habit: I would do it on trains, in stores, and in other public places, and it was not unusual for me to become separated from whomever I was with because I was so busy listening to a conversation among strangers that, in the end, was of no interest.

I'm sure my confusion about who I was and where I belonged was one of the reasons I became an avid reader. As soon as I learned to read, I turned to books for answers to the mysteries of grownups, always hoping to learn the secrets of adulthood and the answer to why I felt so left out. I loved to read about families, especially when there was a moral message—when good triumphed over evil and everyone ended up living happily ever after. I started with fairy tales and other children's classics but moved to adult fiction as soon as I was old enough to understand most of the words. We had sets of many of the classics in our living room—Dickens, Kipling, Thackeray, George Eliot—and I read them all when I was much too young, skimming and skipping the parts I didn't understand. My lifelong love of novels, memoirs, and biographies may have started in a search for answers to questions about human behavior, but by the time I was eleven or twelve, reading had also become a necessity—a glorious escape from a puzzling world, far better than movies, theater, and even music. And throughout my life, this would always be so.

People remember me as a sunny child: all the old pictures show a smiling little girl. I can't be sure but I think I learned at an early age that this was the best way to get the approval and attention that I so desperately craved. My early childhood was privileged, and, looking back, I realize that I was isolated from other children until I started school. We were rich and therefore different. I didn't understand then how my family's lifestyle separated me from others: until I was twelve years old, I attended a private school. My two brothers and I took tennis, swimming, and diving lessons. At the age of nine or ten I could do a jackknife, swan, and back dive. I started piano lessons at the age of seven, although it didn't take long to see that I had no musical talent. And, for several years, I went to social dancing class, where the boys wore white gloves and the girls wore party dresses and Mary Janes.

My happiest early childhood memories were solitary, outside the house, even outside the family. I had certain favorite outdoor spaces. One was our wonderful, expansive front lawn which extended down the hill to the end of our driveway. It was a child's paradise. I was forever looking for four-leaf clover and loved rolling down the delicious, soft, sweet-smelling grass in the summer. In the winter, I never tired of sledding to the bottom of the hill and then trudging, over and over again, to the top. Another favorite place was a field across from our driveway, with tall wavy grass and clumps of colorful wildflowers. One of my favorite pastimes was lying down, entirely hidden by the tall grass, and looking up at the clouds and blue sky. This was where I felt safe and serene.

As soon as I was old enough to wander off by myself, I found the woods. I loved the cool summer silence, interrupted only by the crunch of leaves as I walked, by small unseen animals darting about, and by birds chattering high above in the trees. There was a well-traveled path between our house and my grandmother's that ended at what we called the summer house. This was a simple gazebolike structure with half walls, picnic tables, and a well-used outdoor fireplace. It was the site of many large and small family picnics and also a place where my grandmother often came on hot summer afternoons to sit and catch up on her correspondence. From the summer house and also from a large, nearby rock—high on the hill—I could look through the trees and see the housetops below, feeling powerful, yet protected. This was where I escaped from the tensions at home, where I daydreamed about what it would be like to be in a loving family, and where I imagined how different it would be when I grew up and could understand all the things that seemed so mysterious to me now.

Other paths went deep into the woods, passing several brooks, which had to be navigated carefully—by jumping across or hopping from rock to rock. I always felt excited each year around the middle of March as I walked through the mud and the snow to the place where I knew I would find the first spring flowers. What a thrill it was to find a tiny hepatica or anemone pushing up through the snow and to know that, in another week or so, the trees and shrubs would awaken and begin to sprout leaves and buds.

Aside from the village tailor, I believe our family—including grandparents, aunt, uncle, and cousins—were the only Jews in Pleasantville. I knew nothing about any Jewish holidays or rituals, and we were never told anything about our American Jewish heritage. When I was a little older, I went to synagogue with my grandmother whenever I was spending a weekend with her in New York City.

From time to time my mother spoke to us about religion. She told us that she and my father—and my father seemed to agree although he never added to what she said—found organized religion narrow. They defined religion as a broad belief in God put into practice by doing good deeds, particularly for those less fortunate. She said we needn't worship in any church, temple, or synagogue; she acknowledged that we were Jewish, but I was given to understand that this was some kind of an indeterminate label that she and my father had decided to remove. Then, we would practice this wonderful, amorphous "religion" that transcended any sect. None of us asked any questions or talked about it with each other, but it added to the confusion I had about religion and where I belonged.

Until I went to school, I didn't give this weighty matter much thought. I did notice that most of the household staff took going to church on Sunday very seriously. And, on occasion, I went with my father or the chauffeur as they drove Maggie, Brownie, or one of the others to and from Sunday morning services. I was always impressed by the sight of the large numbers of grownups and children dressed in their Sunday best, streaming in and out of church. I think there were four churches in our village, and, in the eyes of a little girl, they were all very beautiful, distinctive buildings.

I loved the holidays, and we celebrated them all vigorously, that is, all except the Jewish holidays, which we completely ignored. I couldn't wait for the holidays because, during this time, most of the strict rules that governed our lives were relaxed, and we children were allowed to stay up late, eat what we wanted, and participate in the festivities. There were picnics and parades on Memorial Day, Fourth of July, and Labor Day. I still adore picnics: they bring back memories of hard-boiled eggs, cold chicken, and delicious desserts, all of which always tasted different because they came out of the picnic basket. And, even today, watching a parade stirs up some of the excitement I felt as I watched my father march with the other volunteer firefighters in those village holiday celebrations.

Although we never observed the religious parts of Christmas and Easter, we threw ourselves into the spirit of these Christian holidays in every other way, starting with our letters to Santa Claus sent weeks in advance. Equally important was making or buying gifts, with saved allowances, for everyone in the family. One of my mother's favorite sayings was "It's the thought that counts." I would spend hours at Bells, the village variety store, fingering and finally selecting fifty-cent treasures, which I would then carefully wrap in Christmas paper. Hanging up stockings on Christmas Eve and staying up late to help decorate our huge Christmas tree created an excitement that was topped only by the thrill of rushing downstairs early Christmas morning to see if Santa had come. We always first looked for the empty glass and plate—a sign that Santa had come and taken the milk and cookies that we had left for him.

Each holiday brings back special memories. On Easter morning, while most of the community was at church, we hunted for eggs that we had colored and that a grownup had hidden in different, secret places all over the grounds. The Fourth of July was wonderful; my parents always invited many guests for a picnic supper and a spectacular display of fireworks, which we watched from our prized hilltop—the best location in town. We were given sparklers to twirl and stayed up till the fireworks were over and everyone went home.

Then there was Thanksgiving. Thanksgiving dinner was a large family affair, held either at my grandmother's or at our house. Cousins, aunts, and uncles from both sides of the family gathered. I always felt a little awkward when the children were told to go and play, and I found myself with cousins I barely knew. This was particularly true of four cousins, children of one of my mother's sisters, who lived close by, in the old Homestead at the bottom of our hill. For some reason I never quite understood, my mother and her sister Mabel were not close and didn't encourage normal play among their children, even though we were of the same ages. My mother spoke condescendingly about Aunt Mabel and Uncle Irving, who always seemed to be struggling to manage. They certainly didn't enjoy our affluence and they were not part of the many social gatherings at our house. Although my mother frequently mentioned how "good" she was to the Lachenbruch family, I think she meant by this that she gave them castoff clothing, toys, and, on occasion, money. Whenever I went out, I had to pass their house. It was painful to hear Aunt Mabel sometimes call her children inside just as I was passing by the backyard where they were playing. I wondered if this had something to do with me, although I never dared to ask my mother about this.

From the very first day I loved school. Starting in kindergarten, I went with my older brother and, when he was old enough, my younger brother to the Scarborough School, a progressive private school. A twenty-minute drive from where we lived, the school was located on a beautiful old estate overlooking the Hudson River. My memories there, for the most part, are happy ones. I made friends, visited other children, and saw houses and staffs as large as ours, which made our style of living seem less unusual. My best friend was Margaret Flook, a tall, thin girl with straight light brown hair with bangs. I loved going to her house for sleepovers. She lived in a house with spacious grounds, much larger than ours, and everyone there—her mother and father and all the staff—was friendly and welcoming. Margaret radiated a serenity that I envied.

The children who attended the Scarborough School came from all over Westchester County, although we seemed to be the only ones from Pleasantville. We were also one of the very few Jewish families at the school. Being Jewish, however, was not really something I thought about—or at least not until I was in fifth grade, when I had my first experience with anti-Semitism. One day in the classroom, before the teacher came in, I noticed that notes were being passed around and children were whispering and pointing at me. Then one of them said, "You're Jewish, and my mother said I shouldn't play with you." I was dumbfounded; I looked around, but no one came to my rescue. I finally said, "I'm not Jewish. I don't have to be if I don't want to." Some of my classmates then began taunting me, and, by the time the teacher arrived, I felt sick. She sent me to the nurse's office, where I vomited. I was sent home, and I told my mother what had happened. My mother explained that yes, I was Jewish, but this didn't make me any different from anyone else, and that the children were just teasing. The things she said didn't really help; what I wanted was for her to come to school to talk to the teacher or to the principal. But I couldn't ask her to do this, and, once more, I was left feeling confused and uneasy. The next day I returned to school, but I never talked to anyone about this incident. Although the experience was not repeated, I suspect it helped foster my sense of being an outsider.

My grandmother, Rachel Hays, was a remarkable woman and deeply important to me. Feisty, energetic, independent, and somewhat self-centered, she loved her large family and was particularly proud of her sixteen grandchildren. If she didn't see us for a time, which was often the case since she traveled a great deal, she would write us long letters and postcards in her distinctive, beautiful handwriting. Her interest in her individual grandchildren really didn't blossom until they were old enough to fend for themselves, and, so, my close relationship with her began when I was about nine years old.

When I started spending time with her alone, either in Pleasantville or in her New York City apartment, I felt that she was including me in her life. She made it clear that she loved having me around. She took me for walks and short excursions, telling me stories about her activities, the family, and her travels. She assumed that I would be interested in anything she wanted to tell me, and I was. She had a large wraparound veranda at her summer home in Pleasantville, and she would often say, "Let's walk around the piazza." As we walked, she recounted her latest experience on the Board of the Lenox Hill Neighborhood Association or how Grandpa had just been honored by Temple Israel. If I had something interesting to tell her, she would listen attentively, but she also made it clear that she didn't want to hear any complaints about family members. She was fiercely loyal and proud to the point of assuming the mantle of my grandfather's pre–American Revolution heritage. In fact, the only time I ever heard her criticize anyone in the family was when she told me the story of her six children's marriages, which she ended by saying regretfully, "And they all married foreigners." By this she meant that they had all married first-generation American Jews.

Although my grandmother was very warm and inclusive, I sensed that she had a special affection for me, and this made me feel secure and loved. She used to tell me that of all her grandchildren, I was the one most like her. By the time I was eleven, I would occasionally spend a weekend with her in New York City, meeting some of her friends and accompanying her on her various errands and appointments. Saturday morning we always went to temple, and I loved watching Grandma participate in the service—singing, praying, and carefully listening to the sermon. After the service she talked to everyone, introducing her grandchild in a way that made me feel very important. I think she was disappointed that my mother and father didn't practice Judaism, although she never mentioned this. We would then take off for an afternoon treat. It could be a movie, a play, a visit with one of her friends, or an event at one of the many organizations my grandmother was affiliated with. Riding on a Broadway trolley, she would sometimes embarrass me by asking the conductor where he would suggest taking a grandchild visiting from the country. Once Grandma took me to Hunter College for her class reunion, and I don't know who was prouder, she or I, the only child at the event.

When I was fifteen, I spent a month alone with her at the Hays fishing cottage on Rangeley Lake in Maine. She must have been eighty by then, but she had as much energy as always. We regularly walked the five miles on dusty roads to Rangeley Village; when someone we knew stopped to give us a ride, she always refused, saying we were just taking a little walk. We rowed across the lake together, picked wildflowers, and sat on the porch where Grandma kept up her famous correspondence. She really believed one could do whatever one set out to do. She did just that until she fell and broke her hip while visiting a sick friend twenty years her junior. She slipped into a coma from which she never recovered. She died at the age of eighty-three. She was a wonderful person who was an important role model for me.

After his father's death my father brought in a brother-in-law, a man with no business experience or aptitude, to be his partner. The two of them continued to run what had been a very successful business. Profits gradually began to decline, due no doubt to a combination of two inept partners and a generally deteriorating economic picture. By the time of the stock market crash in 1929, the business was in serious trouble.

The Great Depression dramatically affected our lives; yet there was never any discussion at home of our declining fortune or of what was happening in the larger world. Nevertheless, I could sense the rising tensions between my parents and could see the gradual change in the way we lived. The household staff was cut to a bare minimum, and my mother took on many of their tasks. By the time I was nine, we were sent to school on the school bus, and my mother and father started driving us to our after-school dates and other appointments.

The big change came in 1930, when I was twelve, and we transferred to public school. My father told us that this would only be for one year, until his business improved. I announced this proudly to my eighth-grade classmates. About six weeks into the first semester, a group from my class approached me saying that they had formed a club but that I was not invited to join since I was a snob. They told me they wished I would go back to private school. While this shook me up, it made me determined to adjust to this new school. By the end of the first year I would have resisted any attempt to move back to the Scarborough School, although, by then, it was also very apparent that I would remain in public school. At home there was still no discussion of the family's severe financial reversal.

Going to school in the community where we lived, within walking distance from our house, and making friends with classmates who lived in the houses that I passed every day were new and wonderful experiences for me. Although there was a "crowd" that I was never truly a part of, I did make a few close friends. One of these was Catherine Bellman, an easygoing, unpretentious girl. I spent hours at her house and loved the informal hospitality her family extended to me. She and I talked about school and also gossiped about who was popular and why. I never talked about my problems, and she didn't seem to have any, which I envied. The way Catherine's family accepted me—invited me to stay for dinner or to sleep over when they were going out—made it harder for me to understand the rigid rules in my own home. In our house, everything had to be arranged ahead of time. My mother would plan beautiful parties for special occasions like birthdays, but never encouraged the casual and often more spontaneous gatherings that I saw elsewhere.

During early adolescence and on through the next four years of high school, my goal was to be included in the social activities of the school. I did well enough in my studies, but academic success was not the key to popularity. My weekly trips to the public library continued but became secretive. God forbid that I should be called a bookworm! Being popular, being part of the mainstream, was almost all I cared about. I tried to look and sound like the other girls: to wear whatever was in vogue and to do everything I could to be accepted by the crowd. To be accepted became an obsession. I hated living in a big house at the top of a hill and wished we could live in a "regular" house with a front and backyard, surrounded by houses just like ours. I felt we were conspicuously different. My desperate need to be liked by everyone—to become like everyone else—was tantamount to waving a red flag in front of my mother. It signaled a war between us that was to last throughout my adolescence.

I must have been impossible as an adolescent. The lengths I went to in order to conform were ridiculous, but seemed deadly important. The girls I admired wore silk stockings and makeup. They even plucked their eyebrows. They went out on dates, and, by the time they were fifteen or sixteen, they went with boys who were old enough to have driver's licenses. They went to Sunday night church socials for teenagers. They had house parties when their parents were not home and stayed at school dances until midnight when their dates drove them home. Some of them even smoked.

By the time I started high school, I was very conscious of the opposite sex, and boys started asking me out to movies, parties, and various school functions. There was a new ingredient in my life: I began to experience strong new feelings that I didn't fully understand and felt I couldn't talk about with anyone, least of all my mother. When I started to menstruate, my mother took me to see our family doctor and, in his presence, she talked a little about sex, but in a way that didn't invite further discussion. I could see how difficult it was for her to talk to me about this, and finally the doctor gave me a book about the birds and the bees. That was all the help I got from them about understanding sexuality.

I wasn't allowed to do any of the things that my friends were doing socially. Mother said she didn't care what other people did. She had her own standards and wasn't interested in keeping up with the Joneses. My father used to come and fetch me at school dances or house parties at 10:00 or 10:30 P.M., compounding the humiliation I suffered for being the only one in a short dress, so different from the grownup, long gowns worn by all the other girls. Even when I was a senior in high school, I wasn't allowed to go out with the same boy more than once a month—anything more than this would signify "going steady," which my mother strongly disapproved of. I would sometimes get around this by having another boy come to the door to escort me and then switch dates when we got into the car.

I wore silk stockings under the lisle cotton stockings that my mother made me wear, and removed the outer stockings when I got to school. I also put on lipstick when out of sight of home, although I never plucked my eyebrows or used rouge or eye makeup. How chagrined I was when my mother drove by as I was walking home with friends, and she saw me wearing lipstick and silk stockings. For a couple of years the worse deprivation was not being permitted to go to the Sunday night church socials. It reinforced the confused feelings I had about religion and underscored that I was different.

I hated the endless pronouncements my mother made about "who we were" and about how she wasn't going to stoop to the standards of "ordinary people," even though we now went to school with the sons and daughters of local merchants, plumbers, and electricians. She placed great weight on being an active member of the local chapter of the DAR (Daughters of the American Revolution) and was pleased to have her house and gardens used for occasional meetings. One day I came home from school and found a lively group of women, all in costumes dating back to the days of the American Revolution, having tea in the garden. At the time I didn't grasp the significance of being a member of the DAR and viewed this as further evidence of our difference. I thought my mother was a snob and linked her DAR affiliation with her general attitude of superiority. It took me many years to acknowledge that my family heritage was an interesting one.

Those years when I was growing up and rebelling were difficult for all of us. During that time my father was struggling just to eke out a living. My older brother was becoming more withdrawn and beginning to show symptoms of paranoia. These symptoms became more pronounced in his late teens, and, after a year and a half at the University of Michigan, Louis dropped out and then couldn't keep any of the several jobs my father found for him. At the age of twenty he was institutionalized in a private sanitorium. When it became clear that he was mentally ill, Louis was moved to a public institution, a good hour and a half from our home. My mother visited him weekly until he died.

During those years, my mother carried the enormous burden of keeping the house and garden going with very little household or outside help. How she managed, I will never understand. She seemed to have conquered all her earlier physical problems and showed amazing pluck, energy, and determination. She tried to sustain the style of living we had grown accustomed to. As long as we lived in the big house, appearances were important. We still used linen napkins and individual butter plates on which my mother placed perfectly made butter balls, which she had carefully rolled with wooden butter patters.

Neither of my parents ever talked to us directly about their financial problems, and I turned my back on what was happening at home. I was too self-involved to think about these changes and the meanings they held. I overheard arguments between my parents, mostly about money or about Louis, and this made me uncomfortable, but I never spoke about these feelings. I was seldom asked to help with household tasks; the message I always received was that these were grownup matters.

The next few years brought major changes in our lives. The big house, once grand and palatial, became an albatross around my parents' necks. In 1934, when I was completing my junior year in high school and had just turned sixteen, my parents told us that we would have to move. The bank was foreclosing on the house. My mother was devastated and my father was clearly upset, but, in his usual manner, he said things would be all right very soon and that there was nothing to worry about. He had lost his business and was trying to make a living as a sales representative for a national cookie company—an unlikely occupation for this diffident, somewhat ineffectual man. He was to spend the rest of his working life tramping through city streets with a heavy bag of samples, trying to sell cookies to restaurants and to grocery stores. That this took place in the middle of a depression, which affected the lives of millions of people, didn't seem to reach us or to ease the pain in any way. I simply don't remember seeing other families in trouble. This was before the days of television, and the stories we read in the newspaper and heard on the radio about soup kitchens and long lines of unemployed seemed very remote.

By the time we were told the news, my parents had found a four-bedroom house in Briarcliff Manor, a small community a few miles from Pleasantville. I was perfectly happy to leave our house, but I was distressed that we were moving to a new community. This meant that I would have to spend my senior year at a different high school making new fiends.

Our new house was, by normal standards, more than adequate, although my mother saw it as a large step down. It was situated on a pleasant, tree-lined, hilly street and was surrounded by other well-kept houses. At the top of the hill was an exclusive boarding school for girls. When school was in session, there was a constant parade of chattering young women walking up and down the street to the little village at the bottom of the hill. From time to time a few of them would stop and sit on the edge of our front lawn to listen to my brother Bob practicing and playing popular songs on his saxophone.

The rent was moderate enough to substantially reduce our living costs. We were to live there for six years, until our next move to an apartment in New York City, where we could live for considerably less money by giving up a car and cutting commuting expenses. My mother, for the first time, showed her feelings: her despair, her shame, and her displeasure with my father, whom she blamed for this change in fortune.

As an adolescent, I never understood the depth of my mother's distress or why my father was unable to honestly look at his finances. I knew that we were no longer rich and that life was difficult for both of my parents, but I connected wealth with all the values I hated and showed little sympathy for any of the changes our family was experiencing. In fact, I remember secretly vowing that I would never care about material possessions—a vow that, like many others, would become muted and modified over the years.

I spent my senior year at Briarcliff Public High School making new friends and devoting a good deal of time and energy to my studies in preparation for applying to college. It was a hard year but not without high points. I won the Briarcliff Manor women's tennis tournament and also received my driver's license, which enabled me to occasionally drive our Model A Ford with a rumble seat.

Despite seven years' difference in age, my sister and I were very close. I adored her; I loved reading to her or telling her stories, and, as she grew older, she became an important, quiet ally. In her eyes I could do no wrong. Anne was neat; I was messy. She always picked up after me as I rushed out. She loved hearing about my escapades, and I could always count on her to cover for me whenever necessary. When she was an adolescent and our family moved to New York City, I was able to help smooth her way as she confronted new, strange experiences.

In a way Anne experienced the best and the worst of our family. She had a much closer and warmer relationship with our parents than the rest of us had had when we were young, primarily because the extra layer of household help had all but disappeared by the time she was three or four years old. Also, so much time and energy had been spent fighting over the social rules that, by the time Anne came along, Mother was much more flexible. Both my parents had much more important things to worry about than simply rearing exemplary children. Anne, however, was not spared the mounting tensions in the house, since she was at home more than the rest of us. She was exposed to Louis's outbursts. And she was privy to the simmering hostility between our parents as they tried to adjust to a very painful relationship and a radically changed lifestyle.

When the family finally moved to New York City in 1938, Anne was thirteen, an awkward age for changes. The move was difficult for her: a new home, a new city, and a new school. My parents were too enmeshed in their own problems to give her the attention she needed. She was sent to Julia Richman, a large all-girls' high school. My older brother had been institutionalized, and my younger brother and I were both at college and living away from home.

I worried about this difficult transition for Anne. I went to see a private camp director and arranged a scholarship for Anne at an eight-week summer camp in the Adirondacks—an experience she loved and repeated for several years. I made a similar arrangement for her to participate in a social dancing class, which I hoped would open the door to new friends and also provide her with a social life in this strange, impersonal city. Throughout her short adult life, which ended tragically at the age of thirty-seven, Anne was the one who kept us all in touch with each other, smoothed things over, remembered all the birthdays, and saw that we all got together for the holidays.

3 ■
COLLEGE YEARS

Despite our family's severe financial problems, my father was determined that I go to college. Mother was too distracted with all the problems she faced to take an active interest, and I suspect that she may even have welcomed seeing my father assert himself for one of the children. He wanted me to have the chance to go away to school, an experience that he had missed. He had gone so far as to enroll me in Vassar and Wellesley when I was born; this simply meant submitting my name to reserve a place for me when I was ready, a lovely but meaningless gesture. When the time came, college seemed out of the question. Since we didn't live in New York City, the public colleges were out of reach—although my grandmother would have loved to see me at Hunter. My father "borrowed" from an old friend the $400 for one year's tuition at Barnard College in New York City and suggested that I commute daily, as he did to work. My father spoke vaguely, as he always did, about my transferring to some out-of-town college in a year or so, but I was wiser then and knew better.

I applied to Barnard and was accepted. But soon after, I heard about another college that sparked my interest. A childhood friend of my mother's came to visit and described an interesting, young, experimental, progressive college, called New College, which was part of Teachers College, the graduate school of education of Columbia University. I sent for the catalog, read it, and knew this was where I wanted to go. Completely different from Barnard or, for that matter, from any college that I knew about, New College was established in 1933 to implement the teachings of John Dewey. Combining scholarship with experience and emphasizing "learning by doing," the founders of New College hoped to teach undergraduates to think rather than simply to amass information. Their course requirements were extremely broad, and teacher evaluations took the place of grades. The curriculum included academic work, fieldwork in factories and on a farm owned by the college in North Carolina, and two semesters of European study—all leading to an M.A. in education. Students could learn at their own pace and could take a year or two off to work; it usually took about five matriculated years to complete the degree. Many of the students, I later learned, were like me; that is, they were attracted by the school's experimental philosophy but had no intention of becoming teachers. New College also had an unusual admissions policy; the college welcomed students who may not have been accepted at more traditional colleges—students who were outstanding in one field such as music, art, or even physical education. The combination of a progressive educational philosophy, a broad curriculum, and flexible entrance requirements produced a truly diverse faculty and student body.

All I knew about New College was what I had read and the somewhat incidental but comforting thought that my mother's friend's daughter was happy there. Still, I found the description of the courses and experiential program so compelling that, with my parents' approval, I applied, had an interview, and was accepted. Why I selected a college so unlike anything I had ever known suggests that, even at sixteen, I had an adventuresome spirit and a strong drive for independence. I was outgrowing my need to conform.

New College, with its own small faculty and student body of some 400, never had its own physical facilities. It was housed in Teachers College, an imposing brick and stone building that occupied an entire block between 120th and 121st Streets, extending from Broadway to Amsterdam Avenue. The only outdoor campus space was a small cement courtyard that, in good weather, held a few round tables and chairs, where my friends and I used to gather before or after classes. There were no separate facilities: we used the classrooms, laboratories, auditoriums, and dormitory rooms that were all part of Teachers College.

I started college in the fall of 1935 and, from the very first day, it was all I had hoped for. I found myself in an entirely new setting and, initially, I was overwhelmed by the student body, many of whom were passionately interested in a wide range of political, social, and economic issues. They came from diverse backgrounds; many were first- or second- generation Americans. Very few came from wealthy families. The students were probably not unlike those attending the public city colleges in those years—Hunter, City College, and Brooklyn College— but, given my cloistered suburban life, very different from anyone I had ever met before.

The students were friendly, unpretentious, intellectually curious, and amazingly knowledgeable. Through discussions, political meetings, demonstrations, and picket lines, I was introduced to the realities of the Depression, the growing militant labor movement with the right to organize and strike, entitlement issues surrounding Franklin Roosevelt's New Deal, and the rise of fascism in Spain, culminating in the Spanish Civil War in 1936. After years of trying to fit into a bland environment where my goal was to look, act, and think like everyone else, this was a completely welcome turnabout.

From the beginning no one seemed overly concerned with status, upbringing, or heritage. In fact, my new friends found my background as interesting as theirs, even a bit exotic. Through these new friends I was even able to learn more about my own roots. More than a third of the student body was Jewish; I had met few Jews up until then, and, for the first time in my life, I heard Yiddish words, phrases, and jokes that I didn't understand, yet hesitated to question. At first I mimicked some of these Yiddish sayings for my family, but I was brought up short when my father pointed out that I sounded anti-Semitic. All of this forced me to explore my own Jewishness. And, as I made more and more friends, that old, uneasy feeling of being Jewish but not knowing what it meant started to lift, and I became more comfortable with my Jewish identity.

College was my personal introduction to the Great Depression. Most New College students worked, and finding a part-time job was just as important as arranging one's courses. Job listings of all kinds were posted on a large bulletin board, and, after the first week, I found myself starting to think about work. Every Sunday night my father gave me three dollars to cover commuting and other expenses. I hated to ask for this money since it was clear that even this small amount created an extra burden for him. The hour-long train commute also made it difficult to participate in many college activities. After the first month I applied for one of the several room-and-board jobs posted on the bulletin board. To my amazement, the family hired me. To my further amazement, when I presented this to my parents, practically as a *fait accompli,* they, too, accepted it— saying again that it would be only for a few months until my father got on his feet. I suspect that they were secretly relieved.

At the age of seventeen, in the second month of my first year at New College, I left home and moved in with a quirky couple and their four-year-old daughter. They were Russian Jews, and both worked. Walter Walden, a short man with bushy black hair, was a WPA (Work Projects Administration) stage designer, and his wife, Doris Silbert, a plain, older, weary-looking woman, was a social worker. There were two different names on their mailbox, and they lived in an old apartment with all the rooms opening onto a long, narrow, and dark hall on 122nd Street, just two blocks from college. I had my own tiny room and was paid fifteen dollars a month plus board in exchange for helping with the care of little Nora: taking her to and from a neighborhood nursery school, babysitting, and helping with assorted household chores and errands. I often found a dollar or two on top of the refrigerator with a note telling me to plan and shop for dinner for the four of us. This was perhaps my largest challenge, especially since I had never really bought or prepared food before. Slowly, by trial and error, I learned how to plan dinners for the four of us for a dollar or so.

It was an ideal arrangement: I felt I had my own place and, even more, an unusual introduction to the adult world. In some respects I was treated as a member of the family. I had every other weekend off and was permitted to have my friends visit whenever I wanted. I also had complete independence over what I did, who I saw in my time off, and what decisions I made concerning my courses and other vital matters. Both Walter and Doris were out most of the time, and, by trusting me and by treating me as an adult, they gave me the gift of letting me figure out things for myself. I knew that Walter perceived me as little more than a child in the ways of the world; he would often bring me a glass of hot tea with jelly on a Sunday morning and talk to me about how I should experiment with my personal life as well as my academic life. I never knew exactly what he meant.

My two years at New College turned me upside down in every way imaginable. Learning to think for myself was exhilarating, and the constant discussion of new ideas—particularly political issues, which could be actively addressed, spilling over from the classroom into social gatherings and onto the streets—was an integral part of my education. Despite serious social and economic problems in the United States and throughout the world, there were many signs of hope—this hope was evident in the formation of a number of radical political parties that advocated dramatic social change. Although I was recruited by the Young Socialists, the Young Communists, and the Trotskyites, I never joined any party. I didn't know enough and simply couldn't add another activity to my life, but I often joined activist students when they demonstrated on an issue that I understood. One time when we were marching in front of Teachers College on 120th Street, protesting the United States embargo during the Spanish Civil War, I looked up and on the steps was the principal of the Briarcliff Manor Public High School. He looked shocked, then smiled at me, and stepped down to tell me this would be our secret.

New College offered a truly dazzling array of courses, the most important of which for me, a wide-eyed freshman, was Leo Huberman's course on the history of class struggle. This course introduced me to a totally new way of looking at society and to questions of social justice. Huberman, a Marxist labor historian, viewed history as a record of the struggle of the poor against the rich, and somehow, despite my privileged background, I identified with those without power and found Professor Huberman's lectures inspirational and challenging. I also remember a stimulating introductory course on literature taught by Charles

Obermeyer, who was then fairly well known for a course he taught on literature and insanity at the New School for Social Research. For this course I struggled with the assignment of writing a twentieth-century adaptation of Plato's *Symposium,* without understanding the sexual connotations of the *Symposium.* A course on the history of Western music renewed my appreciation for classical music, and I began attending concerts, purchasing standing-room-only tickets at the last minute.

Like many young people in late adolescence, I was a mass of contradictions. I was discovering the passion of learning, and I was determined to complete college. I savored my new independence, yet craved companionship. Dating became an important part of my life. Being able to go out with whomever I wanted without having to listen to my parents'—particularly my mother's—questions about so-and-so's background and to be spared my mother's comments about my date's looks and manners was a wonderful, new experience.

During my freshman year I accepted every invitation that came my way. To the amusement of some of my new friends, I even went to two college weekend house parties with boys I knew from high school, one at Yale and the other at Bowdoin College in Maine. I went out with a handsome Columbia track star, with whom I had little in common and who told me, on several occasions, that I was the only Jew at his fraternity house party. I even had several dates with one of the most extreme radicals at New College, who spent entire evenings lecturing me on the "coming revolution."

Gradually, I started to grow up, and I became more selective. I outgrew some high school friendships, and I stopped dating boys I found boring or irritating. Although I wasn't ready for a serious relationship, there were always young men in my life—some more interesting than others, and some just plain good dancers. I loved to dance and seemed to have unlimited energy. In between my studies and my jobs, I always found time to go out—to parties, to football games, to Marxist discussion groups, and to dance to one of the popular, big-name bands such as Tommy Dorsey or Benny Goodman.

For the first time in my life I had close women friends with whom I could talk honestly. There were seven of us—Sue, Ruth, Laura, Mitzi, Royce, Olga, and I—all with busy school and work lives. We compared notes on courses and college activities: I learned about political issues from Royce and Laura, who were activists. As we got to know each other, we talked about our personal lives. Olga was the practical one, and she always made fun of me when I said I was going to wait to marry until I fell in love. Her view was that college would prepare her for a career should she need to work, but these years were also important for finding a husband who was a good provider. Ruth shared my ideals and became a lifelong friend, partly because, a few years later, she married Norman Simon, a young doctor completing his residency at Mt. Sinai. A year after their marriage, I married a close friend and colleague of Norman's—although I had met my husband quite independently.

With the exception of Sue, who commuted from Long Island and was more like the girls I had gone to high school with, all of these women were Jewish and lived with their families in the city. I was often invited to their homes, and, for the first time in my life, I saw how middle-class Jewish families lived. I observed the close family relationships and the emphases on children, education, and Jewish ritual. On occasion, I was present at a Friday night Sabbath dinner, where I felt privileged to join an observant Jewish family at a table set with a white linen tablecloth, candles, and the sparkle of fine china and good silver. My family reserved such settings for grownup company and major holiday dinners, such as Christmas or Thanksgiving. I went to my first Seder in one of these homes and left appreciative and reflective—contemplating the special meaning of Passover. Through these new friends I glimpsed the rich cultural heritage that, with the exception of the infrequent visits to Saturday morning temple with my grandmother, had been completely absent from my life.

As my life centered more and more around college and New York City, I went home less frequently. I found these visits different from my earlier, more painful experiences at home. My mother was trying to hold the family together in the face of seemingly insurmountable problems, but she seemed to have given up trying to control me. In fact, in 1939—my last year in college—I was so incensed about the refusal of the DAR (Daughters of the American Revolution) to permit Marian Anderson to sing at Constitution Hall in Washington because of her race that, through sheer persistence, I was able to persuade my mother to resign from the DAR in protest. She did it primarily to keep family peace and often told me afterward that she regretted having listened to me.

My main pleasure at home was seeing my sister Anne, now ten years old, who waited patiently for my visits. She loved to hear about my life in New York and poured her heart out about the troubles at home. My brother Louis was being evaluated by a private institution, and there were mounting tensions between our parents as my father's financial situation continued to worsen. It was difficult for them to give Anne the attention she needed. When we moved to Briarcliff, Bob had elected to finish high school in Pleasantville, about four miles from our new home. Most days he bicycled to and from school. He left early in the morning and, with his many extracurricular activities, he was home very little. He kept busy with school, sports, and friends and managed to stay clear of family problems. The main contact I had with him during those years was teaching him how to dance. We spent hours in our sun porch practicing the two-step and the big dip. He turned out to be a fabulous dancer, and I was proud of this accomplishment.

During this time my relationship with my father changed in important ways. I sensed his pride in me and his genuine interest in my intellectual and political growth. Always given to descriptive nicknames, he teased me and called me Pinko, but, to my surprise, he also started subscribing to the *New Republic,* at that time a progressive newsmagazine. When I came home, he greeted me with articles that he had clipped and saved to discuss with me. I also occasionally had lunch with him in New York. At these lunches he usually described his unhappiness with my mother and even talked vaguely of leaving her. These discussions made me feel uncomfortable and frustrated. At the same time, he continued to encourage me to complete my education and maintained his usual optimism about being able to help more in the future. He offered one piece of advice over and over: "Don't rush into marriage; you have plenty of time. The best marriages are made when you are thirty-five or older."

With the exception of tuition, provided by my father's old friend throughout my four years, I was completely self-supporting from the time I was seventeen. I loved feeling in charge of my life, and I'm sure I learned as much from working as I did in the classroom. I held a variety of jobs, always working at least twenty hours a week. I sold clocks at a department store during the Christmas season; I waited on tables at a neighborhood luncheonette; I did clerical work for a well-known, much older professor of psychology until he made a pass at me and I quit. There were other jobs, but I always considered my room-and-board jobs to be my main sustenance. In truth, they were my bread and butter. I stayed at the first one for one academic year and the next one for two and a half years.

The job I found the summer after my freshman year at college tested all my patience and required all my resourcefulness. I was hired by a lawyer and his wife to take care of their three-and-a-half-year-old daughter Susan at their summer house in Montauk, on the eastern tip of Long Island. For three months, I lived in a large house with the little girl, a maid, and her parents, who came every weekend. Owned by Arthur Brisbane, a client of my employer, the house was magnificently located, close to the Coast Guard Station and overlooking the ocean. It was designed by the famous architect Stanford White and was filled with furniture bought at an auction at the old Waldorf Hotel. There were six other Stanford White houses on the road, spaced about a quarter a mile apart; all seven houses originally shared a common building in which the dining and cooking facilities were housed. By the summer of 1936 the common building was long gone, but the other houses remained—some in disrepair but all still distinctive. It was said that Carl Fisher, the real estate developer who had built up Miami, tried to develop Montauk in the early 1930s but failed. His dream of another large port for ocean liners and a new lavish resort was a depression casualty, and I learned that Fisher was very ill and was spending his final days living in one of the Stanford White houses. In 1936 Montauk was a beautiful spot, essentially undeveloped, with an eerie feeling—with unfinished and vacant buildings, deserted beautiful beaches, a few large houses, a small fishing community, a beach and a yacht club, and no tourists to speak of.

It was a difficult summer, but I was determined to stick it out. Susan was not an easy child nor fun to be with. The only other person to talk to was the maid, who clearly showed no interest in being friends and socialized almost exclusively with the other domestic help. I had Thursdays off, but it was too far to go to New York, and, with no place to go and with no local friends, I felt trapped. By the middle of the summer I had met Woody Evert, a young man who managed the local upscale surf club. He had gone to Scarborough School and remembered my older brother; he felt sorry for me and gave me the use of a cabana at the club on my day off. So, once a week, I hobnobbed with the rich and famous. I tried to make friends there but I didn't. Woody occasionally took me out for an evening, but he had a steady girlfriend and tended to treat me as if I were a child. Had I been more assertive, I might have asked him to introduce me to other young people.

The weekend visits of Sue's parents didn't help ease my loneliness. The father, a remote, shy man, always brought an overstuffed briefcase and worked all weekend. His wife was clearly terrified of the child and spent the weekends giving in to Susan's manipulative wishes and discussing Susan with me in tiresome detail. When I took the job, I was told that Susan was being psychoanalyzed, and I was sent to talk to the therapist before we went to the country. The therapist explained to me that Susan had difficulty accepting directives and that, therefore, I should let her do what she wanted as much as possible. When it was time for some activity—going to bed, having lunch, or going to the beach—I must be sure to give Susan options. I was instructed to always ask her if she wanted to do whatever it was that I wanted her to do now or in ten minutes. The only trouble was that the therapist never told me what to do if she turned down both options, which she usually did.

The days dragged. We went to the beach and we occasionally found another child to play with, but Susan preferred to be by herself. It was a decidedly long and lonely summer. Although I thought of leaving, I was proud that, at the end of the summer, I had saved most of the $150 I had earned for school expenses and clothes.

What saved me were books and the ocean. I found a library in the village of Montauk and spent hours there. I must have taken out every children's book in the library to read to Susan, along with as many books as I could find for myself. I read Mann's *The Magic Mountain* and Tolstoy's *War and Peace*. Hoping to understand little Susan's behavior, I even dipped into Freud's *Introduction to Psychoanalysis*. And I took long walks by the ocean, marveling at the many subtle and dramatic changes in color, mood, and intensity of the waves, the horizon, the clouds, the sun, and the sand.

One of my mother's favorite aphorisms was that adversity was good for you because it helped to build character. As I grew older, I came to realize that this puritanical notion was probably not true. Besides, I reasoned, by now my character was strong enough to weather most difficulties. My own view about life, which probably had no more validity than my mother's, was that good things often happened when you least expected them—sometimes just when you were ready to give up. So, when I found a wonderful room-and-board job, which I kept for the two and a half years until I graduated, I thanked my lucky stars.

From the moment I met Sue Rafalsky, a composed seven-year-old with sparkling eyes, I knew we would hit it off. Her parents had just divorced. They were hoping to find a college student to live with Sue, her mother, and a live-in maid in a roomy, sunny apartment on Central Park West.

Sue was a darling, mischievous, yet reasonable little girl, and we took to each other immediately. On the day I moved in, she sat on my bed, watched me unpack, and asked all kinds of questions about my possessions, my family, and my personal life. From that moment on we were friends: in fact, Sue often told people we were sisters because we both had dark brown hair. The boundaries between work and play became blurred. I often took Sue with me when I went home for a weekend or out walking with a date on my time off. We giggled a lot; it was an unusually happy time for me. Life became lighthearted, even fun.

Sue's mother—everyone called her Hans—was a vivacious, attractive woman of thirty-four, who had a full to bursting social life. She was also an active member of several philanthropic boards. She used to tease me about my dirty brown-and-white saddle shoes, which were the style on college campuses; about my serious interest in my studies; and about my concern with social issues. She was always on the phone and loved to tell me how she enjoyed bantering with the young men who called me. A few months after I arrived she started a job in public relations, which permitted her to work flexible hours but frequently took her out of town.

Sue's father was a gentle, undemanding man who came to visit at least once a week, often taking Sue out for lunch on Saturday. I didn't understand then, but I realized years later that having me there gave both parents peace of mind and the freedom to come and go, knowing that a caring person was responsible for their daughter. A bond developed among all of us that was to become a permanent one, and I finally felt that I had a home in New York City.

My job worries were over. Through a contact of Hans I found a good summer job in New York City that I held for two years. I did intake interviews for a social service agency that sent underprivileged children to camp for two weeks. Hans and Sue went away every summer, and I stayed in the apartment, rent free. I earned a respectable salary of seventy dollars a month, fifty dollars of which went into the bank. I learned to skimp on food and to live on the remaining twenty dollars. I would often stop at a cheap restaurant on the way home and have a fifteen-cent bowl of soup with a package of crackers for supper, knowing that I could wait for a "real" dinner until I went to someone's house or was taken out.

In 1937, at the end of my second year at New College, I decided to transfer to Barnard College. Although I was happy with the academic and social life at New College, I realized that I didn't want to be a teacher, and I found the thought of fulfilling the nonacademic requirements overwhelming. I had a job that was comfortable and secure, and I wanted to complete my studies in New York City. Since I had been accepted at Barnard initially, and since both Barnard and New College were part of Columbia University, I thought it would be a simple matter to transfer. Little did I know how wrong I was!

Barnard turned me down, along with five other New College women who had applied at the same time, on the grounds that they could not evaluate our two years of academic work since the course structure was so unconventional and we had not been given grades. I was heartbroken. I knew I had to find a way. I remembered hearing my mother talk about a cousin, Arthur Hays Sulzberger, whom she had known well when she was young but hadn't seen in many years. He had married Iphigene Ochs, the daughter of the founder and owner of the *New York Times*. In time Sulzberger become the publisher of the newspaper. I knew that Iphigene Ochs Sulzberger was a graduate and trustee of Barnard, and I decided that I would try to meet her and see if she could help me.

I mustered up my courage. I didn't have qualms about using family "pull" since Barnard had accepted me two years earlier and I had done well at New College. But it was not easy going to see a relative by marriage when the members of the family were not in touch with each other. It was not easy going as the poor relation, fearful that she would think I was asking for money. I need not have worried, for she couldn't have been more cordial.

She lived in a spacious, beautifully furnished brownstone on the Upper East Side of Manhattan. I was ushered into a charming room, and she greeted me warmly. Mrs. Sulzberger was a pleasant-looking, gray-haired lady with sharply chiseled features, who put me at ease immediately. She listened to my story and asked me lots of questions. When I finished, she said, "My father would have been proud of you. He started out selling newspapers on the streets of Chattanooga." She promised she would do what she could, and, within a few weeks, I and the five others who had applied were accepted by Barnard. She was a gracious, generous person whom I went to visit from time to time—that is, until I was married and moved to the Midwest, during the war years, when we lost touch.

My New College experience was important—both personally and intellectually. It opened my eyes and my mind to new ideas and new ways of learning, all in an unusual, supportive environment. The basic philosophy of New College encouraged students to think about large questions, issues, and themes. But it was also assumed that students, on their own, would dig out all the basic background facts necessary to understand the material. This assumption was not always realized.

I knew that there were serious gaps in my education and that transferring to Barnard in September 1937 was a wise move. I was ready for more rigorous study. Because I had lost some credits in transferring, I was unable to graduate with my class. I left Barnard after two years, in 1939, and took a brief secretarial course over the summer in preparation for a full-time job starting that September. I completed my course requirements the following year by taking one graduate course each semester at Columbia at night, and I received my B.A. in June 1940.

Physically, Barnard was not unfamiliar to me. It was a small, but pleasing, urban college campus, extending from 116th Street to 121st Street, between Broadway and Claremont Avenue. I knew my way around. I had, on occasion, visited the campus and gone to events in one of its auditoriums.

Since I came to Barnard with a busy outside schedule, working at least twenty hours a week—taking Sue to the Lincoln School every morning and picking her up at 3:00 P.M.—and with a full social life, I didn't take advantage of all the college had to offer. I came to Barnard every day for my courses and to use the library, but I didn't participate in any extracurricular activities. Unlike my first year at New College, when my room-and-board job was two blocks from the college, I now lived outside the college neighborhood and seldom came back to school for evening or weekend events. Like many transfers who were commuters, I made a few friends and got to know one or two professors, but never felt part of the college community.

Because of my interest in people and social behavior, I decided to major in sociology. I got to know the head of the department, Professor Willard Waller, reasonably well. He gave me lots of encouragement and seemed intrigued by my background, expressing disappointment when I pressured my mother to resign from the DAR. He often urged me to take advantage of my genealogy and join the DAR so that I could "bore from within," a suggestion I vigorously rejected. I took Mirra Komarovsky's famous course on the family and struggled through a course on statistics and a deadly economics course. I loved a survey course in anthropology given by a wonderful professor, Gladys Reichard. I even found time to audit a course on Brahms given at Columbia.

These were good years. I did well at Barnard and, for the first time in my life, I had a real sense of satisfaction and direction. As a senior I did an independent research project studying how German refugees from the Nazi regime were adjusting to American life. I interviewed a number of Barnard students who were refugees, as well as others referred by these students, about details of their life in America and about whether living here measured up to their expectations. I was surprised and pleased at my intellectual involvement during these years and dreamed of continuing my studies. Graduate school, however, was not an option for me then.

■ 4

MARRIAGE,
THE WAR YEARS,
MOTHERHOOD, AND
THE SEARCH FOR WORK

By the time I left Barnard in 1939, my family had moved to New York City, to a pleasant six-room apartment on the Upper West Side. My mother viewed the move as a humiliating step down. She adopted a martyrlike stance; she did all the cooking, cleaning, and laundry, and went to visit my older brother once a week—an hour-and-a-half bus trip. My father clung tenaciously to his certainty that things would be better soon. The worst part was that they wouldn t talk honestly with us about their problems, and I doubt that they even did with one another.

My main concern was for my sister. I worried about the way she had been uprooted—in early adolescence—from school and from friends, and, without any preparation, sent to a huge girls' public high school where she didn't know anyone. I tried to spend more time with her, and, occasionally, she would tag along on outings with my friends. It was also painfully clear that my father s income was hardly enough for the family to live on. Although my mother had never held a paid job, for a few years when finances were at rock bottom, she worked during the Christmas season in the credit office of a department store, a job my father found for her—a job that she did well and even enjoyed.

Although neither of my parents asked me, after agonizing for months, I decided that I had an obligation to help financially, no matter how modestly. I found a secretarial job, started work in September 1939, and moved home, giving a substantial portion of my small salary to my mother for household expenses. I lived at home this way for two years until I married.

My first permanent job was as executive secretary to the vice president of the ExLax company. He was a friend of Hans, the woman whose child I had cared for during my last two years at college, and he hired me with the stipulation that I learn shorthand and typing. Jobs were scarce then, and, unless you were willing to work long hours as a trainee at a department store, if you were a woman, you had to learn typing and shorthand for any entry-level office job. Salaries of eighteen dollars a week were the norm.

I considered myself fortunate to earn the munificent salary of twenty-five dollars a week. When I reported this to Miss Doty, the director of the place-ment office at Barnard—a formidable person who had been in her job for many years and held rigid, limited views about jobs for women—she expressed surprise that any employer would pay that much money to an inexperienced beginner.

Before starting my job I spent eight weeks at secretarial school, where the require-ments for graduation were typing at sixty words per minute and steno at 120 words per minute. I had no trouble with typing, but I left before completing the course and barely managed to pass the eighty-words-per-minute steno test. Alas, I worked for a man who dictated at almost double that rate of speed and wouldn't slow down, so it was clear that I was in trouble from the start.

It was a dreadful job, and I lasted less than a year. My boss was an impatient, neurotic man who had worn out fourteen secretaries in the previous two years. Still, I was devastated when he fired me and told me that he thought I would make a good wife for someone. This was followed by another frustrating job as secretary to a radio advertising agency executive, where I spent most of my time fetching coffee and taking telephone messages for my boss.

My experience wasn't unique. I had a few friends who were teaching in pub-lic or private secondary schools. But most were enduring tedious jobs, just as I was, with little hope of moving on to more challenging work. We complained to each other, but, in truth, we had other matters on our minds.

We accepted the routine nature of our jobs because we knew that, within a few years, we would be married and starting a family. This was our prima-ry job: any other was unthinkable. We shared engagement announcements, went to each others' weddings, and agonized over a few young women we knew who were in their late twenties and still single. Some of them would end up compromising and marrying more for expediency than for love. We hoped this wouldn't happen to us.

I considered myself one of the lucky ones. I met and fell in love with Bernard Schwartz, a brilliant young resident at Mt. Sinai Hospital who was prepar-ing for a career in internal medicine. I met him at the home of a Barnard friend, Miriam Wechsler, whose father was chief of neurology at Mt. Sinai. Dr. Wechsler made a practice of entertaining the interns and residents on his ser-vice. He encouraged his daughter to include a few of her friends at these gath-erings. When she invited me, she made it clear that she had her eye on one of the residents who would be there and she told me which one. Any of the oth-ers, she said, were fair game.

I was drawn to Bernie immediately. I liked his looks and the twinkle in his eye. He was slim, a few inches taller than I, with dark hair and brown eyes. I thought of him as good looking, although according to conventional standards, he probably wasn't. We talked a lot that evening, and he asked for my telephone number. We had our first date about two weeks later, and, from then on, I saw him about once every ten days until we realized that we were falling in love. It wasn't an easy courtship. Bernie's training was intensely demanding; he often worked around the clock, and many dates were canceled or even forgotten because of his work or his exhaustion. Nevertheless, over the next year and a half, we found time to get to know each other.

He was an unusual person with broad interests, ranging from medicine to literature, science, music, and mathematics. He had a number of intensely satisfying hobbies, including bird watching, chess, astronomy, and playing with the theory of numbers. At the time I met him, I didn't know any doctors socially and assumed that Bernie's wide breadth of interests was typical of all doctors. I was later to learn how unusual he was as I met other physicians whose time and energy were so consumed by medicine that they knew little about culture and politics.

We had different temperaments, but we shared the same social values. He was somewhat reserved and used to say he enjoyed "my sparkle" and my outgoing nature. He hated small talk, yet loved collecting jokes, which he would tell with spirit and style. He had a sweetness about him that became particularly apparent when we had children. In his quiet way he was deeply committed to social change. He was an active member of the Interns Council, a progressive national organization created to improve the status of interns and residents. He later joined the Physicians Forum, an organization established after World War II to press for quality, affordable healthcare for everyone. Throughout his life Bernie believed in the promise of socialized medicine in the United States.

After Pearl Harbor and the United States declaration of war, Bernie interrupted his residency and volunteered to serve in the armed forces. We were married in August 1942 when I was twenty-four. By then, Bernie was a lieutenant stationed at a hospital at Scott Field, an Air Force base in Belleville, Illinois. Our wedding was a typical wartime marriage, held in our apartment, with just family present: no wedding dress, no wedding presents, no honeymoon, and Bernie in uniform.

It was a difficult wedding to plan. Both our families were disappointed in the match and showed it. My mother had never met anyone like Bernie's mother, Fanny Terris, a practical, garrulous woman from a deeply observant Jewish family. On the few occasions when the two families were together, my mother was barely polite. Bernie's mother was a stout, plain, gray-haired woman with large eyes that were magnified by her glasses. My mother, by contrast, was her opposite: trim, attractive, and coolly ladylike with well-coifed gray hair.

My father didn't say much, but he tried to show his support for me by smoothing things over. Bernie's father had died when Bernie was very young, and his mother had remarried. His stepfather, Lou Terris, was an affable man who seemed to accept me, although, as with my family, he didn't have much to say. Bernie's mother made the important decisions. She had set quite different sights for her son and said so repeatedly. She wanted him to marry a wealthy Jewish woman, not one without money and from a family that, in her opinion, was hardly Jewish. She viewed her son as a good catch and felt that he was saddling himself with an unnecessary burden by marrying me. My mother, meanwhile, looked down on Bernie's family and would have preferred my marrying someone from a less Jewish family, even a non-Jew.

Despite the polite hostility between the two mothers, we had a Jewish wedding in my family's apartment and were married by a rabbi of Bernie's mother's choice. What started as a rather tense event shifted when the rabbi recognized my mother's family roots. When he realized who my grandfather was, he told us that he had known him well, and he spoke glowingly of my grandfather and of his work in Jewish affairs. This created a slight bond between the two families and made the wedding a happy occasion after all. We spent our wedding night at the Waldorf Astoria in New York, which at that time was an exceedingly glamorous thing to do. Then, using the rest of Bernie's weekend furlough, we drove to Belleville, Illinois, where Bernie was stationed.

As an army wife, I spent four years living close to Air Force bases—first near St. Louis, Missouri, and then in Madison, Wisconsin. In many ways it was an idyllic beginning to married life. We were a thousand miles from home, in a completely strange setting. We lived from day to day, always waiting for that order to be transferred or the order for flight surgeon special training, which was required for overseas assignments.

We weren't burdened with possessions, not even a car, and we enjoyed such make-do arrangements as using orange crates for bookcases. We didn't miss the usual social obligations and found we could keep military-related social activities to a minimum. We had each other and the promise of a future after the war. We rarely spoke about starting a family, but, when we did, we agreed that we would wait until the war was over.

Although we were living on a military installation, constantly seeing men and women in uniform, and even reading a good daily newspaper, the *St. Louis*

Post Dispatch, we often felt quite detached from the war. There was an air of unreality to it. Among the people we saw socially, there was little talk about the war. Strangely, it was on the rare visits home during Bernie's leaves that we came most to grips with the impact of the war on peoples' lives. In New York we heard war news: news about concentration camps; invasions; friends, and children of old friends, volunteering or being drafted, being killed or wounded; talk of rationing and air raid drills; and the many war-related jobs that New Yorkers were doing.

I didn't question the traditional division of household labor and found I enjoyed learning all the housekeeping skills that went with being a wife: cooking, cleaning, doing laundry, and even ironing. I was determined to do these tasks well. We laughed the first time I pressed the crease in the wrong place on Bernie's khaki army slacks. I never expected Bernie to do anything around the house, at least nothing more than take the garbage out. His days at the hospital were full, taking care of sick patients at the Scott Field base, many of whom were Air Force personnel wounded in action.

It didn't take long for me to realize that being a full-time, supportive army wife simply wasn't enough. I had lots of time on my hands, but it was more difficult than I had anticipated to find engaging work. At each base the commanding officer's wife usually set the rules for social etiquette and acceptance. Paid work was unthinkable for an officer's wife at Scott Field, but not at Truax Field, our next station. After my first officers' wives luncheon, where we spent a half hour learning the Air Force anthem, which opened with "off we go into the wide blue yonder," I withdrew from the luncheons, the bridge games, and even from the volunteer work that many did at the base hospital. When I first arrived, I enrolled in the short training course to qualify as a Gray Lady and joined the corps of volunteer officers' wives who pushed trolleys through the wards, bringing patients library books and amenities from the local PX. I knew that this volunteer work was important, but there seemed to be a glut of women volunteers, and it was hard to feel useful. More time was spent gossiping than serving the wards.

I realized that I needed substantive, meaningful work. Bernie was busy contributing all he could to the war effort. When I first expressed my need to do something worthwhile, he surprised me by saying, "If all that will keep you stimulated is a nine-to-five job, you are in serious trouble." This gave me pause for a brief period, but not for long. Within a few months, I was volunteering as a case aide for Travelers Aid, the only social agency in Belleville, an overcrowded army town with a civilian population of 60,000. Located in the bus terminal, which was the social hub for soldiers and their families, the agency offered information and assistance with travel, housing, employment—catering to the special needs of the largely transient military population that was unfamiliar with the community and its resources.

I loved this job. I was not paid, but the agency was so overburdened and understaffed that, within a few months, I was working almost full time and carrying most of the same responsibilities that several of the professional social workers did. It was always busy, sometimes frantic. I would arrive in the morning to find a line of soldiers, wives—some with small children—and civilians who worked at the base. There were no private offices; almost all transactions were done at the counter. People seeking help stood in line on one side of the counter, while those of us who worked there stood behind the counter, talking to clients, answering telephones, and making necessary calls—trying to provide needed information and resources. In addition to answering questions, we looked up railroad and bus schedules, called around for rooms to rent, and even called doctors, dentists, or one of the hospitals in St. Louis to secure help for a member of a soldier's family. On occasion, when a client desperately needed money, I would get permission to borrow from a cash reserve fund that Travelers Aid had put aside for such purposes. Establishing and maintaining contacts with the chaplains on the base, as well as with the health and social service providers in the community, were central to our work.

No one seemed to mind the confusion and the noise; our clients were grateful for whatever help we could offer. Along with the normal arrivals and departures of buses, soldiers came with overseas orders, or with word of a dying parent or news of a baby's birth. Learning how to help a soldier make connections to get home in a hurry, to find a soldier's wife who was on her way to meet a husband who wouldn't be there when she arrived, or to find someone to care for a child while a soldier's wife went to work were all part of my daily work.

In 1944 my work at Travelers Aid ended when Bernie was transferred to the Air Force base hospital at Truax Field, Madison, Wisconsin, where we would remain until the end of the war. Madison was a jewel of a town to live in during those years. We found a small apartment just one block from the beautiful large lake that graced the city and just one block from the University of Wisconsin. Madison not only housed an excellent university but also was the state capital, and, for the first time in almost two years, we were able to attend concerts, theater, art exhibitions, and lectures and discussions.

Finding work, however, was still a priority for me. I walked into the campus radio station, which had lost much of its staff to the armed services, and the program coordinators seemed to think that my background working at a radio advertising agency in New York City was sufficient qualification for the job. I was never asked to describe my actual experience and was delighted to be offered the position. I spent two joyous years working at WHN, one of the oldest educational radio stations in the country. I was hired to plan classical music programs and to write commentary for the announcer to read between musical selections—work completely unrelated to anything I had ever done before. Although my knowledge of classical music was limited, I discovered that I had a good ear and a good sense for programming. I did my job well, and I sometimes fantasized that, after the war, I might approach some of the major classical record companies for freelance work promoting new recordings.

We loved Madison, and, when it looked as if the war was nearing an end, I started to talk about settling there permanently. I was pregnant and it seemed like an ideal place to raise children. But Bernie was reluctant to consider permanently leaving New York and relocating. Bernie thought it also might be difficult for him to find a job in Madison since there was a medical school attached to the university, and many graduates stayed on, feeling as strongly as I did about settling permanently in Madison. Besides, his ties were in the East, and he planned to return to Mt. Sinai Hospital. As we argued, he asserted that wives go where their husbands wanted them to go and where their husbands could make a living. This silenced me. I had accepted a traditional marriage arrangement: my husband would support the family, and I would stay at home with the children.

In 1946, with the war over and with our first child on its way, we returned to New York and focused our attention on creating a life: finding and furnishing an apartment, starting Bernie's medical practice, and beginning a family. In April of that year, a month after moving into a pleasant apartment on the Upper West Side, we had a baby girl whom we named Nancy. For the next three years I felt fully occupied and satisfied with caring for a much-loved, happy baby, with furnishing our home, and with seeing that all went smoothly for my hardworking husband. Bernie adored Nancy and quickly took to calling her Kugele, which meant "little pudding" in Yiddish. The time he spent with her, though limited, was very special and brought us closer than ever.

Since Nancy was the first baby in the family, everyone showered her with attention. Bernie's mother lived around the corner at the time, and she was in her full glory, shopping for clothes that Nancy didn't need and cooking goodies, most of which Nancy wouldn't eat. Many afternoons I pushed the stroller to the East Side to sit in the park with my mother, who, by that time, had moved to a smaller apartment. She liked to be with us and showed more tenderness to my daughter than she ever had to me. She was still prone to criticism, only now it was directed at my style of parenting. She couldn't resist telling me, on occasion, how I was spoiling my daughter. Also, in her own inimitable way, she couldn't refrain from telling me how much nicer it was to live on the East Side, a neighborhood that she believed to be more socially acceptable than the Upper West Side. I still laugh about the time my mother called and said, "The sun is shining here so why don't you come over and sit in the park with me?" I couldn't resist pointing out that when the sun shone on the East Side, it shone on the West Side too.

Bernie worked long hours in those early years, often seven days a week—making house calls and taking telephone calls from patients at all hours. In addition to his private practice, Bernie covered for an older doctor nights and weekends, was an attending physician at Mt. Sinai, and was engaged in a research project. He was part of a group of young doctors at Mt. Sinai that was formed, shortly after the war, to develop The Central Manhattan Medical Group, one of the original participating groups in HIP (Health Insurance Plan of Greater New York). A new concept in prepaid healthcare, the plan was chosen by Mayor LaGuardia in 1947 to provide healthcare for all city employees.

Then, when I was pregnant with our second child, disaster struck. At the age of thirty-four Bernie had a major heart attack, following the diagnosis of an uncommon disease called *polycythemia rubra vera*, a disease characterized by a preponderance of red corpuscles. Although this condition was not fully understood in 1949, if it went untreated, it could be extremely serious. Now it is known as a form of blood cancer. Ironically, Bernie and a hematologist colleague, Dr. Daniel Stats, had just completed an early, classic article on *polycythemia rubra vera*, which was published in the *New England Journal of Medicine*. That he was subsequently diagnosed with this illness seemed truly bizarre.

Bernie was assured that his heart attack stemmed from lack of sufficient medication, and so, after he recovered, he increased the dosage and returned to his more than full-time professional work. Arsenic was the only course of treatment recommended then, and although Bernie always believed that it might have serious side effects, there was no alternative. I suspect that he knew that his life might be shortened—something which cast a shadow on his remaining years. Bernie died, at the age of fifty-one, of a second heart attack in January 1967.

After the first heart attack Bernie spent eight weeks in bed at home, a serious blow for all of us. I had never been around anyone so ill, and, in the beginning, I was extremely frightened. For the first few weeks around-the-clock nurses and frequent doctors' visits interrupted our household with their essential, and somewhat comforting, attention. I suspect it was hardest on Nancy, who was three and a half. I was pregnant, but decided not to tell Nancy since she might interpret this as another threat. It was also an unbearably hot summer, and I often felt beside myself but desperately tried to suppress my feelings. I prided myself in being like my mother—behaving stoically in the face of any calamity.

At the insistence of our friend and doctor, Danny Stats, we sent Nancy to stay with a close friend whose children she knew well. Nancy protested vigorously, but Danny wanted to ensure complete quiet for Bernie. I acquiesced reluctantly, thinking it was a huge mistake—too disruptive for both Nancy and myself. Nancy stayed a little over a week and then insisted that she be brought home. At home she stayed in the apartment, refusing to go out until her daddy could go out. We tried everything we could to lure her: family members and close friends begged her to accompany them for ice cream, to the park, to one of her grandmas' houses, to the merry-go-round. She never wavered. She was adamant; she would not put one foot outside the apartment door. She even refused to go out with me. She waited the whole eight weeks, unwilling to risk being away while her daddy was so ill.

Bernie recovered from the heart attack and went back to work. David was born in October 1949, only three months after Bernie's heart attack. He, too, began life as a darling, happy child. With two young children and with a husband who needed serenity and plenty of rest at home, I concentrated my energies on making a comfortable home for my family. We were part of the togetherness generation of the 1950s. I was proud to be Bernie's wife and Nancy and David's mother. I worked hard at these roles, and most of the time I felt good about them. I took mothering very seriously; I took the children to the park, to nursery school, to play dates, and to the children's library, while carrying full responsibility for the household and a deepening concern for Bernie.

Bernie possessed an amazing inner strength that enabled him to live out the next eighteen years practicing internal medicine and providing leadership in the field of prepaid group healthcare. I did notice that he stopped doing research and spent more of his time on solitary hobbies: bird-watching, playing chess by mail, and working on Fermat's last theorem, a famous mathematical problem finally solved in 1994. He refused to talk about his health and insisted that we live a normal life. It was not, however, what I would call a normal life, but it seemed to be what Bernie needed. When, on occasion, I tried to get Bernie to participate in family activities such as going to the park or for a family drive on a Sunday afternoon, he begged off. When I interrupted him when he was working on a chess problem, he told me I was jealous of his chess. I began to feel excluded and lonely.

For close to six years I lived almost exclusively for my family. Whenever I had moments of frustration or dissatisfaction, I felt a great sense of guilt. To ease this guilt, I added more tasks: baked more brownies, cleaned more closets, and planned more special outings for my children.

Twice a month the Child Study Association book review committee met, and these meetings, and the books I read for them, were the high points of my month. The committee, composed mostly of professionals, selected books on child rearing for a widely distributed national reading list. These books all upheld the importance of the mother in rearing children. The writers assumed that the mother was at home taking care of her children. Of course, this was dramatically reinforced in Dr. Benjamin Spock's *Baby and Child Care,* the child-rearing bible of the time. It didn't ever occur to me that this was a middle-class view. Naturally, millions of women with children worked full time out of economic necessity, most of them in low-level, dead-end jobs.

My work with the Child Study Association came through my aunt Alene Auerbach. She was an influential person in my life, and I had followed her work history with great interest. She had started as a volunteer at the Child Study Association and, after a few years, moved on to a paid position as a family counselor and parent educator in the same organization. She held this position for many years, taking on more and more responsibilities until she became assistant director. Her husband and two children seemed happy and proud of her. But my mother never missed an opportunity to criticize her sister-in-law for selfishly neglecting her children and her household to pursue her own interests.

Although I loved my husband and my children, something was wrong—something was missing from my life. I felt that part of me was going to waste. I couldn't always contain my frustration, as one painful incident testifies. One Saturday, I rented a waxing machine, while Bernie took the children and his binoculars to bird-watch at a nearby sanctuary. After they left, I set to work waxing the dining room floor. In between waxings I started to drink, constantly refilling my glass with scotch, to the point where I could no longer stand up. When the family came home, they found the waxing machine in the middle of the dining room floor and me fast asleep on my bed.

Never a drinker, I was mortified, and grateful that not a word was ever said to me about this incident. Although it never happened again, this experience made me realize that I needed some sort of fulfillment outside the home.

The message to stay home and be a full-time wife and mother was very strong in the 1950s, and sometimes it was carried to ridiculous extremes. I remember attending a lecture at the Ethical Culture Society when my children were very young to hear a psychiatrist speak about children's behavior. He ended by saying, "It would be better if you were home with your children now rather than listening to me." I had even given up tennis, since it entailed hiring a babysitter and being away from the family for an hour or so just for my own enjoyment. I didn't play tennis for twenty-five years, and, when I finally did start to play again at the age of forty-nine, I found it hard to understand why I had ever given up a sport that gave me such pleasure.

The mainstream media also helped keep women "in their place" by idealizing marriage and the family. Newspapers, television, and feature articles in women's magazines endorsed women's primary function as wives, homemakers, mothers, and consumers. The typical image portrayed was that of a devoted wife thoroughly occupied with housekeeping, bringing up children, gardening, sewing, cooking, shopping, entertaining, and—when children were off to school—doing some volunteer work. For self-indulgence and to keep their husbands' attention, it was expected that women would be keenly interested in fashion and in youthful beauty tips, but that was about all.

In the spring of 1953 with Nancy happily settled in a neighborhood public school, David at nursery school, Bernie seemingly well, and a part-time household helper, I could, at times, begin to see a clearing in the clouds. It was on one of these afternoons that I had my epiphany. The thought that I had reached my peak at nineteen shocked me into action. I knew I needed fulfillment outside of family life—a goal that I could begin to work toward immediately, even while my children were still young. Although I didn't yet know the specific shape of my goal, or the dimensions it would assume, I knew I was beginning to think about returning to work.

I hesitated to discuss this with Bernie; I knew I would sound fuzzy and I was keenly aware of how hard he worked and the enormous burden he carried. The first time I spoke to him about my discontent, he was puzzled. He couldn't see that there was anything missing from my life. When he suggested that I arrange to take a little more time away from the children, I could see that he didn't understand. Although I didn't know then what I wanted to do, I was careful to emphasize that, should I go to work, it would be part time and would not interfere with any of my domestic responsibilities. I assured him that he would not be asked to share any tasks that had been mine. For the time being, we left it at that.

It took me almost a year to take the next step. I knew that simply finding a job that fit my family schedule was not enough. It had to be more than that. And one day it came to me, as clear as a bell. I realized that I wanted to help women, women like myself, find career direction and learn how to prepare for work—be it through purposeful education or through productive work. I felt that my experience was probably typical of many middle-class women's experiences; surely others felt limited, and perhaps a bit trapped, by full-time family life. The more I thought about it, the more certain I was that I was on to something important. Although I had no idea how to begin, this didn't seem to be a stumbling block. I knew I would find a way to acquire both the skills and the necessary training.

I sent for catalogs for graduate programs in counseling but found no mention of vocational counseling for women, let alone for women who might want to return to work, and there were also no part-time graduate programs available during the day. Reading the want ads in the *New York Times* was enough to discourage the bravest soul: the ads were segregated under male and female, and the jobs for women were different from those listed for men. Most of the listings for women were for receptionists, clerks, and secretaries: full-time, routine jobs with no chance for advancement. The better jobs were girl Friday, executive secretary, and administrative assistant. Almost all of these "better" jobs required shorthand and typing.

Early in the spring of 1954 I went back to Barnard and talked with Ruth Houghton, the director of the placement office, a lovely, gray-haired woman near retirement, who was sympathetic with and supportive of my ideas. She said that she occasionally saw alumnae who were exploring starting graduate courses, completing a graduate degree that they had forsaken for marriage and children, or seeking interesting part-time work. She agreed that there could be strong personal incentives for work, but expressed the view that it might be difficult to find employers who would accept women who "didn't need to work." We talked about the job market for women, and she observed that employers and graduate and professional schools seemed to have accepted the conventional viewpoint that middle-class women belonged at home, certainly when their children were young. After that, they were considered too old for anything but the most routine jobs.

Ruth Houghton's experience working with alumnae told her that married women with young children didn't work; that there were practically no part-time opportunities at undergraduate or graduate schools, except attending evening courses; and that there were no interesting part-time jobs. Finally, she knew of no graduate programs or courses that would provide the training I thought I needed.

It would have been easy to stop right there. The hurdles were formidable. But then I relived the humiliation I always felt filling out any kind of application when I came to the question of occupation. I always hesitated before reluctantly writing "housewife." Was this to be my identity for life?

I couldn't give up. A few weeks later I went back to see Ruth Houghton again, and, when she understood my determination, she gave me the names of three people she thought might be interested in my ideas and might even be in a position to help me. She thought the only way I would learn what I needed to know was in a job. Although she understood my unwillingness to consider anything more than a part-time position, she was pessimistic about the possibility of my finding an appropriate job which was less than full time.

The next thing I needed was Bernie's approval, especially now that I was about to go on job interviews. Although Bernie may have had some misgivings, he gave me his blessings. I was to learn later on that not all men were this supportive. I told him again that I wouldn't change any part of our family life, that I would continue carrying all my usual responsibilities, and that I would only work part time. I can't imagine what I would have done without his approval; I know it wouldn't have boded well for our marriage.

I have often wondered whether Bernie's illness was a significant motivating force in my decision to return to work and whether his own awareness of his mortality contributed to his acceptance. We never spoke of these things. I had been unsuccessful in my earlier attempts to talk with him about how he felt about himself, his illness, and our future. Later I was able to get him to see a therapist on a regular basis so I knew he had someone with whom he could speak freely. Years later, when Bernie died, I received a touching condolence note from his therapist, saying how much he admired Bernie for his courage and for his determination to continue living a full life. He found Bernie to be a role model. As the possibility of real work became imminent, I was also grateful that Bernie never complained that it might cost him money for me to go to work, a cry I was to hear, again and again, from the women I counseled in the years to come.

In the spring of 1954 I took a big step. I went to see the three people suggested by Ruth Houghton. Two of them were Barnard alumnae who worked in jobs that put them in close touch with the labor market. The first was Marguerite Coleman, Director of Counseling of the New York State Employment Service, a woman who struck me as a forceful person, probably close to fifty. She listened with interest as I told her what I hoped to do and she acknowledged that I was on to something important. She took my ideas further and observed that there were beginning to be labor market shortages, which might be remedied by turning to new sources of talent. She offered to help me secure a position as a job counselor in the New York State Employment Service, which would provide some necessary training and information. Unfortunately, these jobs were all full time, and I couldn't consider working full time.

The second was Gertrude Stein, a Barnard alumna and social worker who ran an employment agency specializing in social work and allied fields. She was a strong, outspoken woman of independent means who had left social work, because of persistent anti-Semitism, to set up her own employment agency. She was not particularly interested in what I had to say and told me that any woman who was not ready to work full time was wasting not only her own time but also the time of potential employers. These two interviews heightened my resolve and also illuminated the difficulties I could expect to encounter. The prevailing message was that women belonged in the home. In fact, women who worked were regarded as unfortunate not to have husbands in a position to support them financially.

I then went to see Alice Gore King, the third person on my list, with a certain amount of trepidation but also with a determination to make whatever compromises were necessary if there was a suitable opening. She was the executive director of the Alumnae Advisory Center, whose offices were on the top floor of a quaint five-story building in midtown Manhattan. An oddity in the midst of high-rise office buildings and the smart shops and boutiques on Madison Avenue, the building exuded a quality of old-world charm. It was owned by the New York Exchange for Women s Work, a venerable organization, established near the end of the nineteenth century, devoted to helping women display and market their crafts. There was a very popular restaurant on the first floor. Like the building itself, the restaurant was a throwback to an earlier, more genteel time, with delicious home-cooked food and excellent service by Irish waitresses. At noon chauffeur-driven limousines would deposit regular customers, many of them older matrons with retired husbands, who waited patiently to be seated. There was always a line, for the restaurant took no reservations. The second and third floors of the building were devoted to the display and sale of beautiful handicrafts, the fourth floor was the general office, and the fifth floor housed the Alumnae Advisory Center and a small baby-sitter and mothers' helpers agency.

A short, neat, and compact woman, just a few years older than I, Alice King radiated competence and confidence. She had been dean at the Brearley School for girls and had given up this job in 1950 to co-found—with Grace Epstein—the Alumnae Advisory Center. Some fifty colleges throughout the country paid a modest membership fee for the privilege of sending their women graduates to this small nonprofit organization for help securing jobs in New York City. Almost all the women who used this service were recent college graduates, most from outside New York, and many seeking that "perfect" first job that would permit them to live in New York, enjoy a new experience, and perhaps find a husband.

Alice listened patiently as I explained the reason for my visit and what I hoped to learn and to accomplish. She drew me out and expressed genuine interest and approval. She also admitted that nothing was being done to help mature women seeking interesting work, and she doubted that employers would be receptive. She also stressed that all the job openings she heard about were full time.

She then described the workings of this fledgling organization: the board of directors, the listing of college members, the seeking out and development of contacts with employers, and the actual placement process. The Alumnae Advisory Center was established primarily to help women find positions with potential, rather than dead-end receptionist or secretarial jobs. Alice described the vocational library she had started, with material on fields of employment, along with fact sheets with information about training opportunities and specific jobs in fields in which young women had expressed an interest. She stressed the fact that many young women didn't know much about the world of work and that, at the same time, employers tended to think of this talent pool as a temporary stopgap, both for their organizations and for the inexperienced employees.

She worked on a tiny budget but was just beginning to think about hiring an assistant. She broached the idea of my coming to work for her on a part-time basis. She went on to say that if I took this job at hours that were suitable for me and if I would work at the pittance she could offer, I would be in a position to learn about employment opportunities, techniques of placement, and the strategies women needed to get jobs. She added that she would not be opposed to my starting to bring in older women when I had learned enough to be helpful. At the same time she emphasized that the substance of my job was essentially clerical, at wages only slightly above the official minimum wage. Hardly a glamorous way to begin!

I left her, lighthearted and excited with this first glimmer of hope. It was surely an opportunity worth serious consideration. I thought about it carefully; it would mean doing mostly tedious clerical work in the beginning, but there were no limits set on what I could learn and do. And I knew of no other way to get started. My interview with Alice King took place in April 1954. We agreed that, if I took the job, I would start in the fall and begin by working twenty hours a week, with summers off.

I knew I would take this job. Perhaps I was just grasping at a straw, but I saw that I had interested Alice King, and I felt certain that I would learn many of the things I needed to know. Before the summer holidays approached I told her I would start in September. I never mentioned salary again; in fact, I made a special pact with Bernie never to divulge what I was being paid. This was a wise decision. Many times during the next decade I would be asked by some woman what I was being paid, usually under the guise of "I just want to have some idea of what part-time jobs pay." I never told, knowing that, in our society, much of what we do is judged by the amount of money we are paid.

Over the next four months I began to feel differently about myself. I felt that a new dimension had been added to my life; I practically skipped through my household tasks, enjoyed my family more, and found myself reading newspapers and magazines differently. I began to notice articles that mentioned women at work; I paid attention to employment opportunities, including the help-wanted ads. I even began to look at my friends differently, noticing those who completely submerged themselves in their homes and families and those who obsessed over one small problem. I began to see that those who had added some outside interests and pleasures for themselves seemed happiest. I also began to streamline certain household tasks, even to eliminate a few.

I didn't know then that I was to become part of a pioneer movement that was to change many women's lives and, over the next decade, would break down many stereotypes about what women could and couldn't—should and shouldn't—do. At the time change seemed to come very slowly. The myths were not easy to puncture. Women who entered or reentered the labor force, often without pressing economic need, were almost consistently rebuffed or, at the very least, not taken seriously. It took unswerving determination and the establishment of new kinds of institutions and support in both work and education to achieve success. Looking back, it now seems clear that this surge of women seeking to return to school and to work was an important underpinning in the rebirth of feminism in the middle and late 1960s. Without a doubt this movement changed many lives, including my own.

■ 5
MY CAREER BEGINS

When I started my new job in September 1954, I felt as if I were taking a little-traveled fork in the road. Most of my friends were still at home with their families. I took for granted that I was blessed with unusual energy and good organizing skills, and I was proud that I could still handle all my usual tasks. Nancy was in third grade and David was in nursery school until 2:00 P.M., which meant that they would have the same care from me as before.

One of the first things I did was to time the trip to my new office by taxi. I found it reassuring that I could get home—should I be needed—in eleven minutes, barring traffic or other unforeseen obstacles. Secure in this knowledge, I began my new life, making light of it to friends and family. How could I tell anyone that I might be inconveniencing my family, even the slightest bit, to do clerical work at a less-than-livable salary? This remained my secret for a long time. I still wanted to be perceived as a good wife and mother, and, in my circle, this meant staying home. Years later, a friend told me that, during this period, when her children were small, she had worked out of necessity and that the subway stop for her rather routine office job was also the stop for New York University. She felt so declassed that she often pretended that she was going to school rather than to work.

I loved going to work. The office was spacious with three rooms: an office for Alice; a large room with a desk, a sizable table, chairs, files, and shelves, which served as the vocational library and the reception area; and a narrow third office that had been carved out of this large space. This skinny room, fronted by four windows, overlooking Madison Avenue between Fifty-fourth and Fifty-fifth Streets, was to be mine. Alice had created this extra office by placing a partition across the width of the large reception room, preserving the light by choosing a partition that was mostly glass. In the beginning there were just the two of us and a part-time receptionist. We later added a full-time secretary.

Although my office was small, I had the prize spot. I had the view of the city below me from my windows, and the fifth floor was just low enough to see everything on the street below, even, on occasion, to recognize a familiar face. I never tired of watching people, most of them walking purposefully along the avenue. I could also watch reflections in the tall glass building facing ours of the daily cavalry of police going by on horseback. I loved browsing in the many small, exclusive shops and sometimes shopping at one of the nearby department stores—Bloomingdale's or Saks Fifth Avenue. I could also walk to the Museum of Modern Art and to the Donnell Library, one of the best branches of the New York Public Library. Excited by the aura of these institutions, I felt the vibrance of the city in my bones.

The economy during the 1950s was expanding rapidly. After the war there was a sharp shift from producing for the war effort to meeting pent-up demands for homes and for consumer goods. It was a decade of relative full employment; there was a sharp jump in the birthrate, with a mass movement to the suburbs; and many families were able to live on a single income.

New York City in the 1950s was a mecca for young women. They came for a variety of reasons, ranging from the desire to carve out a career to simply finding a job so that they could live in New York. The baby boom had completely transformed the American economy. Now kindergarten and secondary school teachers were in demand and labor market-shortages existed in all areas of education, as well as in the nonprofit and public sector, retailing, and all the service fields. But the young women who visited the Alumnae Advisory Center at that time weren't interested in these opportunities. They came for help in finding jobs in such glamorous fields as public relations, book and magazine publishing, radio and television advertising, market research, and entertainment—and, since there was a desperate need for office workers in all fields, most were willing to take low-level jobs.

Within months I was talking to employers and job applicants. Most of the women we saw were recent college graduates, many of whom were coming to New York for the first time in their lives. They were, by and large, looking for pleasant jobs in prestigious organizations, where the name of the organization was often more important than the actual jobs or the opportunity for growth. Hoping to build a social life, most of these young women accepted jobs as receptionists, typists, or secretaries—titles that were often dressed up as editorial, research, or production assistant. Most of them planned to work only for a few years, an attitude that suited their employers' needs precisely: these attractive—yes, even smart—young women, most of whom came from other parts of the country and often from elite colleges, would fill these low-level jobs, stay a few years, and add a touch of class to their organization. There were a few job listings for women with some experience, but, even here, the word assistant was usually included in the job title.

It was part of the Alumnae Advisory Center's mission to influence employers, to convince them to broaden their training opportunities for women, while, at the same time, to help job applicants raise their expectations. These were indeed noble goals, but I soon came to see that employers would respond only to the pressures of employment shortages and to the legal directives that would come a decade later, and I also came to realize that change depended, to a large extent, on the expectations and demands of women. These changes in expectations, fueled by the rebirth of feminism in the middle and late 1960s, would also come later.

Discovering the limited scope of job opportunities for young women was both sobering and instructive. As I thought about women in my situation, it was clear that older women who wanted to return to work would not fit the parameters of most of these categories and could easily be, and generally were, dismissed as inappropriate candidates for employment.

Initially I set aside my own special interests and worked intensely at the task at hand, absorbing new information about the job market in New York. I listened carefully to what employers told me and to what job seekers said they wanted; I read descriptive and recruiting literature; I tracked down other resources for finding jobs, as well as information about jobs and careers, such as private and public employment services, trade associations, vocational libraries, and conferences, meetings, and publications about employment for women.

Early in 1955 Ruth Houghton invited me to come to a meeting of the Barnard Alumnae Advisory Vocational Committee. She was beginning to see alumnae who wanted information about returning to school and to work, and she thought that this committee, which worked closely with her office, would be interested in hearing my story as well as my thoughts about what I hoped to achieve. I was pleased and accepted the invitation with great anticipation.

The committee was composed of six or seven Barnard alumnae, all about my age or a few years older, all professional women with interesting backgrounds. We met in the late afternoon in the Barnard deanery, a suite of rooms attached to one of the dormitories, which had been Dean Virginia Gildersleeve's apartment from the time it was built in 1925 to when she retired in 1946. The college had taken great pains to keep the apartment as it had been when she was alive. It was a period piece, a perfect setting for teas, dinners, and meetings.

Ruth introduced me, and I was immediately put at ease by the friendly reception and expressions of interest. Tea and dainty sandwiches were served in the living room by Margaret, a frail-looking Irish woman who had become some-what of a fixture at Barnard, waitressing at most of the college functions until she retired. As I started to speak, I realized that this was the first time I had ever spoken about my life and my experience to a group. This realization unlocked some part of my consciousness, and I found myself telling the com-mittee my whole story: my discontent, my frustration, even about Bernie's ill-ness, and how—after I realized I had to add some productive activity outside the household sphere for my own personal development—I decided that I would make helping women find their way to work my career, no matter what I had to do to learn the things that I needed to know.

I knew I spoke emotionally: the words poured out of me, and I could tell from my colleagues' expressions that they understood what I was saying and were interested. I spoke for forty-five minutes, explaining how, with Ruth's help, I had found the job at the Alumnae Advisory Center and how I was now learning about employers, employers' attitudes, job openings, job-hunting strate-gies, and resources in the metropolitan area. I dwelt on the positive, making a strong plea for the rights of educated women to lead fully productive lives and for the larger social rewards to be gained from tapping this unused talent. I didn't allude to the somber realities of the limited job opportunities for women, which I was learning about on a daily basis, or to the realization that the goals I had hoped to achieve were much more difficult than I had ever imagined. As I spoke about a future that would be different for women like me, I did so hoping the committee would respond positively.

It was an extraordinary experience. When I finished, I found myself wiping a tear away. Something happened that day that convinced me I was on the right track. The committee members were extremely receptive; they listened carefully and never hurried me. They kept encouraging me to say more, asking questions about points they didn't think I covered. Marguerite Coleman, chair of the com-mittee, whom I had gone to see a year ago when I was first job hunting, asked me if I thought that these women seeking part-time jobs were serious and would become good permanent employees. Eleanor Furman, director of personnel at the Fashion Institute of Technology, a vivacious woman who would become the chair when Marguerite's term was over, asked if women working part time would be willing to start at low-level jobs. I couldn't be sure, I said, but answered affir-matively because I believed that they, like me, would become an important part of the labor force. There were other questions, and discussion went on in this vein until we had to close the meeting. The committee thanked me for coming and agreed that they wanted to further explore these topics and issues.

Soon after that visit, I was invited to join the Barnard Alumnae Advisory Vocational Committee. Over the course of the next two years I attended meetings focused on what could be done to help Barnard alumnae who wanted to prepare to return to work. Some committee members pointed to labor market shortages, which might make reentry for these women easier, both in clerical and administrative jobs and in certain service fields where women had long played a dominant role—especially social work, teaching, counseling, and library work.

In the spring of 1957 the committee initiated what I believe was the first program of its kind: a pioneer program for Barnard alumnae who had not been recently engaged in paid employment, and now were seeking information about returning to school and work. It was a committee project, done in cooperation with the Barnard Placement Office, and we all participated, attending all the workshops and alternating as leaders of the sessions. We called them the Job Finding Workshops. Although we were somewhat uncertain about the shape of these workshops, with just one mailing, we were fully subscribed. The women who came were also somewhat uncertain, and, after our initial meeting, we took our cue from them and designed the workshops to respond to their needs and concerns.

The workshops consisted of three consecutive weekly evening sessions. The first session began with a group discussion to evaluate personal and family considerations: reasons for wanting to work, family attitudes—particularly those of husbands—necessary home arrangements, and financial aspects, including how a wife's work affected her husband's income tax. In the second session we presented occupational information both on fields with a labor shortage and on fields in which participants had expressed an interest. In this session we included information about the availability of part-time opportunities, discussions of employers' reactions to women returning to the labor market, and some general job-hunting strategies. In the last session each participant met with a member of the committee for a short, individual counseling interview.

We worked hard to make the program a success. And it was a success. There were so many requests for future workshops that we held a series each year from 1957 to 1960. Initially most of the participants were from New York City, but we then had so many inquiries from suburban alumnae that in 1958, in addition to the workshop we held in New York, we went on "tour" to Westchester and held an extra series. The committee drove up together and met with a group of women in the home of an alumna. It was clear that there were women who didn't feel able to make a forty-minute trip to New York City once a week for three evenings just for themselves, although most of them, whenever the opportunity arose, would easily make arrangements for an evening of dinner and theater with their husbands.

By 1960, responding to expressions of interest from the other Seven Sister colleges, we opened the door to alumnae from Bryn Mawr, Mt. Holyoke, Smith, Radcliffe, Wellesley, and Vassar. We also invited their placement directors and representatives of their alumnae associations to come as observers. Once again, the series was well attended and enthusiastically received. We realized then that it was time to consider establishing a more structured, formally organized program.

Between 1957 and 1960 about 150 women registered for one of these informal job-finding workshops. Some came to all the sessions; others attended only one or two. Only a few registered and failed to show up. In those early workshops, we found ourselves confronting the "problem that has no name," which, a few years later, was so passionately described by Betty Friedan in her groundbreaking book *The Feminine Mystique*. We didn't provide answers, but we posed questions and began exploring solutions. By gathering together a group of women with certain common frustrations, hopes, and questions, we started something that would lead to many women taking decisive action a few years later. Women told us how wonderful it was to hear other women express the same feelings they had: feeling trapped and then guilty. The realization that they weren't crazy, selfish, or uncaring to think about fulfillment outside of the domestic sphere lifted an enormous burden and enabled them to more concretely analyze their goals, as well as the impediments to these goals.

Our original goal was to help each participant realistically evaluate her situation, not necessarily to place her in a job. Most of the women who came to these workshops weren't ready to go back to work, but they were eager to start thinking about their futures and found our information extremely useful. Many returned home determined to figure out a way to go back to college or graduate school or to sharpen some skill. Others realized they could gain experience by taking more active leadership roles in their volunteer activities. A few were in the position to start a freelance service or some small-business venture from their homes. Most left knowing that they had taken the first step and that people and resources would be available when they were ready.

None of the women in these early workshops needed to work for economic reasons. All were white, middle-class women, hoping to convince employers and graduate and professional schools—and even themselves—that there were valid reasons for working other than financial ones. In retrospect I realize that there was much we could have learned from women who had always worked full time out of economic need, but we didn't look to them then. It seems a bit arrogant and painfully shortsighted, but we didn't extend ourselves beyond this small, homogenous community of alumnae from private women's colleges. We never asked a working-class woman, or even a single mother who worked to support her family, to share her experiences with us. No woman of color attended our workshops or came for individual counseling. One workshop participant wrote in her evaluation, "I felt that the questions and attitudes revealed by those of us who don't need jobs might be offensive to women in financial difficulty who work at jobs beneath their capacity. Possibly the problem could be faced directly." Regrettably, it never was. Years later, at a meeting on common goals in the women's movement, I heard women of color say, "What is this white, middle-class fantasy about working? We have always worked and would love to stay home and take care of our families!"

I gradually increased my hours of work; although I was still only working part time and I continued to keep my summers free. The summer months were for family. Bernie always took a month off when the children were young, and we rented a house near a beach: first in Connecticut, then in Long Island, and then, for several years, in Martha's Vineyard. These vacation months were precious. We spent most of our waking hours at the beach—sunning, swimming, walking, playing. We would even come out to the beach at night. Bernie loved to show us the stars and constellations and tell us stories about how they were named and how different cultures viewed the heavens. Many nights the four of us stretched out on a blanket, our eyes on the sky, while Bernie treated us to the sky's geography.

By the late 1950s we had a household helper who came five days a week at 2:00 P.M. and stayed until after dinner, which made it possible for me to go to whatever evening meetings I needed to attend. My family seemed to be doing well. David remarked that I planned especially good dinners on nights when I wouldn't be home. I conscientiously kept up with all my household duties: keeping in touch with everyone in the family, doing the normal entertaining expected of a physician's wife, and attending all the children's school functions. When I observed that, on the rare occasion when I said I was tired, Bernie's immediate response was, "Why do you work?" I quickly learned never to say I was tired. On the other hand, my daughter gleefully told me that she was glad I worked: it meant that I was up in the morning before she went to school. Many mommies, she said, slept late and their children didn't see them until the end of the day.

Looking back, I know I overdid being "good." Yet, at the time, it seemed the only way to preserve my marriage and to be accepted in a society that insisted that women be domestic paragons, putting the needs of their families ahead of themselves. Perhaps, with a different kind of childhood, my need for approval might not have been so strong. Perhaps I might have been more assertive. I know that at the time I saw no alternative, and, on occasion, I felt selfish making work an important part of my life.

In 1958, when I was forty, I sent for the catalog for the Columbia University Graduate School of Arts and Sciences. I was beginning to think about working toward a Ph.D. in sociology. I felt that, with my interest in women and employment, a graduate degree would expand my options. As I leafed through the catalog and read the requirements—courses in statistics, proficiency in two foreign languages, and the need to publish the dissertation—I sensed the magnitude of what I was considering. I showed the catalog to my husband, who said ruefully, "I admire your optimism." I was painfully aware of his health problems—although he never discussed them—and the ways in which they affected his thinking about the future. I closed the catalog and never mentioned it again. I knew that I couldn't embark on so ambitious an undertaking without his full support. Since he refused to talk with me about his health, about what he saw as the prognosis, or about his fears, I found it difficult to discuss my own future. His silence silenced me.

There were other painful overtones of sadness in my life. In 1951 my sister Anne was diagnosed with lymphoma. At that time most doctors didn't tell their patients that they had a terminal illness. For eleven years, only three of us knew: Anne's husband, Bernie, and I. We carried this huge, silent burden as we watched Anne undergo radiation each time a lymph node was affected. Anne lived in a Connecticut suburb with her husband and two children and seemed completely unaware of what lay ahead. When she talked about her illness, she always repeated what the doctor had told her—that she had a glandular problem that came and went. When she was in remission, which was most of the time, she lived fully. I think this made it possible for her to accept the medical explanation that she was given. She never asked any of us about her illness, not even Bernie. She continued her normal activities until, during the last few weeks of her life, she was hospitalized. She died in 1962 at the age of thirty-seven.

My father developed Parkinson's disease, and, although he kept working as long as he could, it simply confirmed his belief that he had been a failure. It got harder and harder to cheer him up. He died in 1954 at the age of sixty-nine.

Initially, I concentrated on playing down my job, wanting to show that I was still primarily a wife and mother. When Bernie and I were introduced to other couples, Bernie was often asked what his occupation was, but no one ever asked me that question. I was his wife, and that was enough. I made sure I was available for the children whenever they needed me at school or at home. And, on occasion, usually a school holiday, I would even take one or both of them to the office where they would sit at my desk, try the typewriter, and look out my window at the wonderful view up and down Madison Avenue. Despite my efforts, I received little encouragement or credit. My mother never asked me about my work and often complained that I no longer had time to see her. In truth, I was careful to see her as often as I always had. My mother-in-law used to walk straight to the kitchen when she came to visit, pulling off the covers of pots cooking on the stove, to see if her son's family was suffering because her daughter-in-law was away part of the day working. Nevertheless, when my husband died, she was one of the family members who pointed out how lucky I was to have a job.

From time to time a few friends asked me to describe what I actually did, and, when I offered a few specifics, I would often hear, "I wouldn't bother going downtown just to do the things you do." Later, when my responsibilities expanded and I began to become known, I was amused that some of these same friends would talk wistfully about working and say, "Oh, you know, I'd like a job like you have. I enjoy being with people." I never reminded any of them that they wouldn't have been willing to start where I did.

I read everything I could about college-educated women in the work force in the 1950s. I was troubled by the unquestioned assumption that women's primary responsibilities were marriage and rearing children. A few prescient thinkers did write about women, education, and work and pointed to the waste of human resources, the drop in the average marriage age for women, the marked decrease since the 1920s in the percentage of women completing degrees at all levels, the increase in life expectancy, and the growing labor market shortages. But even these few seemed to accept without question that—unless there was a pressing economic need—women should stay home until their children reached adolescence.

During that period there were four books that I found particularly insightful. As early as 1953, Mirra Komarovsky, in her classic *Women in the Modern World: Their Education and Their Dilemmas,* suggested that

> [Y]oung women who have the inclination and resources for graduate, professional training should be encouraged to take it, even

if they retire from the professional world for the years of child rearing. What society loses in the apparent waste of training facilities, it may regain later if we develop ways to bring these women back to their professions after child rearing responsibilities are over. (287–288)

In 1956 Alva Myrdal and Viola Klein, in *Women's Two Roles,* proposed that women divide their adult lives into two parts, the first twenty years raising children and the next twenty years in the work force. They strongly advocated that this lifestyle be prepared for through education, training, and even some work experience before marriage. Mabel Newcomer, the eminent Vassar economist, in *A Century of Higher Education for American Women,* worried about the need to encourage more talented women to use their education to enter the professions, even if they must do so later, when their family burdens had eased. The National Manpower Council, established in 1951 under the leadership of Eli Ginzberg, devoted its sixth volume, *Womanpower,* to an exhaustive examination of women in the labor force, documenting the large number of women working, mostly in low-level jobs. This book focused on the need to bring more women into the labor force, at higher levels, with recommendations for employers, universities, and the federal government to implement this major task. This study, however, also accepted and, to some extent, endorsed the public view that men were the family breadwinners and thus had superior claims to available work and that, barring economic need, women with young children should not work. The book was very much a reflection of the times; public opinion was split as to whether mothers of even older children should work.

One other book made a deep impression on me at the time: Anne Morrow Lindbergh's *Gift from the Sea,* a wise, beautiful, poetic volume, eloquently describing the need for women to find some time alone, "some solitude, in order to find again the true essence of themselves: that firm strand which will be the indispensable center of a whole web of human relationships" (50). In l955 *Gift from the Sea* struck a deep personal chord. It impressed upon me that women must learn to value themselves and to think of themselves as independent individuals even as they recognized the need for institutional changes. Perhaps this awareness was my first conscious step toward a feminist understanding. I have reread this book several times since then and find it significant that I included it in a bibliography I prepared in 1962 of books and articles for women considering returning to work.

By 1957 the Alumnae Advisory Center was thriving enough to hire a secretary;

I was thus relieved of most clerical duties and could devote my energy to speaking with job applicants and employers. Most of the women I saw were young, many were just starting out, but I was also beginning to see women in their thirties and forties. We never found the perfect name for them; we settled on "returners," even though some had never worked for pay.

One of the first of these women arrived for her appointment a half hour late. She was an attractive, well-dressed woman of about forty, married to a successful businessman. She had trouble finding a place to park her car, and the first thing she did when she sat down was to ask if she could phone her husband and tell him she had arrived safely and ask him what to do about her car. We had a very simple application form that baffled her. In the end we filled it out together. She lived in the suburbs with her husband and two school-age children. She wanted to explore the possibility of working. She said emphatically that she didn't need the money, but she was fed up with volunteer work because, no matter what she did, she never had a feeling of accomplishment. She was obviously not a leader. She had neither skills nor experience, and the fact that she didn't need to earn money actually made her quest more difficult. She hadn't yet discussed with her husband the possibility of working, although she said he knew she was at "loose ends." She imagined, she told me, that she could drive door to door to some nice part-time job that would primarily be talking to people. She added that she hoped to find a job with enough flexibility that she could take time off whenever her husband wanted to travel or whenever her children needed her.

Although she may have sounded somewhat unreasonable and certainly naive, I could empathize with many of her feelings, even some of her ambivalence. I was to see many women like her. I quickly learned that I couldn't always tell from a first interview whether a woman was serious about wanting to work or whether she was so unsure of herself that presenting unrealistic aspirations would simply reinforce her sense of inadequacy.

At the other end of the spectrum, I started counseling women who had worked or had done some graduate study before starting their families. Some wanted to pick up where they had left off—to complete that unfinished graduate training or to return to work in a field they knew. Some were leaders in volunteer organizations in their communities who wanted to transfer this experience to a paid job. A few of these women had attended the Barnard Job Finding Workshops and had already given serious thought to how they would manage their home situations and even had ideas about what they would like to do. Still others wanted to go back to college, but needed clarification about their vocational goals. All these women shared one large handicap: they were only ready to think about part-time work or education, and there were practically no part-time job or employment opportunities.

As I saw more would-be returners, I became preoccupied with learning how to best help these women and started by being a good listener. I observed certain common characteristics: an insistence on part-time jobs; a lack of knowledge about work and about fields of work; a denigration of any volunteer work that these women may have done; a personal timidity that was strangely coupled with inflated ideas of the kinds of jobs they might secure; a belief that—because they didn't need to earn money—it would be easier to find a job; a need to talk to a sympathetic person; a need to build up confidence; and—above all—a fear that they were too old to learn new concepts and too old to start working except in low-level, dead-end jobs. Along with these conflicted conceptions concerning work and personal esteem, I often sensed a strong determination to succeed.

I knew there were shortages in several professional fields and an acute need for office workers in all fields, but I also knew that the big stumbling block was women's insistence on part-time work. I talked with managers of private and public employment agencies, including temporary agencies, and, although employers expressed a desperate need for new employees, they stubbornly refused to consider flexible hours. A few women managed to gain some experience by registering with a temporary employment agency and by working a day or so a week at different offices. On rare occasions a women was able to prevail on a former employer to take her back on a part-time basis, usually at a lower-level job than the one she had left.

A major problem during the 1950s was that most employers believed that mature women who had been away from school and work for a period of years couldn't learn new concepts or even acquire new skills. I heard the director of training at IBM, a member of the Alumnae Advisory Center Board, say that, although they desperately needed recruits, she couldn't hire returners for their training program for programmers and analysts because they wouldn't be able to understand the new technology. This ageist attitude confirmed the stereotypes about women's inability to learn math and science, and, though it troubled me at the time, I didn't question it.

Graduate and professional schools were just as regressive. When a twenty-nine-year-old woman who had done well in advertising told me she realized she was in the wrong field and wanted to be a social worker, she tried to apply to the Columbia School of Social Work. The admissions staff was not encouraging, advising her to work in the field for a year or so to prove her seriousness. In addition most graduate and professional programs at that time refused to accept applicants over thirty-five, except in special circumstances, and had no provisions for part-time study, except at night.

These restrictions only heightened these women's insecurities. It would take another few years, acute labor market shortages, and some success stories to prove that women's brains did not atrophy during the few years they spent at home raising children and keeping house. For this to happen, we needed some innovative programs with flexible schedules that would make it possible for women with families to pursue graduate education.

I knew I had to explore new strategies. I knew that women had to present themselves as serious job seekers and I suspected that just talking to me or another job counselor, or even attending one of our workshops, would not be enough. In New York competition for good jobs was fierce. Employers always asked for a résumé, often before an interview was even scheduled. After visiting several résumé clinics, I attended one called the Job Finding Forum, a public service sponsored by the Advertising Club. There I learned valuable techniques for helping women prepare for interviews with potential employers. One evening each week three advertising executives served as a panel of experts as several job seekers read their résumés. There were usually about thirty people in the audience: job seekers, employers, and a few observers like me. Among the job seekers, some were waiting to sign up to have their résumé critiqued, while others, who attended week after week, were too fearful to get up and risk public criticism and hoped to learn enough from listening.

I went regularly for about six weeks and then, over the next few years, would visit once or twice a year. Each session started with one of the three panelists explaining the significance of a good, functional résumé in making contacts and finding a job. The panelists emphasized that a résumé is different from an application form and should be seen as an important tool to highlight the special qualifications of the job seeker. In order to participate in the résumé clinic, a job seeker was required to know what job she or he was seeking and must bring a résumé. After a few sessions I understood why the panelists insisted that a good résumé must be prepared by the job seeker rather than by a professional résumé service. I also saw that the process itself was as important as the finished product.

The procedure was quite simple. After each résumé was read aloud, first the panelists, then members of the audience, gave their opinion of the résumé, asked questions, made criticisms, and offered suggestions. The job seeker—almost always a man with considerable experience—was told to redo his résumé and return the following week. The process often took four to five weeks, and, when the panel finally found the résumé satisfactory, it was not unusual for the audience, which had listened carefully and participated fully in this torturous process, to applaud.

I kept returning to the résumé clinic with the realization that I could use the clinic's techniques to work with the women who were beginning to come to see me. Although I couldn't replicate the group setting, I could use these techniques on a one-to-one basis and also encourage women to visit the Job Finding Forum. Because this was a new group entering the labor force, I added a few steps.

I asked each woman to go home and carefully write down her background: her education and her work experience, with dates, and to start thinking about whom she could ask for references. Then I asked her to start keeping a list of tasks and hobbies that she enjoyed, no matter how insignificant they seemed. Such a list might include such wide-ranging interests and aptitudes as gardening, rewiring a lamp, organizing a school carpool, planning a children's party, designing and making a quilt, keeping the family accounts, gourmet cooking, doing crossword puzzles, reading French literature in French. Whatever went on the list was useful.

Working on a résumé with a returner was a good way to test the seriousness of her intent and to help her assess her background and experience. It forced her to research fields, jobs, and qualifications. If she had a background of substantive volunteer experience, it was a challenge for her—and for me—to present this experience in a professional way so that an employer could see that it might be transferrable. The process not only helped a woman crystallize her thinking about her qualifications and her interests but also helped her prepare for job interviews. When asked about her background, she would be ready to present whatever meaningful experience she had in its most relevant form. She need not stumble over the fact that she had no recent paid work experience. Too often employers told me that they had wasted time with a returner who, when asked about her work background, rather than answering directly, wandered on and on about such family concerns as having two children and having to give up her volunteer work the year "Johnny had the chicken pox."

I was filled with admiration for the women who came in time and again, accepting my criticisms and reworking their résumés. It was not unusual for a woman to need several appointments to prepare a satisfactory résumé. A good, pinpointed résumé, which could be sent to potential employers, enabled these women to establish a network of contacts—even if there were no imme-diate job openings. In the decade between 1955 and 1965 the women who went back to work or school, or both, were pioneers. Most were serious, highly moti-vated individuals who gradually broke down many of the barriers that kept them from living full lives.

The Bachrach engagement picture of my mother and father, 1913

Jane, age two, in the sun porch, 1920.

Anne with the tulips in the rose garden, 1927.

Growing up. Jane, Louis, and Bob, 1930.

Jane, working in New York, 1941.

Jane and Bernie, just married, 1942.

Bernie, Jane, and Nancy on vacation, 1948.

Mom and the children, 1950.

Anne, 1953.

Mother, 1962.

David's high school graduation, 1967. Nancy, Jane, my mother, and David.

Jane, at a Women's Center's conference at Arden House, 1979. Photo courtesy of the Barnard Center for Research on Women.

The Women's Center 10th anniversary, 1981. Left to right: Elizabeth Janeway, Catharine R. Stimpson, Nancy K. Miller, and Jane. Photo courtesy of the Barnard Center for Research on Women.

*Bella Abzug, Petra Kelly, Jane, and Gerd Bastian at a benefit party
at the Gould's New York apartment, 1983.*

*Jane, 1980. Photo courtesy of the Barnard
Center for Research on Women.*

Jay, 1985.

Kirsten and Diana visiting us in Long Island, 1993.

Tom and Emily, Alexa and Aaron in Vermont, 1996.

■ 6
THE BEGINNING OF CHANGE: CONTINUING EDUCATION AND RETURN-TO-WORK PROGRAMS

Twice a year I would empty and wash down all the closets, a formidable task, but that's what my mother always did, and I had to prove I was as good a housekeeper. Because I knew that both my mother and my mother-in-law disapproved of my working, I did everything I could to maintain the image of perfect wife and mother—sometimes carrying this to an absurd extreme. Although it certainly would have made things easier for me, I resisted asking Bernie or the children to share responsibility for household chores and errands. I was determined to prove that no one in the family suffered because I worked. I ran all over New York to find a special book for one of the children's school projects; I gave family parties even when it was inconvenient; I baked brownies for sick friends; and never failed to make my traditional rich chocolate cake for my children's birthdays. It took years and lots of growing up for me to finally relax these standards and learn to let some things go. I wanted approval for adhering to conventions, yet I also wanted a place for myself to grow outside the family.

Likewise, during my eleven years at the Alumnae Advisory Center, adding hours and responsibilities each year, I was careful, here too, to fulfill all my obligations. Although Alice was always at her desk when I arrived in the morning and stayed until closing time, she was also understanding of the rare occasions when I needed to rearrange my schedule for some emergency at home. I took care not to abuse this privilege. From the start, I felt an obligation to show that married women with young children were responsible employees.

Rethinking and reshaping my life deeply affected my family relationships. I always knew that when I had children, I would make sure that they knew that they were Jewish and understood what that meant. Living in New York City, where Jewish culture was part of the mainstream, made my task easier. Marrying Bernie also helped. Coming from a family of Conservative Jews closely connected to the Jewish community, Bernie had a clear sense of his identity. He attended Hebrew school until his bar mitzvah. As an adult, he had fond childhood memories of the holidays, but felt no obligation, or even impulse, to go to synagogue. On Yom Kippur, the Day of Atonement, Bernie would often say he wanted to go to synagogue to hear the *Kol Nidre* sung, but he never did.

Despite his lack of interest in organized religion, Bernie's Jewish identity remained deeply important to him.

When the children were very young, Bernie's mother—now a widow for the second time—lived on the next block. She liked nothing more than having us over for Friday night and holiday dinners, when she'd light candles. She was an amazing woman: I always found her to be somewhat larger than life. Not only was she physically large, but everything she did was on a grand scale. She talked incessantly—about food, family, bargains, and Jewish life. She cooked and shopped with unstoppable energy and passion, and she prided herself on setting a good table—one from which no one could possibly leave hungry. Her meals were gargantuan. A typical Friday night dinner consisted of grapefruit, chicken soup with matzo balls, gefilte fish, boiled chicken, brisket, cooked vegetables, noodle pudding, salad, Jell-o, cake, and cookies. No one could ever finish all the dishes she had prepared, but, no matter how often we protested, she never cut down. And she loved to shop. The minute she heard about a sale, she was off. She couldn't resist buying clothes for the children. Nancy and David had so many more new outfits than they could possibly wear when they were three and four years old, that I used to beg Fanny to wait until the children were old enough to care about clothes. Or she would buy enough underwear, pajamas, and socks for Bernie to last his whole lifetime. During the war, when food was rationed, she bought up a reserve of canned foods to store in her sister's basement in Brooklyn. The basement later flooded, causing all the labels to dissolve, and, for years afterward, she opened cans without knowing what she was going to find. Mom, as we called her, was an extremely capable woman with more energy than keeping house required, but keeping house is what she did for most of her life. When she later married for the third time, to keep house for a widower with a large family in Lancaster, Pennsylvania, we saw much less of her.

Once a year we went to a Seder given by one of Bernie's uncles. In time I learned to prepare a Seder or a Rosh Hashanah dinner and would invite a family of close friends to join us. With prayer books and Bernie's instructions, we had some wonderful evenings. Nancy loved helping with the preparations: polishing the silver, getting out the good china and linens, and making the table look festive.

A yearly Seder, however, wasn't enough. I tried to make up for what I missed as a child, but I fear I passed on some of my confusion. We celebrated both Hanukkah and Christmas. We had a menorah, lit candles, and exchanged gifts on each of the eight nights. At the same time we observed Christmas with my side of the family, hanging stockings for gifts from Santa Claus. The children used to ask why Granny had a Christmas tree, but we—and Mom—didn't. I knew all the Christmas carols but none of the songs for the Jewish holidays.

Our children went to Sunday school at a neighborhood synagogue. Nancy was confirmed and told us how good she felt when the rabbi blessed her. She was a happy child; she did well in school, played the piano promisingly well, and had a number of outside interests. She always attended the New York City public schools, and spent her high school years at the Bronx High School of Science. From a young age she had sharp sense of social justice. I once overheard a telephone conversation she was having with a friend—when she must have been in sixth grade—about whether the children should wait in line outside or inside the school until they were permitted into the classrooms. Nancy made a strong argument for waiting inside, saying that some children didn't have warm coats and would be too cold waiting outside.

David was a quiet child who, at an early age, showed an unusual proficiency in math and science. When he was as young as six, I would often find him pouring over maps spread out on the floor, independently studying all the contours and figuring out longitude and latitude. He was a poor sleeper and would roam the house at night, playing mathematical games and working on problems in the theory of numbers, an interest that he shared with his father. I worried about David's insomnia, but, whenever I raised the issue with Bernie, he always said not to worry, that David had a strong intellectual curiosity and that it would all even out as he grew up.

At the age of eleven David suddenly developed double vision. Fearing a brain tumor, Bernie rushed him to the hospital. For three weeks David endured a series of painful tests. No brain tumor was found, and the double vision cleared up. But in the hospital David developed another alarming symptom: a pronounced and painful inflammation of his joints. He was to be plagued by disabling bouts of swollen joints throughout his childhood and adolescence, keeping him from school for weeks at a time and curtailing his ability to participate in sports. We felt compelled to take him out of the local junior high school and send him to private school. Medical wisdom at the time indicated that he probably had rheumatic fever, which—by the time he went to college—had virtually disappeared.

David was always somewhat of a skeptic. He barely tolerated Sunday school, and, when it came time for him to prepare for his bar mitzvah, he refused, saying he didn't believe there was a God. If there was a God, he insisted, we wouldn't have any wars. We respected his opinion and didn't press the issue.

My relationship with my mother remained difficult, but it was also slowly changing. I learned how to check some of her constant criticism. She was, from the beginning, critical of how we brought up our children, the way we lived, and our friends. She disapproved of my working, although I later came to realize that her disapproval, her resentment, was mixed with a bit of envy. I found this hard to understand, but later, when our relationship had improved, she told me that she, too, had considered a career. When she realized my father's business was failing, she had thought about becoming a landscape architect. Dr. Robinson, our family doctor and friend, offered to underwrite her training, but—at the time—she was beset by too many family problems to consider such a major change in her life. For many years I continued to try to win her approval: calling her every day, showing her attention, sharing the details of my life, and ignoring her scathing remarks. When I learned to stop seeking her approval, the dynamics of our relationship changed. It took years, but, as I experienced some serious problems and hardships in my own life, I came to admire her for her courage, strength, and independence.

By the late 1950s I became known among my friends and acquaintances as a person to talk to about preparing to return to school or work. It started informally; the focus of conversation at the Saturday night dinner parties gradually changed. At gatherings of Bernie's medical colleagues, the doctors would settle into professional gossip while their spouses—almost always all wives—engaged in small talk. Occasionally, a woman doctor would join the "circle of wives." Among the small talk about children, camps, schools, and the like, a new topic of conversation emerged. Women began to express an interest in returning to school or work, and they had questions for me about how to proceed. They often felt impelled to tell me that they were thinking about working or going back to school, but, for one reason or another, the time wasn't right. They were either planning an extensive trip, or waiting for the last child to start school, or hoping to win their husbands' approval. Clearly, I was touching a nerve in many women who were still at home being full-time wives and mothers.

One incident stands out from this period. Lester Goldberg, a close friend and colleague of Bernie's, invited me to lunch. After catching up on family news, we shared concerns about Bernie's health. Then Lester got right to the point. He had observed that my talking about my work at social gatherings upset Bernie, and he suggested that I not initiate or encourage these conversations. When I pressed him for a better explanation, all he would say was that these discussions seemed to make Bernie uncomfortable and he thought he was doing us all a favor by advising me to be more sensitive to my husband's feelings. I was stunned. I hardly knew what to say.

A red light went on. Here it was again—the message to conform. Lester had always shown an interest in Bernie's welfare and I thought in mine too. We had often socialized as a foursome. My work experience, however, was too new to allow me to evaluate his advice. I was also still unsure of how to balance my personal and professional life. I did ask whether Bernie had said anything to him and he assured me that Bernie hadn't. And, so, I am ashamed to say that, without protesting or even asking further questions, I agreed to be more careful. I never spoke to Bernie about this, not wanting to embarrass him. I never spoke to anyone about this. For the remaining years of Bernie's life, when we were with other people, I limited conversation about this new aspect of my life.

By 1960 the young Alumnae Advisory Center was becoming known as the place in New York for women seeking a new kind of vocational help. Alice King was pleased that we were actively involved in a growing movement and acknowledged that what had started as a trickle of a few discontented women in the mid-1950s had become something significant. The growing number of middle-class women exploring the possibility of returning to school and to work coincided with severe labor market shortages, especially in the service fields where women had traditionally worked. At the same time, educators, foundations, and even the federal government acknowledged this phenomenon and began to respond with creative programs, support, conferences, research, and publications.

Almost overnight a whole new field sprang up. Between 1960 and 1963 some 300 programs—all devoted to continuing education for women—were established at public and private colleges and universities, as well as community colleges, all over the country. Although the programs varied considerably—reflecting the character of each institution and the needs of each community—they shared the basic premise that for most women the first priority was to marry and have children. The common threads among these programs were a more flexible approach to education and the acceptance of the premise that institutions of higher education had been designed for men and were not necessarily adequate for developing the potential of women. Some of these new programs focused on undergraduate education, others on graduate and professional training. Some of the programs offered special noncredit courses and conferences. All acknowledged the need for part-time study during the day, not at night, and the necessity for individual counseling and support groups for these returning women. Many of these early programs owed their success to substantial funding from such major foundations as the Carnegie, Rockefeller, and Kellogg Foundations. These programs broke new ground and showed that adult women with rusty academic experience could provide a rich pool of talent and were highly worth educating. The success of these innovative programs and the intense determination of a growing number of women to add meaningful work to their lives added another rich layer to the groundwork for the resurgence of feminism.

The idea of continuing education programs specifically for women was conceived by a few remarkable, visionary women who had institutional clout, including Mary Bunting at Radcliffe, Esther Raushenbush at Sarah Lawrence, Virginia Senders and Elizabeth Cless at the University of Minnesota, Kathryn Clarenbach at the University of Wisconsin, Jane Berry at the University of Missouri, Rosalind Loring at the University of California–Los Angeles, Ruth Osborne at George Washington University, Priscilla Jackson at Michigan State University–Oakland Extension Service, and Esther Westervelt at Rockland County Community College. I met and heard many of these leaders speak at meetings and conferences in the early 1960s; I read their reports with great admiration and excitement and spoke with many of them about their programs and plans.

Probably no single person contributed more to the establishment of continuing education for women than Florence Anderson, Corporate Secretary of the Carnegie Corporation and the only woman officer at the time. Reserved and unpretentious, she was intensely interested in and supportive of the development of this new field and directed Carnegie support to a number of creative programs for women, including funding for three of the early programs. The Minnesota Plan at the University of Minnesota was established in 1960 under the leadership of Virginia Senders and Elizabeth Cless. It represented the first commitment by a large state university to continuing education for adult women. The Minnesota Plan coordinated and made available to individual returning women, at select campuses throughout the state, all the resources of the university so that returning women could choose from a range of programs. For the first time, adult women could sit down with counselors and receive help for planning to return to school through extension courses, summer programs, or gradual reentry into undergraduate or graduate programs.

The second early program funded by the Carnegie Corporation, The Radcliffe Institute for Independent Study, started in 1961. The brainchild of biologist Mary Bunting, the president of Radcliffe College, it offered one year of support for independent work by women with proven potential for outstanding achievement in scholarship, the arts, or some community activity. It was designed to help women who had taken off time for family responsibilities. For the first few years, however, there were so many applications that those selected were women who had pursued their work continuously, but had been denied the prestigious fellowships normally granted to men.

The Center for Continuing Education for Women at Sarah Lawrence College was conceived in 1962 by Dean Esther Raushenbush, who directed the center until 1965, when she became the college president. I first met Esther in the late 1950s, when she served on the board of the Alumnae Advisory Center. Whenever we saw each other, we talked about the changing social climate for women and about creative ways to effect change. In 1969, when she had retired and was working as a consultant for the John Hay Whitney Foundation, we had lunch together. She had just given a speech at Cornell University, sponsored by NOW (National Organization for Women), and she had been criticized by the Cornell daily newspaper for sounding too traditional. As she told me about it, she smiled and said, "I think they were right." We talked about the many changes we were seeing in the lives of women, and she told me that she thought she had learned more about women in the past decade than in her whole life. For someone of her generation—she must have been close to eighty then—she showed an unusual openness and flexibility of spirit. I admired her greatly.

The Sarah Lawrence center focused on helping women who had dropped out of college to marry and rear children return to complete their bachelor's degrees. By evaluating college transcripts—some, twenty years old—and by setting up introductory seminars in areas in which these women had some knowledge and interest, the center provided orientation and a supportive atmosphere so that women might regain their confidence as students. After completing a transitional introduction—two seminars on such subjects as contemporary art, Western literature, or urban problems—these mature students matriculated as part-time students and completed the same degree requirements as other full-time undergraduates at Sarah Lawrence.

In the beginning Esther had difficulty finding faculty members who were willing to teach the introductory seminars offered by the center, even though they would receive extra pay. Initially, those asked assumed that teaching these women would be dull—that these women had been away from the academic world for too long. But Esther persisted, and she loved to tell how faculty discovered, after just one course, that these new students were intelligent, lively, outspoken, and, most important of all, highly motivated.

My old friend Ruth Simon enrolled in this program. As a New College student she had a colorful experience that diverted her from completing her degree. After spending the required semester of European study in England, she went to Paris and was hired by Edgar Ansel Mowrer to report for the *Chicago Daily*

News, an assignment that led to a brief stint in Franco Spain, shortly after the Spanish Civil War had ended. Following this, she returned to New York and found a job in public relations, which she kept until 1941, when she married Norman Simon, a young doctor already in uniform. After the war, and after moving to the suburbs, raising three children, and doing her share of volunteer work, Ruth heard Esther Raushenbush speak at an Alumnae Advisory Center meeting, which I had invited her to attend. The program description interested her so much that she applied immediately. She was accepted, did well, and loved the program. I think she was a bit sorry when it was over. I went to her graduation in 1969, and, as I looked around at the other mature women who were receiving their bachelor's degrees, I marveled at how far we had come in a short time.

A few institutions responded directly to severe labor market shortages. In 1960 Rutgers University designed a retraining program for women mathematics majors—replete with scholarships, counseling, and placement—to fill jobs in New Jersey, either teaching math or working in industry. Around the same time, Wellesley College, with a grant from the National Science Foundation, invited women who had been chemistry majors in college and were now out of touch with their field to participate in a tuition-free M.A. program in chemistry that would lead to a job.

Within a few years a number of professional schools in such traditional women's fields as librarianship, social work, and education opened their doors to returning women, designing special part-time programs that women could manage along with their home responsibilities. So desperate was the need for teachers in public junior high schools in New York City that my son brought home a flyer from the New York City Board of Education imploring mothers who were college graduates to consider teaching. To qualify, all one had to do was to take one or two education courses at a branch of the City University of New York, start teaching, and make a commitment to complete a master's degree over a two-year period.

The willingness of institutions to establish creative programs for women, and of foundations and government agencies to fund them, stemmed from the optimistic climate of the late 1950s and early 1960s and the need for trained professionals in a number of fields. For a brief period we were an affluent society, and, in many ways, these were golden years. Despite the Cold War—which had produced years of above-ground nuclear bomb testing—the Cuban missile crisis, and the specter of the Vietnam War, the early 1960s seemed to promise a better, more humane society for many. With the landmark Supreme Court decision in 1954 outlawing school segregation, a strong acknowledgment of a growing civil rights movement, and a partial test ban treaty negotiated in 1963 there seemed reason for optimism.

John F. Kennedy was elected President in 1960. One of his first appointments was that of Esther Peterson as Director of the Department of Labor Women's Bureau. A strong trade unionist, she expanded the mission of the Women's Bureau, issuing useful publications and sending representatives with research findings to conferences and meetings. Advocacy for the Equal Rights Amendment was building, but Peterson shared Kennedy's opposition to it, fearing that women would suffer without protectionist laws. At Esther Peterson's suggestion, Kennedy established a President's Commission on the Status of Women, with Eleanor Roosevelt serving as its chair, to consider how working women fared in their jobs.

In 1963 two important publications on women appeared. The first was Betty Friedan's *The Feminine Mystique*, giving voice to American middle-class women's deep discontent so eloquently that its readers felt it was personally addressed to them. The other—published eight months later—was *American Women: Report of the President's Commission on the Status of Women*, an equally impressive publication, documenting the large numbers of women in the labor force—mostly in low-level jobs—and the deep discrimination against women embedded in hiring practices, wages, and opportunities for promotion. The long list of recommendations, some of which are still not in place, included universal day care, paid maternity leave, and part-time employment opportunities. The commission was particularly forceful in affirming that the federal government should assume leadership in employing highly trained professional women who were not free for full-time employment on a part-time basis.

The program closest to my heart, the Barnard Job Finding Workshops, also reaped the benefits of foundation largesse in the early 1960s. Under the leadership of two strong Barnard women, Ethel Paley, who became director of the placement office after Ruth Houghton's retirement in 1955, and Eleanor Furman, who was then the chair of the Barnard Alumnae Advisory Vocational Committee, we extended our vision of the earlier volunteer vocational workshops. We decided to broaden the sponsorship and make it the Seven College Vocational Workshops, while acknowledging that Barnard would assume the major responsibility.

With the active support of Barnard president Millicent McIntosh, the Seven College Vocational Workshops were awarded a substantial grant from the

Carnegie Corporation for a four-year program, from 1962 to 1966, on the campus of Barnard College. I never knew Millicent McIntosh well; she was in office as the college dean from 1947 to 1952 (after I had already graduated from Barnard) and she became the first president of the college in 1952, a post she held until she retired in 1962. From everything I knew about her—her public addresses, the few conversations we shared, and the vigorous interest she took in our vocational workshops—it was clear that she was a determined, strong woman more than ready to support and implement programs that expanded women's options.

From the program's inception in 1962, I was intensely involved in all aspects of these vocational workshops. While continuing to work at the Alumnae Advisory Center, I served on the board of directors and the search committee for the director of this new program. I helped plan the curriculum, located outside speakers, and occasionally spoke at sessions. Many of the workshop participants came to see me at the Alumnae Advisory Center when they were ready to go back to work. I also served as the chair of the Barnard Alumnae Advisory Vocational Committee from 1961 to 1965.

When Ethel Paley left Barnard in 1965, I took over her job as director of placement and with it the responsibility for the last year of the workshop series. When the Carnegie funding later ran out, I secured federal funding and ran the program from 1966 to 1968, with a slightly different focus, as the Barnard College Community Service Workshops.

After a small announcement in the *New York Times* in 1962, the Workshops were flooded with applications from women in the metropolitan area and nearby suburbs. We were clearly responding to an unmet need, but I was surprised by how quickly the first workshops filled up, particularly since, unlike the earlier programs, there was a tuition charge. With very little publicity, we closed registration with our quota of fifty women long before the workshops even began. From then on, the word got out, and, for the next six years, the workshops were completely booked—almost always with a waiting list. Over 600 women participated in one of these ten-week programs, held every fall and spring from 1962 to 1968.

The program was designed for women who had graduated from college at least five years before and who had not recently been employed or who had no work history. Participants ranged in age from twenty-nine to sixty-five. Some had no work experience, while others were fully trained professionals—lawyers, social workers, and psychologists—who had either never practiced their profession or had done so only briefly. Most of the women were married; a few were divorced or widowed. Practically all had children. In the beginning most of the younger women were not ready to go back to work, but they were clearly searching for a way to plan for a future that would include meaningful paid employment. They saw these workshops as the first step.

The workshops were held in one of the old-fashioned, once very elegant "parlors" at Barnard College. There was always a feeling of excitement in the room at the start of each new series. We felt like pioneers, although, in retrospect, we were offering a reasonable, ladylike response to the discontent educated women were expressing. Still, the program was truly innovative for its time and probably the only one of its kind. It was upheld as a showpiece and from the start attracted a great deal of attention. There were always a few observers present: deans, alumnae, and placement directors from the sponsoring Seven Sister colleges, as well as educators, researchers, and journalists from the United States and abroad. I was bursting with pride, pleased that Barnard was responding so creatively to a societal need. Over the next twenty years, this feeling of pride and deep satisfaction would surface again and again.

We were fortunate in finding Ann Cronin, another visionary, to serve as the director. She was a willowy, well-put-together, attractive woman of indeterminate age; I suspect she was older than she looked. A Radcliffe graduate, her professional background included managing a successful employment agency. She had all the administrative skills necessary for the job as well as many contacts. She was articulate, had a good sense for public relations, and was an excellent counselor. She also looked like a director; her bearing was almost regal.

She and an impressive roster of speakers, including educators and other professionals and employers from the private and public sector, as well as representatives from a number of federal government agencies, spoke to the group about the realities of the workplace, opportunities, training needed, the impact of work on the family, and the need for spousal approval. All the speakers stressed the lack of part-time work opportunities. Opportunities for volunteer work were discussed by volunteer leaders with particular emphasis on the training such jobs could provide. The sessions also included mock interviews with role playing, résumé preparation, and, finally, an individual counseling session with the director of the program, including recommendations for specific resources to consult.

There were ten consecutive two-and-a-half-hour sessions. Attendance was excellent and most participants never missed a session. We discovered, almost unwittingly, that participants were able to absorb information about job qualifications, family and employer attitudes, and interview preparation in a way that was not always possible on a one-to-one basis. When I spoke with a woman in my office about meeting employer's expectations—that she couldn't, for instance, accept a job and then expect to be able to take off whenever her husband needed her to accompany him on a business trip or to see her son perform in a school play—I often had the feeling that she didn't hear me. She might say, "Well, I'll just wait till I find a job that will give me the flexibility I need." When a woman heard this in a group, however, she paid attention, even if she thought these remarks were intended for the woman seated next to her. Women listened carefully when an employer spoke to the group about a bad experience with an employee described as a "mature woman" who "didn't need the money" and spent too much time on the phone checking on her children and talking to friends. They asked challenging questions: How did an employer know if an employee needed to earn money, and what difference did that make? What did the employer mean by having a "bad experience"? Didn't the employee do her job? Did the employer have these complaints about younger women? How did women employees compare with men? Sometimes, an employer was embarrassed by these questions and didn't answer directly. Participants supported each other's questions and comments; we were using group process without having planned to. It was satisfying to see the interaction between the participants and the speaker.

The workshops provided a forum for beginning to consider returning to work. I think most of the participants felt they received support, useful information, direction, access to networks, and—often—a new way of thinking about themselves. As in our earlier volunteer programs, some women simply enjoyed the workshops and did nothing further. Others waited until the time seemed right to make plans. And others used the experience as a springboard for employment. From time to time during these six years, we tried to measure the results of our program by sending out surveys to participants. The responses to the program were generally enthusiastic, although many respondents were still thinking about what they wanted to do and had not taken any action. We hoped that by having employers and leaders in the professions speak at the workshops we would create an awareness of this new pool of talent, and, to a certain degree, I think this happened. This was particularly true of professional school programs, which were under pressure to produce trained personnel at a time of critical shortages. Over this six-year period, more and more women registered for the workshops in response to the shifting social climate, and, by the time we completed the last two years, which were strongly slanted toward paid or volunteer careers in community service, the demand for this kind of program seemed to have ended. By 1968 reentry programs for women were so much a part of United States culture that information about programs and about jobs was widely available.

■ 7
CONFRONTING
TWO MAJOR ROADBLOCKS:
INFLEXIBLE EMPLOYERS
AND TRADITIONAL MARRIAGE

Where were the part-time jobs? This was to become my obsession. Starting in the late 1950s, the number of women seeking part-time employment who came to see me at the Alumnae Advisory Center steadily grew until, by the early 1960s, they constituted nearly half the women who came to the center. I began asking employers who had listed job openings with the center to consider hiring a well-qualified candidate on a part-time basis. But this, however, was to no avail.

At the time, it was clear that we had hit an enormous roadblock. All the literature about women in higher education and employment from 1955 to 1965 cited the Women's Bureau projections that, in the foreseeable future, the average American woman would marry at the age of twenty and a half and would drop out of school or the labor market when her first child was born. She would have 2.5 children, and, when the youngest started school, she would return to work on a part-time basis and spend the next twenty-five years in the workplace. The bureau's projections underscored for me the need for substantive jobs.

There were a few success stories—mostly of women who combined determination and persistence with some experience and training. One woman, who had been the director of publications for a national membership organization, convinced her former employer to rehire her ten years later, working three days a week in the office and one day at home. Another woman, who had been a volunteer director of a community program in the arts and who now felt ready to seek paid employment, took a different route. She convinced her family of the importance of her enrolling in a six-week summer program for arts administrators at Harvard. This was a big personal step for her; she lived in New Jersey, and her family felt as if they were sending mommy away to camp. After she had successfully completed the course, she prepared a résumé summarizing her years of substantive volunteer experience and recent professional training. After carefully researching possible employers, she found a part-time job running an arts program for a large local YWCA (Young Women's Christian Association). One woman told me she got up at 4:30 every morning to work on her master's thesis for a couple of hours before her family woke up. Another described her commute—two hours each way, twice a week—to a university where she took graduate courses in counseling so that she could complete an M.A. and transfer from her volunteer job to a paid professional job at the same agency.

But such success was not the experience of most women. The stumbling block of course was employers. After much thought, I realized that the center had to learn more about employers. Alice and I decided to reach employers in a more structured way—to explore the reasons for their unwillingness to consider employing college-educated women part time in jobs of more than a routine nature, even when their organizations had critical labor shortages. We needed to learn much more about employers' attitudes and practices in order to effect any changes in employment policies. We believed that, as more employers knew about this new source of labor power, some would be willing to consider hiring qualified women on less than a full-time basis. In this spirit, we prepared a proposal for a year-long study.

In 1963, with a grant from the Carnegie Corporation, the Alumnae Advisory Center undertook a qualitative study of part-time employment, focusing on employers' attitudes and practices with respect to opportunities for the college-educated woman. I was appointed the director of the project and was relieved of my regular duties for a whole year. Given complete freedom as to how I would go about gathering this information, I worked from home, coming and going to libraries, appointments, and the center for secretarial assistance and consultation with Alice. I also had the assistance of one volunteer.

One of the first things I did was to consult with Eli Ginzberg, a summer neighbor and director of the Conservation of Human Resources at Columbia—the acknowledged "manpower" expert at that time. He was helpful and encouraging, although he had no specific advice on how to proceed. He observed that the grant was too small to permit any statistical research and that, since so little was known about part-time employment, whatever information I could uncover would be useful. The only requirement of the foundation was that the study yield a publication with the findings and recommendations.

Initially, I was somewhat apprehensive because I lacked research experience or formal training. As I thought through the questions I needed to ask and started talking to people, I realized that my firsthand knowledge of this new source of labor power, my broad contacts with employers and leaders in the professions, and my passionate interest in the issue were indeed the right qualifications.

During the first six months I conducted 155 open-ended interviews with representatives of organizations in the private and public sectors in five broad fields of employment: commerce and industry; mass communications; education and research; health, welfare, and community service; and special services such as placement, trade associations, business and technical services, unions, etc. I selected employers from organizations and companies in which some college-educated women were employed, although not necessarily part time. Some were employers who had listed jobs with us. Sometimes, for large organizations, I arranged interviews with more than one person. In addition, I interviewed fifty-one leaders in the professions, as well as in government agencies concerned with women. I summarized the findings and recommendations in a sixty-two-page report entitled *Part-Time Employment: Employer Attitudes on Opportunities for the College-Trained Woman,* published in 1964 by the Alumnae Advisory Center.

It was a wonderful year. With Nancy away at college and David in high school, my home responsibilities had lessened. The first half of the year was spent on interviews and the second on organizing my material and writing the report. I wrote the first of eight drafts on the porch of our rented summer house in Martha's Vineyard, while Bernie and the children were at the beach. Completing the report was a long, arduous task but deeply satisfying. Not only did I enjoy synthesizing and processing my findings and recommendations—giving a sense of closure to nearly a year's worth of work—but I also discovered that I enjoyed writing and the whole process of learning how to write well. This was not true of public speaking. The night before I was to publicly present my findings to an audience of about one hundred—employers, college placement directors, Women's Bureau representatives, employment specialists and supporters of the center— I panicked. I was forty-six, and—until then—I had painstakingly avoided speaking in public or chairing large meetings. I was petrified. I momentarily considered saying I was ill and calling the meeting off. Of course, I went through with it; I stood in the auditorium of IBM, began speaking, and somehow carried it off. To this day, however, I am never at ease before a large audience.

The findings I presented were disappointing. Most of the employers I interviewed told me that they didn't employ anyone part time except for routine or highly specialized, often personally tailored, jobs. I doubt that I changed any employer's attitudes. I heard over and over again that any job of substance simply could not be performed on less than a full-time basis; moreover, it was against company policy and thoroughly unprofessional. I heard this just as often from employers who admitted to having vacancies as from those who had no trouble attracting competent employees. Only in such fields as health and welfare, where employers were desperate for employees, did I find occasional flexibility.

On the other hand some employers described with delight their success placing women, mostly housewives, in routine part-time jobs. Employers in banking and insurance companies were particularly proud of their stable, part-time labor force. They admitted that, because they had had difficulty in finding employees who would stay for any length of time, they had intentionally designed jobs that meshed with women's family schedules. Employers in retail reported similar success, perhaps even more so, since women often considered sales jobs more attractive than clerical work. Everyone understood that training and promotion opportunities were almost nonexistent for these part-time workers, many of whom were highly overqualified for the jobs they held.

At the other end of the employment ladder were jobs that required special qualifications. I found some unexpected revelations here. The interviews were unstructured, and most employers were generous in allotting time for the interview. This allowed time for exploration, and I often would find employers altering their initial assertions. For instance, after firmly proclaiming that they had no part-time employees, some employers finally did remember an exception: a part-time employee, almost always a woman, either someone who had formerly worked for the organization for a long period and had developed expertise in an area needed by the employer or who had special skills that could be used on a part-time basis. I found that some employers actually tailored a job for the person they wanted, as in the case of a public relations firm that created a part-time job for a woman in charge of its fine arts department, an expert in her field but available only three days a week. Or a foundation that created a part-time job for a woman whose fourteen-year background with the organization made her invaluable. One large company had a former employee from the personnel department come back each year to revise and update its personnel manual.

But there was general agreement that administrative jobs could never be part time. An advertising agency executive described how they had permitted a vice president to shorten her hours to two days a week by relinquishing her administrative duties and confining her activities to copywriting. Others pointed to using freelance writers, researchers, and publicists, but adamantly refused to consider part-time employment as part of "normal" employment practices—except, of course, for routine, largely clerical jobs.

Most of the employers I spoke to were men, but even the few women executives I interviewed—most of whom were at the operating rather than the corporate level—shared this resistance to part-time work. With the exception of members of the President's Commission on the Status of Women or representatives from education, state, and federal women's programs—not necessarily employers—I found a general inflexibility and even an unwillingness to seriously consider women who were not prepared to work full time. The women employers I spoke to showed little interest in or understanding of the plight of educated women who felt trapped as full-time homemakers. It was clear that these women had struggled, often without role models, mentors, or any special kind of support, and had achieved their success by being twice as good—and working twice as hard—as men. They simply couldn't see how women could expect to find meaningful part-time jobs and made it quite clear that they were not going to risk their status by extending themselves for other women.

I was puzzled by these reactions, just as I was curious to know more about the handful of successful professional women I knew who had families and worked full time. What made them do it? How were they able to manage? I had never seen a study examining this small group, but my analysis suggested that among the reasons for their achievements were their own superstrong egos, their working mothers or other women in their circle who served as role models, their encouraging fathers or unusually supportive husbands, and their special economic needs. A few were divorced women, some with children, who developed successful careers. But in the early 1960s even successful women were situated precariously and were usually of no mind to help other women who were seeking a way back to a career.

That some employers had had some positive experiences with at least one part-time employee on their staff was a significant finding. I tried to use this to convince other employers that such arrangements could work by limiting the number of people each organization could absorb in such jobs and spelling out the kinds of work that could be done on a less than full-time basis. But I still found little acceptance.

Even more discouraging were the negative attitudes some employers expressed about women in the workplace. While it is true that these attitudes may still exist, legal mechanisms no longer permit such prejudiced opinions to be stated openly. In 1963, however, employers still expressed serious reservations about married women with young or school-age children holding a job. I often heard employers say that, if women didn't need the money, they should stay home. Further, the opinion was often stated that women who could only work part time were not a good business investment since they wouldn't be as committed as full-time employees.

■

There was also a deep skepticism about mature women's abilities and competence. I heard that the world of work was a man's world, that women were not capable of holding responsible jobs. Some employers told me that very few women could be objective, that they were too emotional. Again and again, deeply sexist generalizations emerged: Women are poor at motivating others or exerting leadership. Women don't make good executives. Women don't have the drive for success that men have. One employer told me that clients would not be candid or comfortable with a woman, particularly in situations where money was being discussed.

Many employers voiced concerns about mature women who had been at home for many years. They thought it would be hard for women to balance their home and work life and that this confusion would spill over into the office. Several stubbornly clung to the idea that the abilities of a woman who has been out of the labor market would have deteriorated. Some even questioned whether such women could manage the subway rush, could abide by office regulations, and could work with or under the supervision of younger people. These views, all articulated by men, were expressed with such conviction that I sometimes wondered whether such generalizations were based on their views of their own wives. Basically the question I heard over and over and in different voices was, How could a woman make a real commitment to an employer when she had family responsibilities?

A few went out of their way to describe a difficult woman employee who had asked for special arrangements and additional concessions to fit her family needs. Also, although no statistics were ever cited, several said mature women tended to take more time off and stay home longer when ill. In fact, I actually heard a handful of employers say that they had had such a poor experience with a mature woman employee that they would not hire a woman again. Of course, they would never follow this principle in the case of an unsatisfactory male employee. For who, then, could be employed?

My recommendations assumed that part-time employment was, and would continue to be, important for many college-educated women. I emphasized vocational counseling, starting as early as junior high school, with information on careers and the changing patterns of women's lives, so that young girls would be motivated to think about the value of careers. Many of my recommendations were based on continued labor market shortages in certain fields, and I offered suggested guidelines for encouraging women to seek training in such fields as teaching, social work, and librarianship. I recommended that refresher courses be offered by colleges and professional schools for women who had been away from a field for some time and the creation of flexible educational programs to enable women to complete or continue interrupted education. I recommended discussions, conferences, and meetings on the value of using well-trained women in part-time work until such a time as their family responsibilities permitted them to work full time. Several of my recommendations focused on educating employers about the potential of this untapped pool of talent and on encouraging those employers who had successfully used part-timers to share their experiences. I concluded by recommending further study of employers and women who had good part-time jobs. At this time, of course, I had no idea how drastically the labor market would change in the following decade.

Remarkably, most white, middle-class women did not consider, or even acknowledge, the largest barrier of all: traditional marriage. In the 1950s and the early 1960s most of us lived our lives within this traditional framework. Marriage was both our security and our identity. A few years later we would call it "the weight of patriarchy"—a large, invisible weight constantly pressing down on every part of our lives. Until then, however, most of us didn't question the unequal roles of men and women or the extraordinary power that men had over women. Our husbands supported us, and, because of this, it was almost as if they owned us. Even women who were widowed or divorced endured the social repercussions and weight of the patriarchal household.

During those years we affirmed marriage, even as we sought new ways to achieve a small degree of independence. In the six years that we held the ten-week series of vocational workshops at Barnard, we always devoted one whole session to family issues, particularly focusing on "getting your husband's approval." We stressed the necessity of having this approval to return to school or to work, even for just a few hours a week. We explored the kinds of objections women might expect—chiefly that they might "disrupt" the rhythm of home life for their children and their husbands, the hardworking breadwinners. We acknowledged that the husband was the wage earner and the wife the helpmate. On the face of it this seemed fair. This certainly reflected the culture of the time and even my own experience.

Most of the women participating in these vocational workshops lived privileged lives, with all the creature comforts: a home replete with appliances, summer camps for the children, part-time or full-time household help, and even winter vacations to the Caribbean. Even those who couldn't afford these luxuries lived a comfortable life on a single income, and that's the way most men wanted it—they were the providers.

In the two-and-a-half-hour workshop devoted to family issues, we encouraged participants to be as open and frank as they could. We talked about specific objections that husbands customarily raised, and, at the top of the list, were the extra expenditures for buying clothes suitable for work, transportation, tuition, and even additional household help. Women told us that their husbands resisted the thought of their earning money because it would push the family into a higher tax bracket. Husbands expressed concern about what would happen to the children, but women agreed this wasn't a real concern, since it was not a concern when wives filled their days with volunteer work, bridge games, or shopping sprees, which sometimes brought them home barely in time to prepare dinner. Some husbands objected because they anticipated that their wives would not be available for unexpected trips or would not be available for all the routine caretaking errands they were depended on to do. For some husbands, the mere thought of helping their wives find time to study at home was out of the question. For husbands who objected, it often boiled down to liking things the way they were. They had been reared to be men who could support their families, and a large part of their masculinity was defined by their success as providers. They thought they needed a wife at home to ensure their status and success. A few women described arguments with their husbands about their participation in these workshops, and there was always laughter as women described the grumbling of their spouses about the content of the program.

Status remained an important issue. When I spoke to women's groups in the metropolitan area and in the suburbs, I noticed a sharp difference between their attitudes about status as it applied to volunteer and paid work. In some communities women told me there was more prestige in working for pay—no matter what the job was—than holding a leadership volunteer position. In other more closely knit, homogeneous suburban communities, I learned that women couldn't take a paid job because their husbands would feel threatened and, as a family, they would lose status. Conceptions of personal status—often attached to work—and of family status—often attached to the idea perpetuating the patriarchal family—were overlaid in complex and conflicted ways.

Not all husbands had objections. Some regarded their wives' preparation for returning to work as an investment in the family's future. They understood that being productive outside the family could make a woman a happier and more interesting person which, in turn, might contribute to the well-being of the family. It was a relief to hear women talk about husbands who were encouraging and were not threatened by their wives' success outside as well as inside the home. But there were few, and implicit in their approval was the expectation that the balance of power would remain the same—that their own masculinity would not be challenged in any substantive way.

There was, of course, the economic reality. Men were the heads of the household and earned substantially more money than their wives who worked part or even full time, and their position could never really be threatened. One woman I knew, with a husband and two school-age children, worked full time at a job she disliked to supplement her husband's inadequate salary. She got home about an hour before he did and regularly fixed a martini for him so that he could enjoy the evening news while she prepared dinner.

There were other surprises. We had not considered, for instance, that men might also feel limited and burdened by the strong societal pressure that accompanied being the head of the household. At a conference held at the New School for Social Research on women returning to school and work, I was on a panel with a husband selected to show his support for working women. To my surprise, he expressed strong resentment that a woman should have the privilege of changing her life, while men were trapped in jobs and careers that they might prefer to change but couldn't because of their responsibilities as family providers. These remarks intimated that—for both men and women—there were some very real stresses associated with maintaining the "traditional" conception of the family. But, since this view was so rarely expressed and family roles and obligations were so deeply ingrained, it was not something that we addressed.

But working part time and caring for a husband and children were just at the tip of the iceberg. Being married was a double-edged sword, a necessary status symbol, economically enabling, yet a kind of voluntary state of bondage. Although some of us changed the traditional wedding vows from "love, honor, and obey" to "love, honor, and cherish," we didn't question the final utterance by the rabbi, minister, or judge: "I now pronounce you man and wife." Men were men, and we were wives—not women. Those of us who came of age in the 1940s, 1950s, and early 1960s knew that we would marry; this was what was expected of us. We also knew that we would have children because this, too, was expected of us. Most of us shared the consensus that married women who elected not to have children were selfish. Even I thought it was odd and wondered why certain couples had no children or even just one.

Who knows how many women settled for a marriage of convenience after finding themselves in their mid- or late twenties still unwed. And who knows how many women married in response to strong social pressures who, today, perhaps would not have married *at all*. The few women who didn't marry and lived out their lives alone or with aging parents were pejoratively referred to as spinsters or, even worse, old maids.

How well I remember the enormous pride I felt in wearing my wedding ring. I loved the status it implied: the public acknowledgment that I was married. I was *somebody* now; never mind that it was somebody's wife. The thrill of ordering my first personal stationery with Mrs. added to my husband's name is comparable only to the thrill I experienced almost thirty years later when I married for the second time and ordered personal stationery without the Mrs.—although, even here, I still took my husband's surname.

Being a Mrs. gave a woman status and privilege; without the Mrs., she was a lesser person. When a married woman signed a letter, she didn't mind that it was cumbersome that she had to write Mrs. John Smith and then, right above it, sign her own name, Jane Smith. A married name defined one. If you were divorced, you took back your own first name and were Mrs. Jane Smith, but, if you were widowed, you kept Mrs. John Smith. You had to have a Miss or a Mrs. before your name, and, if you were a Miss, people felt sorry for you or at least said things such as "I wonder why she never married."

Ah, but the stigma of being unwed had not always been so strong. In the early 1970s I arranged a panel of distinguished Barnard alumnae, four feisty women who had graduated between 1918 and 1925, to discuss their professional lives. They told us that they abhorred the new appellation for women, Ms., created to de-emphasize a woman's marital status. They had all made a conscious decision to become professional women rather than to marry, and they liked being addressed as Miss. It was their choice, and they felt proud of their lives and their title.

We used to joke and say that all the "unimportant" decisions were made by the wife and all the "real" ones were made by the husband. By "real" we meant the financial decisions and where and how we lived. Women couldn't obtain bank credit without husbands' approval; our charge cards were in our married names and depended on our husbands' credit standing. In our family most of our major decisions concerning summer camp, private school, and major purchases were made together, but, when we disagreed, I knew that Bernie's opinion was the decisive one. It was a painful learning experience when, despite my objections, we moved back to New York City at the war's end. I often wondered how different our lives would have been had we remained in Wisconsin.

Many women were given household allowances and prided themselves on managing to save small amounts from this allowance. For some women this was the only money they could call their own. Bernie and I had a joint bank account, which worked well as long as I was careful. He was a generous person who normally didn't pay attention to petty expenditures, but he always checked the monthly bank statements, and he sometimes questioned a few of my checks, mostly how much I spent on gifts. This questioning aroused uncomfortable feelings of impotence and dependence. When I started bringing in a salary, it went into our joint account. This, however, didn't give me substantially more leverage or independence. My pay check was extremely modest, and, had I pressed the issue, it may very well have turned out that my working was actually costing us money.

It was an era of "togetherness"—sometimes too much of it. Few women vacationed alone, although they might visit an ailing parent or go to a college reunion once in a while. It was, however, quite acceptable for men to go off on fishing or hunting trips and, of course, on the many business or professional trips that were part of their regular lives. When I was first married I met a woman who had been married for twenty years; she proudly told me that she and her husband had never been apart for one night. At the time this seemed to indicate a beautiful relationship, one to be emulated—the perfect model of togetherness.

The expectations of togetherness, of course, placed women at home with their children. Unlike men, when women were called for jury duty, they could be excused if they so desired, the assumption being that taking care of a family was an excuse for almost everything—including avoiding civic duty. Of course, these same women may have arranged to take a two-week vacation with their husbands, away from children, but no one expected them to do the same for jury duty.

There was a sameness, a blandness, and a restrictive quality to how women were supposed to look. Most of us conformed. We wore dresses—for a few years shirtwaist dresses—and skirts and sweaters. Pants were for roughing it in the country or for those few women who didn't care how they looked but wanted to be comfortable. If skirt lengths went up, we shortened our skirts; if they went down, we lengthened them. At least once a year, I would take a pile of clothes to my dressmaker to make whatever alterations were necessary to keep me in style. We all wore girdles, no matter how slim we were; and, of course, we all wore brassieres. If our breasts were too small, we wore falsies. For a few years we wore scratchy crinoline petticoats. All of this was to achieve the perfect figure of the times: big breasts, small waists, and well-concealed thighs. We dressed like ladies when we went anywhere: to school meetings, to social gatherings, and—certainly—to work. The dress code was even more rigid for city dwellers. We were expected to wear high heels, stockings with straight seams, hats, and gloves. For a few years I even wore hats with veils; it was considered feminine and sexy. I had gloves for every season and even carried white cotton gloves in the heat of the summer.

This conformity extended to makeup, hairstyle, and even jewelry. We all wore lipstick, powder, and rouge and kept our hair long or short, bouffant or straight, whatever fashion dictated. If pearl necklaces were the acceptable jewelry, that's what we all wore; when it changed to gold chains, we all bought gold chains and put our pearls away. Looking like everyone else was what was most of us did. I know I ruined my feet by wearing high-heeled, pointed-toe pumps for years. At the insistence of my daughter, who felt we would be more effective if we looked like ladies, I even wore high heels and carried gloves when I went on marches and protest demonstrations in the 1960s.

I confess that I was like most women of my class and generation in taking most of these unwritten social conventions for granted. Despite the 1953 Kinsey Report on women, which found that half of the nearly 6,000 women interviewed said that they had not been virgins when they married, I still abided by the traditional sexual mores that granted men more sexual latitude than women. We called it the "double standard." Not all of us were virgins when we married, but most of us said that we were. Most of us didn't talk frankly, even with our closest women friends, about sex or our bedroom lives. There must have been many women like me who had never been given basic sexual information by our mothers and had scarcely talked about sexuality before our first sexual relationship.

In 1964 I went back to my job at the Alumnae Advisory Center, still on a part-time basis, but with increased working hours. My year spent interviewing employers had been sobering. It gave me a new understanding of how hard it was for all women—even young ones—to find satisfying employment with the promise of training and eventual promotion. I witnessed firsthand how deeply segregated and limited employment opportunities for women were. It was discouraging to find employers, by and large, unwilling to show any flexibility in their hiring practices while admitting to acute labor shortages in many fields.

Although the majority of the women who came to see me were still looking for part-time work, they were more serious than those we had seen a few years earlier. They were younger, more motivated, more goal oriented, and more realistic and knowledgeable about the kinds of preparation and the compromises that they might have to make. I, too, had changed; I was tougher and found myself pushing applicants not only to do their own research on what they wanted to do but also to use initiative in convincing potential employers why they should be hired, even outlining the jobs they saw themselves doing. Sometimes it worked.

Some women, with skills and experience in writing, editing, graphics, fundraising, or in public relations, set up businesses in their homes. One woman read an article in the *New York Times* about a new organization that was still in the planning stage. She wrote to the one person named in the article, the head of the project, expressed her interest, requested an interview, and outlined what she thought she could contribute. She was hired for a job that she helped develop at hours she could manage. Another woman started a much-needed after-school recreation program in her local public school for children of full-time working mothers. After a successful year as a volunteer, she wrote a grant proposal, which included a salary line for herself in the project's budget. When the project was funded, she became the paid part-time executive director.

About this time an organization called Catalyst set up a pilot program for team teachers and social workers—two women sharing one job. The program was privately funded for several years in the hope that it would be successful and that employers would be willing to continue it. I observed the program with great interest, but it never really took hold. Although the pilot program folded, Catalyst continued to serve as a strong advocate for part-time employment and to help women secure seats of power on corporate boards.

By 1964 many women were seriously considering going back to school. Some had been taking noncredit courses for years, intimidated by tests or other course requirements. The thought of taking the GRE (Graduate Record Examination) terrified women who had been away from school for a long period. As special programs for women emerged, some of these requirements were eased: the GREs were not uniformly required; sometimes "life credit" was substituted for some course credits; and a few programs provided special adult education counselors to help returning women complete the application and entrance process.

Women were beginning to express anger about the age discrimination they found and couldn't change, both in jobs and in graduate and professional schools. We were a few years away from the birth of affirmative action, and employers and schools could do pretty much as they pleased. Thirty-five was the cut-off age for a number of professional schools, yet many women who had spent time raising their children were almost, or were already, thirty-five before they could consider their professional needs. One employer told me he wouldn't hire a "mature" woman for the job he listed with us because the company took up two floors and they all used the stairs to go from office to office. When I pushed him on what he meant by "mature," he said not over thirty-two because that was his wife's age, and she didn't like to climb stairs.

Middle-class lifestyles were beginning to adjust to this new cohort of women workers. I began to hear about how family members were being asked to assume household responsibilities. Children were given modest household and grocery shopping chores. Even husbands were asked to stay at home certain evenings to care for the children and to help them with their homework while the new career woman was at a class or a meeting. One woman who had a regular evening meeting once a week right after dinner left the dishes with the understanding that her family would clean up. The first few times that she found the dishes waiting for her in the sink when she came home, she decided to leave the dishes until her family finally did them, even if it took a few days. Other women followed the same principle: If someone forgot to buy the sugar on the shopping list, it was instructive for the family to go without sugar for a day or so, until whoever was assigned this task did it. If children didn't clean up their rooms properly, women learned to close the doors. Women also learned—sometimes painfully—that if they expected help around the house from members of their family, they would have to lower their housekeeping standards. For many it was a worthwhile trade-off.

■ 8
A NEW JOB AT BARNARD

With the Kennedy assassination in 1963, followed by racial conflicts and the seemingly endless war in Vietnam, there was a darkening in the social climate. I became aware of the depth of the historic discrimination against people of color; I supported the burgeoning civil rights movement and applauded the activism on the part of many young people. I watched my daughter and her friends—all students at Oberlin College—not only organize speaking engagements and fundraising events but also go south to work on voter registration. I was pleased that Nancy had chosen Oberlin, which had long been committed to social justice. During the nineteenth century the college assisted slaves through the Underground Railroad, and during the 1960s, the college provided bail money for Oberlin students arrested for civil rights work.

I joined the growing number of Americans, young and old, who regularly participated in marches and demonstrations to register support for the developing civil rights movement and to protest the United States's role in Vietnam. Although Bernie shared my commitment to peace and civil rights, he never went with me on one of these marches. He was overworked and his medical responsibilities took all his strength. As the years passed, he showed less interest in social issues and became a much more private person. Although I understood his withdrawal, it saddened me. It was one more indication of his precarious health.

The struggle for women's rights became part of the tumultuous 1960s. The President's Commission on the Status of Women produced a comprehensive report in 1963 that led to the foundation of the Interdepartmental Committee on the Status of Women, the Citizens Advisory Council on the Status of Women, and the establishment of state commissions on women throughout the United States. This was followed by two major pieces of legislation, the Equal Pay Act of 1963 and the Civil Rights Act of 1964, which included Title VII, prohibiting discrimination based on sex, a last-minute addition by a Southern congressman in a desperate attempt to defeat the bill.

By 1965 I saw dramatic changes in the lives of middle-class women, changes that were happening at a much faster rate than any of us had anticipated. The birth control pill, the Kinsey Report, the sexual revolution, and expanded options for women made the "foreseeable future" referred to in the Women's Bureau projections quite different from what we had been led to expect. Women were marrying later or not at all, and they were having fewer children. There were more divorces, and sometimes these were initiated by women with children, a phenomenon almost unheard of until that time. These changes in the family structure had a strong impact on employment. Although middle-class women with families still admitted to preferring part-time employment, more and more women were willing to work full time to further their careers and, in some cases, to provide for their families. More women were going to professional school full time, and, after completing a rigorous program, it was natural that they would continue working full time, hoping to make the most of their late starts into professional careers. As more women chose full-time study and work, they would be able to consider, advocate, and negotiate for equality in education and the workplace more effectively.

The social upheaval of these years and the new interest in women's equality produced a certain restlessness in me, which translated into some discontent with my job. Although I understood there would always be a need for part-time employment, I saw another struggle coming to the fore as more women decided to work full time. I was still a long way from understanding all the inequities facing women, but I could see that achieving equal opportunities and equal pay were pressingly important. I felt I had gone as far as I could go at the Alumnae Advisory Center, but I wasn't sure what to do next.

I looked to community colleges, most of which were established after World War II to meet the needs of the growing number of students who were seeking an alternative to four-year colleges. Many community college students were from working-class families and a fair number were adult women. I sent my résumé to several community colleges in the metropolitan area, hoping to find a position helping women students and alumnae find jobs. It never occurred to me that I would be rejected without even being granted an interview. But that's what happened. I received a few responses saying that, although my experience was excellent, they couldn't consider me because I didn't have a graduate degree.

In the spring of 1965 I received a telephone call from the office of the president of Barnard College, Rosemary Park, asking me to make an appointment to talk with her. I hardly knew her then, and my first thought was that she wanted to discuss my activities as chair of the Barnard Alumnae Advisory Vocational

Committee. To my surprise, she told me that Ethel Paley, the director of the placement office, was leaving, and she asked me to take over. She commended me on my work at the Alumnae Advisory Center, which she had been following, as well as my activities on the alumnae committee, which, at my suggestion, had recently begun to hold vocational meetings for small groups of students. As we talked at length about my interests and experience, President Park indicated that she was prepared to support the expansion of alumnae services as well as any other new ideas that I might have, if they seemed appropriate.

I had two weeks to decide. My meeting with President Park was so positive that I came away feeling that this might be just the right job for me. Working at Barnard would also permit me to take graduate courses at Columbia when I was ready. I hesitated for two reasons. Although I was ready for a new experience, once again I would be working primarily with middle-class women, the majority very young. Second, I hesitated to take on a full-time job. David was still in high school, and I was constantly trying to spare Bernie further household responsibilities. When we talked about the job offer at length, I was astonished that Bernie encouraged me to accept it. He felt I was ready and could manage the time, and he pointed out that I would gain valuable administrative experience, which I could subsequently use if I wanted to work in a different setting. I would later realize how prescient he was.

When I started working at Barnard in September 1965, I didn't realize that I would spend eighteen years of my life there as an administrative officer in two distinct jobs, first as director of placement for eight years, and then, for the following eleven years, as director of the Women's Center. From 1972 to 1973 the two jobs overlapped, and I spent a year working half time on each. These eighteen years enabled me to work with women on issues that touched the lives of many women, not only the privileged few at Barnard.

Despite my experience first as a Barnard student and later as an active alumna, I was unprepared for my job as a Barnard administrator. Most department heads had been in their jobs for years. There were no personnel department, no handbook of rules for administrators, and little communication among administrators, merely an unspoken layer of tradition that everyone seemed to honor. When I started my administrative work at Barnard, it was a bit like stepping back fifty years in time. Despite the current social unrest in the world outside, I felt a complacency throughout the college. In 1965 Barnard was, for the most part, politically removed. I found little interest in or discussion about activity in civil rights, the war in Vietnam, or even the changing expectations for women.

Walking into this atmosphere, where people did things I didn't understand "because that's the way they have always been done at Barnard," made me feel like an outsider. This wasn't a new feeling, but a rather familiar one—one that had surfaced in my childhood and reappeared, from time to time, when I sensed I didn't belong. I had learned to live with and accept this feeling; in truth, it was a mixed blessing. As a child and as an adolescent feeling like an outsider had been acutely painful, and I would have given almost anything to fit in, to be accepted by my family, my peers, the adults around me, whatever group was popular. But as this feeling accompanied me into adulthood, I sometimes found it sharpened my perceptions. This outsider's perspective enabled me to make critical judgments and important decisions that, as part of the establishment, I might not have considered or had the courage to initiate. It had served me well during the 1950s, when I had dared to question aspects of women's lives at a time when few others did.

Throughout my life I've had ambivalent feelings about belonging. Sometimes the ache to be accepted was so strong that I would actually pray to be invited to a party where I knew I would be bored if I went. When I married a doctor, had two children, and was "just like everyone else," I took a distinct pleasure in "doing the right thing." But nothing was ever enough, and I never outgrew the strong feeling that I was different—an outsider. Gradually, I learned to trust my judgment, while, at the same time, admitting that if I was to be effective as an innovator, I could learn to work within a traditional setting. Coming to Barnard brought back these old feelings with intensity.

A few months before starting my new job, I thought a great deal about the young women that I would be working with. They weren't a completely new constituency; I had been seeing recent graduates at the Alumnae Advisory Center and also groups of Barnard students at meetings of our alumnae committee. The prospect of working with young women who were at the start of their adult lives and, thus, in a position to make better career plans than their mothers excited me. I felt certain that the dramatic changes affecting women's lives in the work world were just the start of vast social changes.

Once I started working at Barnard, however, I realized that my optimism was somewhat unrealistic. I began to understand firsthand something I had learned years ago in an introductory sociology course: it is easier to change a law than an attitude. I was disappointed to find that, even in 1965, the aspirations of most undergraduates and recent alumnae were not qualitatively different from those of my classmates who graduated in the late 1930s and early 1940s. Although I knew that the climate in the broader world of work was improving and that opportunities for women were expanding, most of these bright, young women still considered marriage and family to be their primary goals—even those who had done brilliantly in college and had entered graduate school. There were of course exceptions, but there have always been exceptions. Accomplished and talented artists, thinkers, writers, dancers, and others with strong inner drives all testify to the fact that women only needed opportunities to achieve success, provided that their drive and talent were large enough and that they had the encouragement and support from at least one mentor, parent, or other caring adult. But without a clear sense of their own worth and abilities, most young women still placed internal limits on their aspirations.

I knew something these young women didn't know. I was aching to tell them an important truth if they could but hear me. I wanted them to take career planning seriously; I wanted them not to settle for low-level jobs with no chance for advancement because they were planning on marriage. I knew that many would be returning to work when their children were old enough, wishing they had more seriously reflected on the personal sacrifices involved in this and had considered a career when they were in college. I wished that I could help them avoid finding themselves in the situation of many regretful alumnae. I wanted their lives to be different from the alumna who reported she had been awarded a fellowship for graduate school and had given it up after one semester to get married. Or another who told me she was one course away from completing her course work for her Ph.D. in psychology when her husband was transferred to another part of the country and she dropped out of the program. Again and again, I heard these women say, "Why didn't someone make us finish? We didn't take ourselves seriously. We could have managed." Their remarks haunted me. I knew that, when they deferred to family pressures, they had simply chosen to do what was socially acceptable. It was almost like the child, familiar to all of us, who balked at practicing the piano and quit after a few months, only to grow up and wail to her or his parents, "Why didn't you make me take piano lessons when I was little?" I came to understand that these were personal, very individual, and often painful decisions. It was not easy to break out of the mold.

I started to pay attention to the messages given to these young college women, messages from their families, the faculty, their advisors, their peers, and society at large. Although I don't think young women (we called them "girls" then) came to Barnard primarily to find a husband, it was assumed that, along with acquiring a first-rate education, they would become more eligible for marriage to young men with similar educational backgrounds. Employment was acceptable for a few years, but it was simply a prologue to their "real" work as wives and mothers. In 1965 most entry-level jobs for young women college graduates, with the exception of those in government agencies and in secondary school teaching, were still clerical and secretarial. The message was clear. Each year representatives from large companies and government agencies came to the Columbia and Barnard campuses to recruit talented employees. The recruiters talked to the men at Columbia about management training opportunities, and then came across the street to talk with Barnard women about openings for service representatives in such organizations as the New York Telephone Company or about learning typing and stenography for secretarial positions in such sought-after fields as publishing, public relations, or fashion.

Wherever they looked, students saw women in low-level jobs. Barnard itself was no exception. There were young women in offices throughout the college working as receptionists and secretaries. The college, like other employers, took advantage of the fact that many overqualified women college graduates were willing to take these poorly paid jobs with no futures. This image was often reinforced for students in their summer work experiences where the only women they saw in permanent positions were young women who were clerks, receptionists, and secretaries, and—alternatively—gray-haired women who had been in their jobs for many years training young men to be managers.

One way to avoid the low-level-job trap was to go to graduate school. And many young women did just that. There was a shortage of college teachers and ample fellowship money available. Barnard faculty, who were the most important influence on students' lives, encouraged their bright students to continue their studies and become college teachers. During the middle and late 1960s over half of the graduating class at Barnard applied to graduate school. Some were serious about their goals, but for many who had done well academically it was a prestigious alternative to learning shorthand and typing and becoming just another secretary. It was almost as good as saying you were engaged. Some young women told us they applied because it delayed making any career decisions. Many were accepted and didn't go, often because they had to take a full-time job to support a husband who had received a draft deferment by going to graduate school. Or if they did start, many women didn't stick it out to the end.

On the one hand, Barnard faculty prodded their top students to go to graduate school; on the other hand, some still viewed women through a stereotyped lens. I saw this in several faculty letters of recommendation, which were an important part of a student's or an alumna's record. It was not uncommon to read statements such as "She has a pleasant demeanor," "She is bright but not pushy in class," "She is attractive and well dressed," or "She is someone you would like to have around." Some comments limited expectations and abilities: "She would make a good school psychologist" or "a fine high school teacher." These statements were all made by men, and I find it hard to believe that male professors would write similarly about their male students.

When I looked at some national and international statistics, I was disturbed to find that in 1965 the proportion of women in the professions was lower in the United States than in most countries throughout the world: Women were 9 percent of all full professors (mainly in the fields of home economics, nursing, and physical education), 8 percent of all scientists, 6.7 percent of all physicians, 3.5 percent of all lawyers, and 1 percent of all engineers.

I longed to talk to colleagues about what I saw as obstacles and problems for our students and, even more, to share ideas of what we could do to help them plan for their futures by taking advantage of some of the broadening of options for women. But communication among administrative officers was rare, and even rarer between administrators and faculty.

I gradually began to meet members of the professional network of placement and personnel officers. The most important organizations I joined were the ECPO (Eastern College Personnel Officers) and the Seven Sister college placement directors. These groups, sharing common concerns on procedures and policies, reinforced the status quo I was finding at Barnard. Surprisingly, the membership of ECPO included *both* placement officers and recruiters, although it seemed to me that this could pose a conflict of interest for placement officers. I was troubled, too, that the membership was largely men, due no doubt to the fact that most of the recruiters and many of the directors at large university placement offices were men. This also explained the heavy emphasis at these annual meetings on addressing the needs of employers, with the major focus on opportunities for men.

As with most professional associations, the highlight was the annual meeting, held each fall at a different large summer resort, with a full range of recreational facilities and lots of free time for partying and sports. I dreaded these annual meetings, but I attended to make and to maintain contacts for our students and alumnae. I always felt uncomfortable, but, little by little, I found a few kindred spirits who shared my frustration over the strong male bias of the meetings. The most important of these was Martha Green, the placement director of Marymount College. A Radcliffe graduate, married, and the mother of three children, Martha was a few years younger than I, smart, perky, funny, and slightly offbeat. She has always distinguished herself by wearing an eclectic array of slogan buttons, some political, others cause-oriented, and some just plain silly, ranging from "Reagan for Shah" to "Block Bork" to "Pass the ERA" to "Sleeping Is an Art" to "Funky Is Chic." We met at one of the boring morning sessions and, from that moment, we became allies and friends. We loved to talk about the sexism at these conferences and to make fun of the limited understanding about women's career goals expressed by most of the conference participants, whether male or female. A decade later I was able to lure her to Barnard as the director of career services, and for several years we worked together on a number of projects.

In an attempt to help redress the male bias of the ECPO, I volunteered to serve on the program committee, and, after several years of constant prodding, we invited a woman to be the keynote speaker—a first in the history of the ECPO. We chose a superbly qualified woman, Bernice Sandler, the director of the Project on the Status and Education of Women of the Association of American Colleges. A dynamic speaker, she thoughtfully and realistically described the employment picture for women, emphasizing the new and broadening options. I regarded the half-empty conference room that morning with anger and dismay. Many of the men had skipped this part of the program to play golf. Even some of the women had decided this could not be important and didn't attend.

I never felt at ease with the ECPO and disapproved of their official policy of protecting the rights of recruiters to visit campuses. Considered against the background of rising student unrest and protests directed against such companies as Dow Chemical—which was manufacturing napalm, used in the Vietnam War—this protection seemed unconscionable, honoring corporate values over student and social concerns. With this clear endorsement from their professional association, however, many college placement officers publicly sided with recruiters; a handful of universities and colleges took this protection a step too far, calling the police in response to student protests rather than holding dialogues between students and administrators on recruitment policies.

Becoming part of the Seven Sister college placement directors was another important new experience. I learned that the Seven Sister colleges kept in close touch with each other at several levels: presidents, deans, financial aid directors, admissions directors, and placement directors. From time to time they met to share information and discuss common issues. The groups were informal: no chairs, no bylaws, no formal procedures. I was welcomed into a tightly knit group, most of whom I had met earlier through the Seven College Vocational Workshops. Most were about my age or older, and two were close to retirement. They had all been in their jobs over twenty years, most of them all their working lives. They kept in touch with each other on a regular basis, shared information, and met at one of their college campuses for several days once a year. I was touched that they maintained contact with their retired predecessors and, when possible, included them in the social part of their annual meetings.

Joining this long-standing group was productive though sometimes exasperating. I was eager to learn, ask questions, and work with them. They cared deeply about their students, their alumnae, and their institutions and went to great lengths to represent their constituency and to learn about job opportunities. From the beginning, the group made it clear that they expected me to fit in and to absorb their wisdom. They did their jobs pretty much as they had always done and were proud of the way they functioned and of the contacts they had made with federal agencies, independent schools, and a wide range of employers. As a highly respected, elite group with entrenched conservative convictions, these women exerted substantial power and sent out strong messages to employers and students and alumnae.

They could see no need for change, and, when I made my first suggestion—at the meeting I attended after one year in my job—that we collectively inform recruiters that they must interview women for the same kinds of jobs that they interviewed men for or we would no longer invite them to our campuses, I was reprimanded. The director of the Wellesley office, Joan Bishop, took me aside and told me that I should wait until I had more experience before expressing such radical ideas. Later that same day, she gave me a small gift that she had just purchased for me. I didn't understand this gesture, though I now see that perhaps the gift was to offset her criticism. I cite this as an example of my relationship with my new "sisters" which, while becoming closer, I also found confusing. They accepted me but kept a firm, polite distance, usually opposed my new ideas, and never let me forget that I was a newcomer and had better watch my step.

I had come to Barnard with much to learn about administration and with a determination to see young women make the most of their opportunities. Initially, I felt isolated in my own office, where I and a staff of eight were responsible for a number of functions. In addition to our major purpose—to help students and alumnae of all ages make career plans and to find jobs—we collected and maintained all faculty and employers' recommendations, handled FBI security investigations for Barnard women being considered for jobs in federal agencies, ran a thriving baby-sitting service, did all personnel recruiting and interviewing for support staff jobs throughout the college, and worked with the Barnard Alumnae Advisory Vocational Committee on a number of projects. I was troubled to find some staff members, many of whom had been working in the placement office for some time, doing their specific jobs with little interest in or even knowledge of what else went on in the office and quite resistant to change. As I asked questions about each staff member's work, I could see that I wasn't endearing myself to everyone and that I had to move slowly.

On my first day, when I had asked for a typewriter, my staff looked at me with horror. They told me no director of any department used a typewriter; that's what secretaries were for. There was also just barely enough space for a typewriter; my office was tiny, large enough to hold only a desk and desk chair, two straight chairs, and one small bookcase. The second chair could only be used when the door was closed. Nevertheless, I insisted. I managed to rearrange the furniture, discarding one chair, so that the typewriter would fit—though barely. I was accustomed to thinking and writing on a typewriter, and, until the era of word processors, I couldn't imagine being without one. Word processors didn't arrive at Barnard until after my retirement.

I was fortunate to report to President Park. A petite woman with a quiet, yet decisive, manner, she always listened carefully when I presented my plans for new projects. She made it very clear that, when she brought in new administrative officers, she was prepared to support changes that she approved of. She was a wonderful boss, interested, accessible, and receptive, and I was sorry to see her leave in 1967.

I gradually began to restructure the office. I was able to transfer the collection and maintenance of recommendations, along with the government security checking, to the office of the dean of studies; to make the baby-sitting service a separate, student-run entity; to help students set up their own bartending agency so that they would not have to work for less pay than the men at the Columbia Bartending Agency; and, in time, to move personnel recruiting for the college to a newly created college personnel office. This left us free to concentrate on what I perceived to be our mission: to help students find part-time and summer jobs; to see that students and alumnae received the information they needed to make appropriate career plans; to administer the new federal Work-Study program; and to help graduating seniors and alumnae sort out their interests and needs and to find permanent jobs. Whenever I had a staff opening, I was elated. In a gentle way, I sometimes helped create openings by encouraging a recalcitrant staff member to move on. I slowly began to build a staff that worked well together and that shared my concern about expanding women's career goals. Together we renamed the placement office, created a new identity for the office, and rethought recruitment policies.

I changed the name of the office to the Barnard Placement and Career Planning Office. Traditionally, all career planning offices, for both men and women, were called simply placement offices. This was fine for men because they knew they had to plan a career and, hence, used all the services their college office provided. I soon learned of some distinctions between men and women's alumni/ae services: I learned that most men's college placement offices didn't serve alumni, believing that if an alumnus required further help several years after graduation, he was deemed a loser and not worthy of receiving help from his alma mater. Alumni offices sometimes served headhunters and kept the names of graduates in good jobs who could be lured to better jobs. Alumni clubs, particularly clubs for men's ivy league colleges, had old boys networks, lists of successful alumni who were ready to help fellow alumni find a good job.

I hoped that the renamed office would entice more students to come in for career planning. Seniors were required to attend one vocational meeting and mandated to have an interview with one of our staff to discuss postgraduation plans. No one took these requirements seriously, and many students deliberately avoided our office, either because they thought they weren't ready to think about their futures or because they were too anxious to do more than apply to graduate school.

Then came recruitment. I consulted Athena Constantine, the soon-to-become-permanent director of the Columbia Placement Office, who had successfully run that office for years, covering for the director, who was often ill. I found her to be particularly sensitive to the needs of women, possibly due to her own long experience working in a male environment. She had been in her job for years, doing most of the work of director without the title and salary that went with it, and it took much too long for the Columbia administration to finally give her the recognition that she deserved. Throughout my years in the office of placement and career planning, I could always count on Athena for support and understanding.

I described our meager recruiting program to her and the limited jobs that were being offered to our women. She understood immediately and agreed to include Barnard women in the Columbia recruiting program. This signaled the end of a fully autonomous, but very limited, Barnard recruiting program and offered our young women opportunities to have interviews with a broad array of recruiters. There was, of course, no assurance that the recruiters—who were almost all men—would describe the same opportunities to women, and I was initially disappointed in the small number of Barnard women who took advantage of this new program. It was an important first step, and I was delighted when I heard about the first "real" offer to a Barnard graduating senior for an honest-to-goodness management training job in a large company.

■ 9
FURTHER OBSTACLES: DISCRIMINATION AND WOMEN'S LIMITED EXPECTATIONS

n January 1967 Bernie died suddenly of a second heart attack at the age of fifty-one. I had learned to live with his chronic condition, assuming somehow that he would live out his normal life. Although he seldom alluded to his fragile health, I suspect he knew the truth. On occasion, he would say that eventually the disease would get him, and that his lifespan would be considerably shortened. I would shudder when he said this and try to put it out of my mind. How can one prepare for such a loss?

Initially, I was in a state of shock. My children and I were surrounded by family, friends, and colleagues. What I recall most vividly from those first few days was listening, as we huddled in our grief, to a recording of the *Fauré Requiem,* which David was rehearsing for a school choral program.

Bernie was a remarkable man, highly respected and admired by his colleagues and loved by his patients. Despite his eighteen-year bout with a terminal illness, he lived a full professional life as an internist, successfully combining research and patient care with administration. In addition to his private practice, he was a pioneer in prepaid group medical care. As a founding member of one of the original participating groups of HIP (Health Insurance Plan of Greater New York) and, for the last ten years of his life, as the director of the HIP Central Manhattan Medical Group, he devoted an inordinate amount of time and energy to establishing a new kind of group practice. His major concern was providing top-quality, affordable medical care, and he often said that, although it would take years for the country to be ready for what we now call single-payer healthcare, HIP was a small and noble start.

Although it often seemed as if the professional world had first claim on his time and attention, the children and I treasured special memories of our relationship with Bernie and his expressions of love for us. For me, it was the way he was always there for me when I needed him: in any emergency, no matter how small, he would take over, calmly and reassuringly, canceling professional appointments if necessary. And the children remember the times he spent with them, how they shared interests and hobbies and how he expressed pride in their achievements. Even my mother, who had opposed our marriage, had come to appreciate, admire, and depend on Bernie over the years. In her way, I believe she cared about him deeply and felt his death acutely.

In many ways Bernie was very traditional. He accepted without question the different social roles prescribed for men and women on the basis of sex. Yet, once I returned to work, Bernie was supportive of, interested in, and even proud of me. It may have started with the feeling that my working was a kind of insurance for the family, should something happen to him, but I like to think that his perceptions about women's lives and aspirations had expanded.

I returned to work quickly, perhaps too quickly. I didn't give myself time to mourn. I was grateful that I could immerse myself in a full-time job and in nightly graduate courses, which I had started the fall before Bernie died. But nothing could ease the tremendous ache—an ache that sometimes felt like a physical pain. Although I think I projected the appearance of confidence, my self-image was badly shaken.

Despite the comfort of family and friends, outside of the home I became a woman alone. I experienced all kinds of unpleasantness that I had been shielded from when my husband was alive. The landlord pressured me to move, since large apartments were in great demand. The superintendent would raise his voice unpleasantly when I asked him to fix something. And, when probating the will, my lawyer, who was Bernie's uncle, treated me as if were a child. After a few months I transferred all my legal matters to another lawyer, a difficult move, but one I saw as necessary for my peace of mind.

Those first few months are a blur, but somehow I managed. During this time I decided to buy a bicycle, a small symbolic gesture of independence. Ever since we had traveled to Amsterdam and had seen how many people used bicycles as their means of transportation, even to an evening opera, I had wanted to bike in New York. Bernie had disapproved strongly, saying it was dangerous. Although he never said so, I suspect he also thought it inappropriate for a doctor's wife to be riding a bicycle through the streets of New York. To the amusement of Barnard students and with the occasional "Hi, Grandma" from truck drivers, I rode my bike regularly to work and, in fact, all over the city. After a long day in the office, it felt good to get on my bike, toss aside work problems, and enjoy the wonderful feeling of flying down Riverside Drive.

Two family events drove home our loss with an acute poignancy. Within six months of Bernie's death, Nancy graduated from Oberlin College and David from high school. David and I, and my mother too, went to Nancy's graduation. It was a bittersweet day. How her father would have loved to see her graduate with honors from a college that had suited her so well—a college that challenged her intellectually while providing a base for social activism, a college that enabled her to spend her junior year at the London School of Economics, living on her own, and creating many lifelong friendships.

David graduated from high school, winning awards in math and in poetry. He also elected to go to Oberlin but had a completely different experience from his sister. David was more private, and college was not a good experience for him. At the time he went to Oberlin, the student antiwar movement was at its height. He majored in math, which was easy for him, and took the option of substituting the pass/fail system for grades. His earlier intellectual curiosity seemed to dissipate, and he became another disaffected, antiestablishment student. It was a small miracle that he didn't actually drop out of college.

It was easier to blame David's disenchantment with college on the anti-establishment sentiment that was then pervading many college campuses than to attribute it to David himself, but we were soon to learn that David had psychological problems, which surfaced during his late adolescence. I had worried about David for years, noting small aberrations and his tendency to spend too much time by himself. Bernie constantly reassured me, saying David was a late bloomer and would catch up socially in time. At college he was encouraged to seek psychiatric help. I was not prepared, however, for the news that when David went for his draft physical, he was immediately classified 4-F for psychological reasons.

Nancy decided to defer plans for graduate school and to live at home for a year so that I wouldn't be alone. She found a job in New York, and despite my protestations and my insistence that I wanted to start living by myself as soon as possible, she was determined that we live together. We tried to give each other space and independence in our large apartment, but, after having tasted living on her own during college, Nancy found it difficult to return home, and I didn't readily adjust to the idea that Nancy was now an adult and not a little girl. After a few months we both agreed that it wasn't working out. With my encouragement and blessings she found her own apartment nearby, where she stayed until she went to graduate school.

After Bernie's death, my mother and I grew closer. She extended herself in ways that were new to me: she called me more often than she had; she showed a new interest in my life; and she offered her support. I appreciated her attention, although we still seldom agreed on anything, large or small, personal or political. Her attitude about my working changed: now she could see it was important for me and, on occasion, she came to hear me speak publicly.

Although we shared more than we ever had, it simply seemed too late to fundamentally change our relationship. Still, we saw more of each other than we used to and we were careful to treat each other with respect.

In the fall of 1966, just months before Bernie died, I started graduate school. I was a full-time college administrator, forty-eight years old. I registered in the master's degree program in Student Personnel in Higher Education at Teachers College, the graduate school of education at Columbia University. It was a pared down, yet practical, realization of my lifelong dream to earn a graduate degree. I selected this program because it was accessible and manageable, and I hoped that it would add to my understanding of my work as an administrator as well as to provide new links with people at Teachers College who shared some of my concerns. It took me four years of evening classes to complete the degree.

The atmosphere at Teachers College in the middle and late 1960s certainly didn't reflect the unrest expressed throughout the country. Occasional references were made to civil rights and to the antiwar movements in classes, and there were, of course, notices of demonstrations and actions on bulletin boards in public places. But I heard no mention of women's rights.

I was deeply disappointed in the program and in the institution itself. Not surprisingly, most of the heads of departments and tenured faculty were men. I found no interest in women, no acknowledgment of changes affecting women's lives, and no special attention to the needs of girls growing up in a changing society. I was particularly struck by this in courses on career development. I was dismayed to find that, as late as 1968, faculty members were still teaching the same theory that they had been teaching since the early 1930s, a theory based on the experiences and expectations of men. This was made particularly clear in the discussion of military service and how it affected career decisions. I soon understood that none of these researchers and teachers thought that women were seriously planning careers, even though more than half their students were women.

I learned little that was useful or timely about college administration and even less about career development, though many faculty members commanded wide respect in their fields. When I went to see one of the luminaries in career development to discuss my plan for a term paper in his course, he gave his approval in less than two minutes, hardly looking at me as he spoke. As I was leaving, I spontaneously blurted out that I was disappointed in his course, which didn't speak or seem to apply to women. He perked up and insisted that I come back and sit down and tell him what I found lacking. He made no effort to discuss the issue of women, but he was incredulous that I could find his course wanting, and he said over and over that no one had ever criticized his course before.

Although I was bored with many of the courses and dismayed by the arrogance and limited perspective of most of the faculty, I was determined to complete my degree and to make my graduate experience meaningful. I decided to use what I was learning about the aspirations and the sex-role expectations of Barnard students and alumnae as the basis for my term papers. I also initiated several studies that I doubt I would have conducted without the pressure of school. For this I am grateful to Teachers College. Two of my graduate school papers were later published in the *Journal of the National Association of Women Deans and Counselors,* although they were scarcely read either by the faculty person teaching the course or by my advisor. In fact, none of the faculty for whom I wrote papers on women ever commented directly on this aspect of my work.

The years between 1965 and 1970 were filled with dramatic change for American women. The momentum that had led to groundbreaking legal changes in the early 1960s accelerated and broadened, becoming—almost overnight—a live and healthy women's movement. In 1966 twenty-eight women founded NOW (National Organization for Women) and elected Betty Friedan as president. Initially, NOW focused on discrimination against women in the work place, but, within a few years, it broadened its scope to address sex discrimination in all spheres of life. Over the next decade NOW grew rapidly and, in time, became a strong activist feminist national organization with chapters throughout the country. The next few years saw the proliferation of new women's groups, including task forces, caucuses in professional associations, and expanded agendas for already-established women's groups. Pressure was building for the passage of the ERA (Equal Rights Amendment). This energy was evidence of an awakening feminist consciousness, and it gave me a feeling of great hope in my new job.

My first encounter with feminist activism took place right outside my door at Barnard. In the fall of 1967 two young faculty members, Kate Millett and Catharine Stimpson, picketed our office in support of NOW's first picketing of the *New York Times.* They were protesting the newspaper's policy of separate male and female help-wanted advertisements. I had barely met Kate Millett or Catharine Stimpson at the time, but, as I talked to them, I could see that these two vibrant women—"the two Kates" we used to call them—were passionate about rectifying such blatant inequities. For the few years they were at Barnard, each could be counted on to bring some of the emerging issues affecting women's lives to the attention of the college.

More than anything else, I was amused by the picketing. Although I was in complete sympathy, I felt these tactics were foolish and would scarcely affect a newspaper as important and prestigious as the *New York Times*. To my great surprise, NOW kept the pressure on the newspaper and on the EEOC (Equal Employment Opportunity Commission) until, a year later, both the EEOC and the New York Fair Employment Practices Commission forced all city newspapers to discontinue sex-segregated want ads.

Although I fully supported the movement for women's rights, I separated myself from the more "radical" branches of the women's movement. I questioned some of the issues and strategies advanced by the new women's liberation groups founded by radical women activists in the middle to late 1960s. Many of these women had become disenchanted with the subordinate role assigned to them in both the antiwar and the civil rights movement, and the refusal of these groups to include women's issues on their agendas. I watched with apprehension as groups such as WITCH (Women's International Terrorist Conspiracy from Hell), Red Stockings, and New York Radical Feminists turned their anger into organized public actions. I questioned the picketing of the Miss America pageant in Atlantic City in 1968, which became known as the bra-burning incident (although no bras were burned), the picketing of the New York City Marriage License Bureau to protest the institution of marriage, and the "hexing," "spooking," and other forms of guerilla street theater conducted at such institutions as the New York Stock Exchange. At the time, I felt these were divisive acts, fringe spectacles, that would alienate large numbers of women and men and would compromise the movement's ability to legislate for equality with mainstream support.

I hadn't yet fully grasped the magnitude of the ongoing upheaval. I needed the experience of working, often unsuccessfully, with young women who placed internal limits on their aspirations to see that acting out—however spectacularly—against the inequities experienced by women served a useful purpose and was even necessary. For all my progressive claims, I was still essentially a traditional, middle-class woman who believed that change should be brought about in "an orderly fashion." Although I spent all my waking hours thinking about achieving equality for women in the workplace, I still took pride in behaving like a "lady." Staging a sit-in at a male enclave didn't seem the right way to go about it.

My work with returning women continued to be an important part of my job. Their numbers kept growing and, as a group, they were quite different from those I had seen a decade before. Most of these alumnae were much more knowledgeable about how they would organize their lives to achieve their goals and much less concerned about getting their husbands' approval. Unlike young undergraduates and recent alumnae in the middle and late 1960s, who thought in terms of graduate school—too often with no concrete goal—these returning alumnae were quite realistic, selecting graduate or professional programs that led directly to jobs in fields where they were needed, such as social work, school counseling, librarianship, and teaching. Many were prepared to work or to complete their education as full-time employees or students.

The return-to-work movement was, on the whole, a success, although it never challenged the male establishment in any significant way. By and large, these returners entered "women's fields," where they were finally warmly received because of acute labor shortages. They performed their jobs with deep commitment, having labored long and hard to achieve their professional status. Their success, although largely unrecognized, broke down a number of myths about women's capabilities and was one of the forces that continued to spark the women's movement.

My long involvement with returners, their frustrations, and eventual successes prompted me to focus all my creativity on helping young women take advantage of their new, expanding opportunities. It seemed as if we were on the brink of a new era, and I saw my job as identifying discrimination and encouraging young women to aim high and realize their full potential.

By the late 1960s the professional schools that had refused admission to women or had accepted only token numbers started opening their doors to women. Most were not motivated by simple good will but were reluctantly responding to pressure from the growing number of women's rights groups and the stream of federal guidelines, executive orders, legislation and class action suits in the years between 1965 and 1969. Affirmative action had begun. Accepting women was such a new, unproven phenomenon that everyone understood that women candidates must have exemplary qualifications to even be considered for a job. It was also understood that women should be prepared to answer questions about their families, marriage plans, living arrangements, and other personal matters during their application interviews—questions that, a few years later, would be considered illegal.

I failed, however, to recognize the depth of this discrimination and how the lifting of established barriers in employment and education threatened not only the status quo but also the self-image of men. In general, men appeared to be extremely reluctant to consider including women in their professional lives on anything near an equal basis. For many, such a change was perceived as an attack on their masculinity, which they found unacceptable and frightening. That many women were not ready to take advantage of equal opportunity impressed upon me the powerful forces of fear and traditionalism—forces that would make the struggle against discrimination lengthy and difficult.

I heard many heartbreaking stories during the late 1960s. One young woman applying to medical school told me the admissions officer asked her how she expected to take care of her children: she was neither married nor engaged. Another student at the Harvard Business School, which had recently started admitting women, reported that corporate recruiters who came to the campus were still asking women, but not men, if they could type. One senior with a brilliant academic record recounted the discouraging interview she had when she applied to the graduate program in musicology at Yale. The admissions officer explained that the department was very small and admitted only half a dozen students each year. He was sure she would understand why they couldn't give one of those valuable places to a woman and suggested that she apply to a graduate program for piano teaching in the Midwest.

I shared in the discouragement and the sense of powerlessness that students expressed in the face of such common incidents. We felt somewhat impotent. Within a very few years, however, women enrolled in increasing numbers in all the professional schools traditionally regarded as only for men: medicine, law, business, architecture, engineering, and even music and gourmet cooking. The numbers were small at first, and the professional schools did not always graciously receive this new constituency. Initially, some schools even tried to pit white women applicants against minorities of both sexes in meeting quotas for their affirmative action programs.

Sex discrimination remained a constant problem during my eight years in career planning at Barnard. Sometimes it seemed that employers and professional schools didn't understand what was necessary to attract qualified women. This was particularly evident in some of the recruitment literature that was sent to our office. The copy for an investment bank brochure, whose cover portrayed two men in gray flannel suits, began "This booklet has just one objective: to persuade intelligent, aggressive, hardworking men who are about to complete their formal education to talk to us about a career in investment banking." The same firm repeatedly called Barnard for secretaries. A major airline's packet of recruitment literature, which included a handsome brochure describing management opportunities, opened, brazenly, "For young men on the way up." Throughout the booklet, opportunities were described for men, with photographs of young men in management positions and women as stewardesses, clerks, and secretaries. A special booklet for women entitled *Fun in Las Vegas* featured glamorous pictures of vacation spots where stewardesses might luxuriate between jobs. For a time I wrote directors of recruitment at the offending companies, explaining why Barnard couldn't circulate their literature, and invited them to correct and to broaden their material to include women. I even offered to help them revise their copy. The only response I ever received was one from the airline company informing me that they had sent us the wrong brochure, followed by a second brochure on opportunities for women as stewardesses and reservation agents.

Discrimination, however, was often more subtle. For example, when Columbia Business School started to recruit women, the admissions team held a women's day each spring. Prospective women candidates were invited to a program designed to give them a flavor of the graduate school, the faculty, and the student body. I attended several of these events and watched as students acted out case studies, an important part of their curriculum. I never saw a woman play one of the principals in the cases presented. When I asked the dean of admissions about what I considered a glaring omission, he told me that they used actual cases and that women had simply not been involved in any. He seemed surprised when I asked whether they might not imagine a few women as major players. He shrugged his shoulders and simply said that was the way it was. I could see that this was not a suggestion he was prepared to accept.

In some cases employers rejected women because they were unable to accommodate them. This was the experience of a student who had passed a civil service test for a summer job as a park ranger and was turned down because the federal government didn't have living facilities for women. Fortunately, she came in to report this disappointment, and I insisted that she write to the government demanding that they provide suitable accommodations for her. They did, but there were many other situations that didn't turn out as well.

I observed with impatience situations over which I had no control. Typical of these was the experience of one young woman who, after working as assistant to an account executive in a large advertising agency, was temporarily promoted to acting account executive when her boss left the agency. She performed well and, for over a year, assumed all the responsibilities of the job to the complete satisfaction of the clients. She told me proudly how one of her major accounts welcomed her weekly trip to their corporate office in White Plains. She was replaced by a man and told that she could never expect to be an account executive in that agency. It was simply not a job that could be held by a woman.

Sexist stereotypes about what women could and couldn't do were common. No one seemed particularly outraged over the accepted practice of firing a young teacher when she married on the grounds that she no longer needed to earn money. Similarly, no one seemed to think twice about the fact that, at initial corporate job interviews, prospective employers questioned women about marital plans, about how long they planned to stay, and about whether they could travel or transfer locations. These were not questions typically asked of corporate-bound young men. For one thing, men were not expected to stay. There was a kind of unwritten agreement that corporations undertook the training of young men even though, once trained, these men might leave for a better job or take time off for military service. Corporations were training the next generation of corporate officers and did not count women among them.

In fact, many women were not ready to make a lifelong commitment to full-time work. Compared with what they knew of women in the work force, marriage and having children often looked better. Besides, women could stop work at anytime and by staying home earn more approval from family and the community than by working. During this transition period, it was also probably true that those professional women who had achieved a modicum of success in their fields continued to tolerate—and, in fact, reinforce—the social conventions that defined women's place in the world of work.

In 1968 I proposed that the Seven Sisters college placement directors take group action, this time on the subject of recruitment literature. I suggested that we make an official statement—one that I was confident would receive approval from our college presidents—announcing that, as a group, we would no longer accept discriminatory recruitment literature. Once again my suggestion was turned down. I sensed that two of the women might have acceded, but the group pressure was so strong that they were silenced. The others were committed to maintaining the good will of employers at almost any cost. They were perfectly willing to wait for things to change in the normal course of events, and, besides, several said their students and alumnae were not offended by either the recruitment literature or employer's attitudes

At Barnard we expanded our program of inviting alumnae in the professions to come back to the campus to discuss their careers with students. By and large we found that these professional women had paid such a high price for their success that they couldn't imagine gaining professional status without difficult struggle and sacrifice. At a meeting on careers for women in medicine, an alumna physician spoke about her experience. A student asked her how many women there were in medical school class. She said there were two. Another asked her if she felt comfortable in this male bastion and whether it was true that her credentials had to be twice as good as those required of male applicants. She cheerfully and proudly answered yes to both these queries. She added that she liked being almost the only woman in the class and that she knew she was smarter than at least half the class. Finally, she stressed her conviction that extraordinary achievement was the only road to success in any male-dominated profession. We would later call this the queen bee syndrome. Throughout the late 1960s and early 1970s I was to find similar attitudes as I met and spoke with successful women. Given the realities of these professions and the way the old boys network operated to insure domination of the professions by like-minded white males, I could understand how hard it was for the few women who persisted.

I was reminded of a speech that Millicent McIntosh gave when she served as Barnard's president, which—although I had never heard it—was still remembered and became known as her "inspiration speech." She loved to talk to students about fulfilling their potential. She described her life, her marriage to a doctor who was the head of a department at the Columbia Medical School, her five children, and her more than full-time job. She used herself as an example of achievement, believing it would show undergraduates they could "have it all." But for most students in the 1950s and early 1960s her message lacked relevance. They were overwhelmed by a woman who seemed to be superhuman. Even in 1969, I feared the message would have been lost on most Barnard students.

I focused my attention on young women who were starting to consider careers. I knew that they still faced external limits: that it would take years to eliminate the deep-seated discrimination in kinds of jobs offered to women, in wages, in opportunities for advancement, and in admission to graduate and to professional programs. What bothered me most, however, were the internal personal limits that constrained many young women. Of course, I was in my forties when I became sensitized to discrimination against women, but here were young women who should have been enthusiastic about discovering the wide range of possibilities opening up for them. Why was there so little readiness to take advantage of these new opportunities? Most of these highly intelligent, often talented young women found it hard to envision themselves as independent professionals ready to make long-range plans. Many were fearful of considering careers in traditional male fields. I was dismayed to hear graduating seniors and young alumnae actually say that medical, law, and engineering schools were right to limit their admission of women because women were not a good risk. Even worse, I felt defeated when I heard young job seekers vehemently claim, "I wouldn't work for a woman," or, "I wouldn't want her job; she is an aggressive, unattractive woman, and I wouldn't want to end up like her."

I felt powerless as I saw graduating seniors give up their own career plans for expedient, unrewarding jobs to support young husbands in graduate school. It was infuriating to hear a recent graduate say that she was just looking for a job for a year or so. It didn't matter too much what the job was because she hoped to be getting married soon after that, although, when I pressed her, she admitted that there was no young man in the offing. It was exhilarating to help a graduating senior find a real management training job with a young financial firm. But I felt as if we had all failed when, a few months later, she called to tell us that she was giving up the job to plan her large wedding. But, at the age of these young women, I had chosen the same path. I had wrestled with confusion and pain about my inability to continue the independent life I had lived as an undergraduate. How I wished that I had had the courage and the conviction to oppose the social conventions that had kept me from pursuing a career when I graduated.

In the fall of 1969 I decided I needed to know more about what young Barnard women were thinking about work and its relation to the rest of their lives. I undertook a study of the relationship between what I then termed aspirations and sex-role expectations among a representative sampling of the senior class. My findings were based on extensive individual interviews with seventy seniors, 16 percent of the class. This group included a random selection of those who had come to our office at some point during their undergraduate years to talk about career plans, plus a number of those who had never approached our office but had responded to a letter I sent to all seniors with superior academic records. I compared the first group's aspirations and sex-role expectations with those of a second group of seventeen students chosen from among those who had been elected to Phi Beta Kappa or nominated for one of the prestigious fellowships—Woodrow Wilson, Marshall, Danforth, or Fulbright. Except for stronger vocational goals, there were no clear-cut differences in attitudes between the two groups.

Almost all the seniors I interviewed acknowledged that work would be an important part of their lives. Few, however, had made definite plans. The second group stood out: the same strong motivation that had brought them academic success propelled them to make career plans. Most were applying to law school, medical school, business school, graduate programs in the humanities, the arts and sciences, and had specific career goals in mind. But, when we talked about how they envisioned their family lives, most of them acknowledged that they probably would forsake or at least interrupt their careers—if necessary— when they were ready to have a family.

This common thread ran through all the interviews. Not surprisingly, most of the young women in both groups expressed concern about how they would balance the responsibilities of marriage, children, and work. In different ways they expressed anxiety and ambivalence about priorities and career commitments. Almost all felt that family came first.

Perhaps more important than their career perceptions were the many indications that most were still unable or unwilling to question traditional roles for women. Many valued men's approval more than their own independence. They appeared uncomfortable with the concept of equality. Several pointed out that most men are unable to separate masculinity from success and feel threatened by women who seem their equals. And most expressed concern over the risk of appearing "unfeminine" and "aggressive" by choosing a "conventionally male" career or a way of life that might be different.

Many were convinced that the sexes were *not* equal. Some women told me that men and women are different and that these differences should be maintained at all levels of society. More than once, I heard the statement that women's minds are inferior to men's. Most of these women accepted that men must provide and care for women. Several admitted that they enjoyed having men treat women with courteous deference—opening doors, giving women seats on the bus—and that they were perfectly willing to accept lesser positions in employment. A few volunteered that they enjoyed the "benefits" of being a woman and wouldn't want to risk giving them up.

Most discouraging were the attitudes expressed about the women's movement. Only four women said they belonged to any part of the movement; nineteen others believed the movement was needed but didn't participate. And an overwhelming number disapproved strongly of everything the movement represented. And this was in 1969! Those who approved of the movement gave the expected reasons: the time had come; an organized movement was necessary to exert pressure, and women must organize to bring about change. A few said the movement was making them aware of their own feelings about what women should do and be, and others approved of women beginning to demand their rights. Negative responses covered a wide spectrum, ranging from some views I had heard earlier about biological differences to opinions that struck me as reactionary. Some stressed that they abhorred the idea of group action or protest. Others spoke of the movement as a group of militant, aggressive women they could never support. Many who acknowledged the need for change said women must act as individuals to achieve goals of equality. One young woman labeled the women's movement as ridiculous; another said that women who belonged to the women's rights movement must all be single women who, if they had any expectation of getting married, would not feel this way.

Even among the group with strong vocational motivation, I heard notes of disapproval. One self-confident and optimistic senior felt she could individually overcome any personal discrimination she encountered. She was not interested in other women and thought a women's movement would mean that "mediocre" people would be given opportunities they "didn't deserve." Another expressed resentment that the women's movement might hurt her chance to make it in the business world.

This study was a very sobering experience for me. For the first time, I could see clearly that only a very small proportion of young women were ready to take advantage of these new options. I found that most of them—on the very brink of adulthood—felt ambivalent about their gender roles and this interfered with their career aspirations. Fear of deviating too far from the traditional model of femininity appeared again and again. Concerns about being perceived as aggressive, reluctance to participate in group action even when there was a recognized need for change, and an almost welcoming acceptance of an inferior social status all complicated the difficulties involved in making appropriate career choices. I found it painful to acknowledge that the internal limits most middle-class women accepted were even more difficult to overcome than the external limitations. It was even more painful to realize how deeply ingrained these limits were.

Why was I so surprised by this unwillingness to give up culturally entrenched positions? I had, after all, ample opportunity to observe many of these attitudes during the years that I had worked with adult women seeking to return to work. But I had never expected significant change then. Like my colleagues, I was accustomed to very small signs of progress, was grateful to have moved out of the 1950s, and was satisfied that women were even permitted to enter the male work establishment. That most of these women needed to work only part time had obscured the basic issue of equality. For as long as I could, I had clung to the belief that change should be effected gradually through education and legislation.

Probably no one in those years expressed it better than Alice Rossi, then a sociologist at Goucher College. Since 1964 she had been raising important questions and suggesting new ways of thinking about women's lives. Although her position is obvious today, in the 1960s she was a pioneer, a voice in the wilderness. Rossi set forth a strong case for male-female equality, insisting that equal sex-role expectations must be established at an early age. Although she acknowledged that progress had been made in ending discrimination and inequality in public life, she underscored the difficulties in removing the inequalities deeply embedded in everyday life. She stated unequivocally that, until girls are permitted and encouraged to develop freely as individuals rather than in traditional female patterns, women will continue to be unable to take advantage of all of the new legal guarantees of equality.

Rossi's work confirmed my own findings and deepened my understanding of the breadth of the problems women faced. By 1969 I found myself rethinking some of my earlier reservations about the women's liberation movement. I began to see the need for the actions sponsored by radical feminist groups. Most of the members of these radical groups—dubbed "women's libbers" by the mainstream press—were young women, veterans of the civil rights and antiwar movement. I could see that these young activists understood better than I the internal barriers women faced and were ready to take whatever dramatic steps they felt necessary to gain public attention for their cause.

I continued to feel more comfortable supporting such groups as the Women's Equity Action League, New Yorkers for Abortion Law Repeal, and all the caucuses, task forces, and commissions which sprang up in both the public and private sectors and devoted their energies to women's rights. I observed but did not participate in such public demonstrations as the counter-inauguration activities at the Nixon inauguration, where women activists railed against male chauvinism, or the protest at annual stockholders meeting of CBS (Columbia Broadcasting System), where a few women interrupted the meeting and charged CBS and the media with degrading and misrepresenting women in commercials and in programming, or even the sit-in at the *Ladies Home Journal* to protest the way women were portrayed in women's magazines, as well as the low number of women in good jobs in the field.

My initial confusion, and even disapproval, dissipated, and somehow I found myself quietly approving of issues that I had once thought were peripheral. I came to understand that I had to question all the givens about women. I came to acknowledge that the movement had to receive public attention, even if this meant sometimes behaving in an outrageous fashion. I was beginning to accept the need for a strong, diverse, and inclusive women's movement; I realized that I—a white, middle-aged, middle-class woman—was hardly in a position to decide which groups and which issues had credibility.

In the fall of 1969 the women's liberation group at Columbia University published a report on the status of women faculty at Columbia revealing that 24 percent of all doctoral degrees were earned by women but that only 2 percent of tenured professors at Columbia were women. This led to the Columbia Senate hearings on discrimination against women, and I was asked to testify. Although I was the only administrator speaking, I felt exhilarated to step outside of my traditional administrative role and present publicly some of the information and stories I had collected.

■ 10
A "GENTLE AGITATOR" IN THE TURBULENT 1960s

The first few years after Bernie's death were difficult ones. Although I felt myself growing stronger professionally, developing competence and confidence, taking more risks, and enjoying my work life as an administrator, at home I felt lost. I felt grief, self-pity, even resentment that life had been unfair to me. I seemed to be caught in a time warp. I relived the familiar childhood ache of not belonging, and I felt envious of other peoples' lives. I was ashamed of these feelings and very carefully concealed them from others.

I felt as if I had lost more than a husband: I had lost my identity. Coupled for twenty-five years, suddenly I was alone and bereft. I knew few unattached women, except at work, but, outside of professional functions, we didn't see each other socially. I depended too much on my old friends; I was waiting to be included in the social life I had been a part of for so long. I rarely initiated a call to a friend, even when I was painfully lonely. I never felt that I could ask to join friends for a social occasion. One friend called to talk and to say she was sorry she couldn't invite me to her dinner party Saturday night, for she already had one extra woman and that was all she could manage. I was crushed, but it didn't occur to me to be critical. I think I accepted that this was simply the ways things were. It took many months until I felt at ease enough to invite friends to my house for a social evening.

We had always subscribed to concert series with one or two other couples, but once I was alone, that, too, ended. Fearful of making plans on my own and not wanting to burden even my children, who by now had busy lives of their own at college and graduate school, I solved the vacation problem by going on two summer group tours traveling in Europe. On both trips the group was composed primarily of widows and divorcees, all feeling, like I did, disconnected and out of place. Outside of marital status, we had little in common. Each time I wished I had had the courage to travel alone. On the other hand, I did travel alone in my professional life, to meetings and to conferences held in different parts of the country. But, apart from my job, I shrank from initiating social plans for myself and, even today, I rarely go to restaurants, movies, or theater alone. Although I felt vulnerable and needy, friends later told me that I had projected such an image of strength and independence that no one had really worried about me.

Bernie and I had one friend whose wife had died some years earlier and whom we used to see quite often. On occasion, if Bernie had an emergency or was exhausted, I would invite Franz to use Bernie's ticket and to accompany me to a concert or theater. We were, I thought, simply good friends. I assumed this friendship would continue and make life easier for both of us. But it didn't happen. Franz came to the house to pay a condolence call once or twice and then disappeared. I was disappointed; I had assumed our friendship would continue, and I had pictured Franz accompanying me to an event from time to time. I soon learned that a man alone was sought after socially, while a woman alone was not.

On occasion, well-meaning friends introduced me to an "eligible" man; for the most part, these meetings were disastrous. There were a few evenings when, in the company of two or three couples, I was paired with a semi-retired, successful professional man—usually a doctor—fifteen or twenty years my senior who, it seemed to me, was looking for a younger woman as a traveling companion and, perhaps, a nurse when he became old and frail. Although I was lonely, these blind dates never worked out.

Having my life suddenly uprooted in this manner forced me to look at the way we had lived. Although we had some friends who were not in the medical profession, by and large, the couples we spent evenings with were physicians and their wives, with an occasional physician and her husband. The doctors who worked at the same hospital—many of them in the same HIP group—and who referred patients to each other were the mainstay of our social life for over twenty years. During the winter months there were frequent dinner parties on Saturday nights. As the doctors became successful and as the dinner parties became more formal, Bernie used to joke that the same party helper opened the door, whatever the address. It was, in fact, the same caterer, often even the same menu from one Saturday night to another. There was a regularity and sameness about these evenings that I had come to dread, although, when our turn came to host a dinner party, I rose to the occasion. And without this pattern, I felt lost.

Most physicians enjoyed a privileged status, elevated far above most "ordinary" people. Doctors earned this esteem by healing the sick; by working twelve to sixteen hours a day, close to seven days a week; by taking round-the-clock patient telephone calls; and by making house calls. The doctor's word and discretion were law. It was then common practice for doctors not to tell patients when they were seriously ill nor to explain the course of treatment. Many times I heard Bernie say that terminally ill patients didn't want to know the truth. What better evidence was there of the power doctors held over their patients than this.

Being a helpmate to a doctor who made patient care his priority was a particularly demanding job, and I prided myself on doing it well. Throughout the years, particularly after Bernie's first heart attack, I took full responsibility for the children and for all the details of day-to-day living. I tried to be the supportive wife who never minded canceling plans—even vacations—when my husband was needed by someone who was ill, but I knew that I never quite achieved the status of being the perfect doctor's wife. Some women seemed to give up their identity and became mere extensions of their husbands. Many doctors had married nurses whom they had met when they were interns, and it was easy, therefore, to slip into the same hierarchical doctor-nurse relationship in their marriages. But I had carved out a niche for myself in my work and was pleased that I could manage all my domestic responsibilities without ever turning to Bernie for help.

Now I had to find a new way for myself, alone. Along with the pain of missing Bernie, I slowly came to the realization that it was time for me to examine the way I had lived for the past twenty-five years, to see how much energy I had devoted to being a wife and mother, and to begin to start a new life. I was no longer a doctor's wife and I couldn't bear the thought of being identified solely as a doctor's widow or even as a college administrator. I was forced to build a new identity for myself. Part of the process was learning to trust myself, to speak up when I had strong convictions, and to take the initiative to meet people. I slowly began to enjoy a more spontaneous way of living. Little by little I gave up the life I had outgrown. I made new friends and nurtured old friends. I felt energized in my work and in my graduate studies.

My job was more challenging than I had anticipated, and I became obsessed with how to motivate more Barnard students to seriously consider career plans. A critical source of support for me was my office staff, particularly the two or three young women who shared many of my professional responsibilities: helping students and alumnae make appropriate career plans and find jobs, talking with employers and researching opportunities in emerging fields, establishing contacts with faculty members, maintaining a current vocational library, and planning vocational meetings and new programs. When I had a job opening, I shied away from the pool of candidates with placement-office experience who were locked into the status quo. Instead, I looked for bright young women, sensitive to the questions and demands of the women's movement, who would normally not apply for these low-paying jobs. I asked for a two-year commitment.

I was able to find highly gifted young women with some work experience, who were able to share the concerns and the experiences of students and alumnae in an immediate way. I offered them a chance to gain valuable experience in an interesting job with an opportunity for growth. Other administrators often asked what was wrong in my office: Why couldn't I keep staff for more than two or three years? I always responded that I wanted the kind of person who, after two years, would be ready for my job. I was willing to put up with whatever temporary inconveniences this caused; the rewards were far greater.

I consciously and successfully gathered and nurtured a staff not only willing to question women's traditional roles and expectations but also willing to initiate innovative programs—a staff close enough in age and in experience to bridge the gap between students and administration. I learned as much from them as they learned from me. I discovered I loved the challenge of training young women—a challenge I was to enjoy for the rest of my professional life. I have always been willing and ready to delegate, and it was gratifying to see how quickly these young women took hold and became colleagues. I learned to tolerate the slight discontinuity of changing staff, and I learned to send my employees off graciously when they were ready to go to graduate or professional school. I have maintained friendships with most of the dozen or more who worked for me. Several are now lawyers, one a clinical psychologist, another a social worker; others are college professors, and one a college dean. I am intensely proud of their achievements.

I held weekly staff meetings, initially to describe the work each staff member was doing, to discuss office procedures, and to create a less-hierarchical office structure. We later used these meetings to decide how to offer more vocational help to students and alumnae and also to explore new ways to help these women think about their lives and futures in the context of the growing women's movement. Some of our most innovative programs were conceived in staff meetings.

These meetings helped to create an atmosphere of trust among a friendly, informal staff of eight who worked well together. This made a difference not only to students and alumnae but it also made a tremendous difference to me. I no longer felt the isolation that had enveloped me during my first year of administrative work at Barnard. I still was disappointed in the meager communication among administrative offices throughout the college and in the great gulf between faculty and administrators. I still found many college rules and customs inflexible and even incomprehensible, but I had slowly come to accept most of these procedural regulations and had even begun to figure out which ones I could change or challenge. Against the background of this impersonal, administrative climate, I was determined to build a collective, supportive feeling within my own office.

My office became known as a place that welcomed students, with or without an appointment. This would come to serve us well, at unexpected moments and in ways I hadn't anticipated. In the student turbulence of 1968, when Columbia was nearly shut down, we became one of the few Barnard administrative offices that students trusted. At staff meetings we discussed student participation in the Columbia/Barnard antiwar movement, and, when the crisis came, we voted to support the student moratorium. We publicly endorsed this action on our large bulletin board right outside our office, where announcements of meetings and special opportunities were posted. Since we were part of the administration, however, we didn't close our office. Instead we relieved each other, using lunch hours or vacation time to attend meetings and demonstrations taking place all over the campus. This was in sharp contrast to the official college position of "business as usual" coupled with additional administrative meetings, which were often held at the precise time of the demonstrations.

Months later, I was called into President Martha Peterson's office. She was a large woman with premature white hair and a youthful face, probably in her fifties. Although I reported to her and had regular meetings scheduled with her during the year she had been at Barnard, I was uncertain of the depth of her support. She had called me in to tell me that the college was closing for an extra day on the day before the Fourth of July in appreciation of the cooperation the administrative staff had provided during the troubled days of the early spring. But, she added, it had come to her attention that my office staff had "not behaved well." She understood that some of my staff had publicly shown support for student demonstrators. She deemed this inappropriate behavior for an administrative office. She went on to say that some administrators had pointed out that our staff did not, therefore, deserve this extra vacation day.

I had often had fantasies about what I would say if called to task for not conforming to some directive or rule, and now it was happening. My stomach churned, and I momentarily panicked. It seemed an eternity, but, after a moment of hesitation, I swallowed hard and explained calmly how we had made the decisions we arrived at and how we had kept our office open and functioning throughout the crisis. I also pointed out that all time spent at meetings and demonstrations, other than lunch hours, had been vacation time, reported as such to the comptroller's office. President Peterson made no further comment and terminated the meeting.

My heart pounded as I left her office, but, as I walked down the long hall to my office, I felt elated. I had done something I had never done before. I was aware of a new feeling of strength, accompanied by a new self-esteem. My outrage at injustice had always been part of my nature, but, knowing Bernie's disapproval of public expressions, I had always been careful not to embarrass him. Now that I was alone, I could take actions I had never dared to take before.

A few months later a letter arrived from the Columbia Faculty Committee Against the War in Vietnam asking if I would sign a petition that was to appear in the Columbia daily newspaper. After serious consideration I decided I wanted to be a part of this public dissent. I went to see my lawyer, a good friend, to discuss whether this was a wise thing to do. We considered all the angles, particularly how this might affect my job. I did some research and learned that all administrators at Barnard received an annual letter of appointment, stating their salary for the coming year. The letter, however, was not a contract and, unlike tenured faculty, I learned that the president of the college could fire an administrator at will. By now, I was a self-supporting widow and could hardly afford to lose my job, but I felt this was a moral decision and a risk that I wanted to take. I signed the letter. What a letdown it was to see the list of faculty in the *Columbia Spectator* and my name not among them. The letter was sent in error. The committee had never intended to include administrators, perhaps knowing how vulnerable they were.

Threading my way through the turbulence of the late 1960s at a traditional institution was incredibly exciting. As the Vietnam War continued, I noted a strong resistance on the part of students—both women and men—to working for the establishment. We saw the beginnings of the alternative-work movement, and, listening to students, we started to collect information on all kinds of nonestablishment programs, from the Peace Corps and Head Start to training in midwifery and teaching in alternative community schools.

As the women's movement progressed, our office responded with a range of bold new approaches and programs. We were somewhat naive, but, at the time, I was convinced that significant changes were just around the corner. Once again I turned to Athena Constantine at Columbia for help. She readily agreed that the time had come to share job listings, which would enable women students to apply for jobs listed specifically for young men and permit graduating male seniors to look into jobs as secretaries or girl Fridays, should they be so inclined. Our students and alumnae reported difficult interviews with uncomfortable employers who were so taken aback with having to interview women for management training jobs that they often tried to lure them into secretarial jobs. One young man who wanted an entrée into a public relations firm applied for the only job available, a girl Friday, and was told that they wouldn't dream of having a man answering the phone and fetching coffee.

We experimented with a series of informal group meetings for students, well before their senior year, to provide an opportunity for young women to share vocational concerns and expectations and to raise questions about the pressure and ambivalence they felt as potential career women. We sought out successful Barnard alumnae and young women faculty who were willing to speak to undergraduates about their professional experiences in such a way as to raise student consciousness to the growing opportunities for women. We expanded our vocational library to include material on *all* fields of work (including those traditionally deemed "male"), professional school catalogues, and information on the current legal and economic changes in women's lives. We aggressively pursued employers in a broad range of fields for job listings, descriptions of training programs, and summer and midwinter internships.

It was a slow, frustrating process. Where I used to be sympathetic, I began to question—even to goad. Thus, to a brilliant senior who wanted to shelve her plans for graduate study to support her husband who had just received a fellowship, I asked, "Shouldn't you at least consider yourself too?" To another who expressed an interest in a management training program in business, I asked whether she thought it valid to refuse to accept traveling assignments. And, for the student who wanted to be an architect but was hesitant because a dean of admissions of a graduate school in architecture questioned her motivation and an uncle in the field told her women were never given good jobs, I found a woman architect for her to talk with and urged her to persevere. Although these were all steps in the right direction, I sometimes felt as if I was faced with a Sisyphean task.

One day in the early spring of 1970, I had a visit from a courtly, Southern gentleman representing the Yale Alumni Club. He came for advice on how to handle Yale's new female constituency, which posed problems for the Alumni Association. "Successful alumni," he pointed out delicately, "were accustomed to helping young Yale graduates get started in careers. But what to do with women graduates?" I secretly enjoyed observing his obvious discomfort, knowing full well that forty recently admitted women undergraduates at Yale had, a few weeks earlier, picketed Yale president Dr. Kingman Brewster as he spoke at Yale Alumni Day. They chose this occasion to express their outrage about the small number of women Yale was currently accepting and the lack of a concrete plan to enlarge the number of women admitted in the foreseeable future. They were also responding to Brewster's statement, which he made repeatedly whenever he spoke to Yale alumni groups throughout the country and which had received considerable press coverage: that Yale had a commitment to produce 1,000 potential leaders each year. Since he never mentioned Yale's newest constituency, it was clear to everyone that he meant 1,000 male leaders.

My visitor opened his attaché case and took out a long computer printout. Each sheet bore the name of a firm and a list of alumni, scattered all over the country, who were officers or in responsible staff positions in firms. All these men, he pointed out, understood what was expected of them: when called upon, they would pave the way and lend a helping hand to young alumni who were beginning their careers. For the first time I understood the special meaning that the "old school tie" had for men, who were quite used to helping each other move up the career ladder through informal, but well-established, networks.

What should he do? Since I worked with women, he was turning to me for help. He was quite ready to admit that he knew nothing about women's employment, and, although he didn't say it directly, it occurred to me that he thought he might turn the women graduates over to a women's placement and career services office. I pretended not to notice his barely contained horror at this new situation and gently pointed out that Yale's commitment to this new constituency must include providing whatever special help was necessary to ensure equality.

I told him that this was a great opportunity to introduce Yale women to alumni employers. I suggested that the Yale Alumni Association might start with a letter to all its members, introducing and describing this new pool of talent, while outlining the special help the college and its career services office were prepared to offer. I stressed the importance of emphasizing that Yale was serious about accepting women on an equal basis. I suggested that the letter ask alumni to welcome Yale women in this spirit and to give the same kind of help in opening doors for these young women that they had been doing so graciously and successfully for their young men. As the visit drew to a close, I offered to help by speaking to alumni groups and by sharing our experiences with their career services office. He barely maintained his civility; it was clear that treating these new Yale women as equals was unthinkable to him. He left, probably more uncomfortable than when he arrived. That was the last I heard from him.

This incident gave me a glimpse of how elite power is used to control entry into corporate positions. Men knew they had a more efficient way of filling key jobs and helping young men get started than those provided by employment agencies, placement offices, newspaper ads, and personnel departments. They made and exchanged contacts in gathering places for men: over a double-martini lunch, on the squash court, at the club's bar, and in the locker room. Even in academe—affirmative action programs notwithstanding—chairmen of academic departments continued the time-honored practice of calling colleagues on other campuses or in their professional associations to ask whether they had "a good man" to recommend for a faculty opening. It was not only white women who were kept out but members of minority groups and others who were different. A successful white man could look at an untried, white young alumnus and see his younger self. The old boys network really worked.

It was a revelation to me. This kind of informal assistance was virtually unknown for women, since few women had achieved real power. Those women who had traveled a lonely road to the executive suite were, moreover, often reluctant to help other women. To be identified with other women might jeopardize a hard-won position. Besides, the standards successful women had set for themselves were so high that they could only recommend another woman with superior qualifications—one who would be a sure winner. What could I do to introduce the idea of having successful women help the young and inexperienced find appropriate entry-level positions as men did? I watched approvingly the early establishment of caucuses, task forces, and other women's groups within professions, fields, and even within a few large firms, which, in time, would teach women the importance of helping other women.

In the early 1970s I tried to create an "old girls network" for the Barnard community—though we never called it that. I introduced the project with an article in the *Barnard Alumnae Magazine,* through several talks to alumnae clubs both in the New York area and in other parts of the country, and by a mailing to all the alumnae clubs asking for their help. I included a suggestion that internships be arranged in different fields in different parts of the country to provide women with the opportunity to explore unfamiliar careers. This marked the beginning of a women's network that the Barnard Alumnae Association has nurtured over the years. Barnard now has an active Alumnae Business and Professional Club in which many successful women serve as mentors and door-openers to young graduates.

One of the tasks I inherited and disliked intensely was reporting annually on young alumnae six months after their graduation. The faculty loved this report, but I thought it bore little relation to what these young women would be doing a few years later. The report listed each alumna under her major, and faculty eagerly scanned the lists to find their former students. They also liked comparing the six-months-after-graduation achievements of students from their departments with those from others. For my office, it was a tedious chore, tracking down members of the class who had just graduated—who by now had fanned out all over the country—and tabulating their responses: graduate school, job-hunting, jobs, marriage, traveling, or just doing nothing.

After several years of these reports, I realized that it might be much more useful to find out what alumnae were doing after five years. In the summer of 1970, with the help of a graduate student, Abby Pagano, I sent a questionnaire to the 365 members of the Class of 1965. With only one mailing, within six weeks, I had received 163 responses, almost half the class—a surprisingly good response. I asked about occupations, salaries, graduate and professional training, marital status, and children. I included some open-ended questions on experiences and attitudes about discrimination and the women's movement. The responses to this survey were so different from anything I had heard from undergraduates that I realized that powerful forces were affecting women *after* graduation.

An analysis of the replies revealed extremely high achievement levels, in both advanced training and employment, often in combination with marriage and having children. It may very well have been that I heard primarily from achievers (those in paid employment, graduate or professional school, or both), whereas others preferred not to reply. Even so, the achievement level was impressive. Three out of four were either working or attending graduate or professional school. Of those employed, almost three quarters were in the professions, the largest number in teaching: nineteen in colleges and universities, and seventeen in secondary schools. Over three quarters were married and half of those married had children.

The most important finding of the survey was that the higher the level of professional or educational achievement, the greater the sensitivity to discrimination. Over two thirds of the respondents reported that they were aware of discrimination, and over half had actually experienced discrimination either in jobs or in graduate schools or in both. It was interesting to find that married women with children, either working or attending graduate school, and women with high salaries expressed concern about discrimination to a degree significantly above average. Those working in women's professions such as social work, librarianship, and secondary school teaching, those with low salaries, and those not working had either never experienced discrimination or showed the least awareness of it.

The few open-ended questions on discrimination, which I had added almost as an afterthought, yielded the most significant information. I was amazed by the lengthy replies, suggesting that these women welcomed the chance to describe their experiences. The many individual stories of discrimination included accounts of salary differentials for men and women in the same job, barriers to receiving deserved promotions, discrimination in graduate school admissions, and restricted opportunities in some professions. Situations and attitudes that many, as recent undergraduates, had accepted without question were found to be frustrating and intolerable five years later, particularly by those struggling to build a career. It was the difficult road to achievement that had sensitized many young women to sex discrimination in the work world.

Most respondents expressed bitterness and disappointment in discovering that their bachelor's degrees had proved to be no insulation from an employer's interest in their typing skills. They also noted that women seemed to start and finish in dead-end jobs. Men were research assistants, while women in similar jobs were clerk-typists. One woman put it bluntly when she wrote, "If one could feel confident, as a man does, that a subordinate position would lead to advancement sooner or later, one wouldn't mind."

Pervasive inequities in salary were reported: "An office position of comparable responsibility held by a man usually pays fifty to seventy dollars per week more." One woman told of applying for a job as an actuarial trainee and being offered one hundred dollars a week because "all our girls get that. Men get more." A woman who was supporting her graduate-student husband and herself on a marginal wage reported that supporting wives were used "almost as slave labor" in the university town where they lived.

The stories of discrimination in the professions were frequently moving. One alumna, who had recently earned her M.D., reported that women were considered unsuitable for certain fields such as surgery. Women doctors, she wrote, were believed to be "more conscientious, more intelligent, and more hardworking than men," but they were also supposed to be "weaker and unable to think in a crisis." Another wrote that women speakers at the scientific meetings she attended were not considered seriously unless the women were "tough and older." And several women observed that they had to prove themselves to be "twice as good as men" before they were treated with the respect they deserved.

Reports of discrimination in employment in academe were common and included prejudice against married women, nepotism, and obstacles to being hired and receiving promotions. A typical story was that of an instructor who had been in her job for three years. Although she had received the average annual increment, she remained an instructor, while men with the same qualifications had been promoted. At the same time she watched the number of women in her department of thirty-five drop from twelve to three.

The largest number of complaints centered on experiences as students in graduate and professional schools. There were stories about admissions quotas, difficulties in getting fellowships and teaching assistantships, lack of encouragement from professors, and the generally disdainful attitudes of male classmates. A recurrent theme was "I find the prejudice insidious—few women in the department, no women on the faculty—the feeling that women will, at most, teach a few years and will rarely be scholars or publish." One graduate student in French was discouraged by the two heads of her department, who believed that women were unsuited to academe, that they couldn't complete the Ph.D. requirements, and that they would never publish. After two years with a good academic record, this woman dropped out of graduate school and applied to social work school, seeking a career that she thought was more compatible with women's role in society.

Some women were told frankly not to apply for admission to particular schools or were informed that they were not awarded fellowships because of their sex. Others observed that, in order to receive grants, they had to do better than men and constantly demonstrate their seriousness as students in a way that was not expected of men. One respondent told of applying for a teaching assistantship at a university that made appointments according to an "objective" point system. Although entitled to a full assistantship, she was granted only half of one, with a proportionately reduced salary. Her professor explained that the department knew that she and another of its graduate students would soon be married to each other. It was decided that since two could live as cheaply as one, or almost, the couple would be treated as a single unit rather than as two individuals. Thus, they were awarded one and a half, rather than two, teaching assistantships: the woman was awarded the half.

More than half of the respondents expressed concern about the inequities confronting women in society. The responses were often impassioned and ranged from pleas for an end to discrimination and nepotism to demands for day-care centers, part-time jobs, and a rethinking of family roles. They asked for institutional changes and a strong women's movement. Several faulted the college for not giving them better preparation.

Some responses were very personal: "I have become more aware of griev-ances that I have nursed within myself for years." Or, "The women's movement has made me realize the extent of my anger and more importantly has made me less fearful of articulating it." Marriage and motherhood were regarded with less urgency and more flexibility, and several felt that women's aspirations out-side the home seemed more feasible as professions appeared much more accessible. One respondent said, "I myself have changed a great deal. I never had much confidence in myself or in my ability to really accomplish something. Now I feel inspired to make something of myself because the outlook is much more promising." Others talked about being closer to their women friends, and a few expressed an obligation to help other women and to work for change.

Although I knew the sample was too small to permit any generalizations, I sensed something important was taking place, even as early as in 1970. Also, quite different from the survey I had done of graduating seniors a few years ear-lier, this study revealed that women's postgraduate experiences compelled them to think seriously about discrimination and about their lives as women. As they had embarked on ambitious careers, these women had been exposed to real-ities that had both raised their expectations and honed their consciousness. The study was published in the *Journal of the National Association of Women Deans and Counselors* under the title of "Sex Discrimination and Achievement."

I no longer felt sanguine and content. I began to chafe at the limitations of my job as a career counselor. I could see that, if women were to make appro-priate career choices, they must free themselves from their internal limits, from the myths and stereotypes that burdened their lives. This work could not be assigned to even the best career planning office. We could organize activities to help women raise their aspirations, gain knowledge and some work expe-rience, and, on occasion, even get good jobs. We could extend our network of contacts, and we could prod young women and help them pursue their career interests even in the face of initial rejections. But the important task of raising consciousness had to come from other sources and must start long before the college years.

Although I believed deeply that women should enjoy equality in choices and access to all jobs, I found myself thinking about more than job equality. Simply ensuring that women would be fairly represented in top levels of management and in the professions would not change things for *all* women. I began to see that true equality required much more than getting women into good "male" jobs, and I wasn't sure that I wanted to spend the rest of my pro-fessional life helping women become bank presidents and corporate officers.

Fortunately, the isolation I had felt for so long was lifting. By late 1969 there was a sense of excitement on the campus, and I found several young faculty members and a handful of students who were as drawn to the reemerging women's movement as I was. Many of us who were involved in the women's movement at that time were also participating in antiwar demonstrations in New York and Washington. Initially, we were a small group, but, as we expanded, I was conscious of a new, exhilarating feeling of solidarity.

About this time I was forced to confront my own insecurities about moving up the career ladder. In June of 1971, at a farewell lunch for my two assistants who were leaving after fulfilling their two-year commitment, one for law school, the other for graduate school in psychology, we talked of our futures. I was startled when both young women turned to me and said, "What about you? You've been in this job long enough. You've made as much of it as is possible. It's time for you to move on." I felt myself growing anxious; I wanted this conversation to stop. I couldn't imagine how I could get a better job. I sensed the truth in what they said, but I wasn't ready to face it. Although deep down inside I knew they were right, the thought of looking for another job was frightening. I couldn't imagine what I would look for. My role, that of a gentle agitator, was tolerated at Barnard. I was fearful of giving up the security I felt I had. And so, I had to face the truth—at least to myself—that my sights were set as low as some of the young women I counseled.

■ 11
BARNARD RESPONDS
TO THE CHALLENGE OF
THE WOMEN'S MOVEMENT

In the fall of 1968 I met a man who was to become my lover, best friend, and partner for the rest of my life. Jay was fifty-three when we met, three years older than I, but his age belied his looks. He was of medium height, taller than I, but not much. He was well built, neither fat nor thin, and without the paunch of many middle-aged men. Brown-eyed and with a full head of brown hair, he was enormously attractive to me, but not only because of his looks. He was quite different from any man I had known. Vibrant and intellectual, his broad interests ranged from tennis and music to economics and politics. Unlike many men of his age who had left their wives for much younger women, Jay sought a relationship with someone close to his age, with whom he could share a common history.

From the start of our relationship, we discovered that we both shared an unshakable optimism about the human capacity for change and the potential of young people. Trained as an economist with a Ph.D. from Columbia University, Jay had just left a secure, well-paying job to start a computer database business that would apply practically the theory of input-output economics. He was a protégé of Harvard professor Wassily Leontief, who won the Nobel Prize in 1973 for developing the mathematical principles underlying input-output analysis. Jay was also in the midst of ending a long-standing but troubled marriage while attempting to maintain a strong relationship with his two daughters: Diana, age twenty-five, and Emily, an adolescent, eleven years younger. It was both a good and a bad time for him.

Despite these stresses, Jay was engaging and generous, and we were able to learn a great deal from one another. Even old interests became new. Jay reignited my love of music, which had become limited to listening to one classical music radio station and a few old records. A lifelong choral singer, with a knowledge of and appreciation for music that outstripped mine, Jay introduced me to choral music. Going to concerts, opera, and choral performances became a part of our lives.

At Jay's insistence, I took up tennis again. After not playing for twenty-five years I dusted off my old racquet. Like many other things we were to do together, my game got better and better. We started playing singles and, later, added a Sunday morning doubles game, continuing to play together for years until an arthritic hip ended tennis for Jay, although not for me. In the same spirit, Jay took up bicycling, an activity that we continue to enjoy today.

An unexpected bonus was Jay's genuine interest in my professional life and the fact that we shared many of the same social concerns. By now my deep involvement in the women's movement permeated every part of my life. When I wasn't attending an evening meeting or a weekend conference, I was working on a paper for my graduate degree. Not only did Jay never complain about how much of my alleged leisure time I chose to spend on professional activities, but he went so far as to observe that I was lucky to have work that was meaningful, even if it interfered with evening or weekend plans.

We spoke constantly about the condition of women. I could scarcely believe my ears when Jay said that he thought that the women's movement was as important a social revolution as any in history. He had read Simone de Beauvoir's *The Second Sex* long before we met, in an effort to understand his own marital problems, and he had given serious thought to the inequities faced by women. Later, after he had attended many public discussions, conferences, and meetings about women, Jay observed that our relationship was enriched by this close contact with the women's movement.

We were married in the fall of 1969. For the first time in my life, I enjoyed a relationship as an equal partner. Here we were, in our fifties, embarking on a totally new life together, leaving behind many of our preconceptions, adjusting and modifying some lifelong habits, and making significant career changes. I learned an important truth: nothing fosters equality more than reality. Jay still had a family to support, an ex-wife and a school-age child, and was in no position to take on additional financial responsibilities. That I was self-supporting was not only important for my feeling of self-worth but also necessary if we were to live together.

In the beginning this new relationship must have been unsettling for all four children. With the exception of Emily, who still lived at home with her mother and was at school in New York, the others were out on their own: Diana was establishing herself as a screen and television writer in Hollywood; Nancy was at graduate school studying political science; and David was completing college. My children saw almost as much of Jay as they did of me when they came home; Jay had moved into our apartment and, almost overnight, became a member of my family. But it took several years for Jay's daughters to accept me and to want to see us together. This was a difficult period for all of us, but Jay showed remarkable patience and was convinced that, eventually, we would rework strong relationships with both sets of children. Although I was less sanguine than Jay, it did finally happen, and my life is richer because of Diana and Emily and their families.

It was hard to know what my mother thought when I married Jay, but she quickly became one of his strongest admirers. She had always shown a preference for men, and she had every reason to approve of Jay. Having lost his own mother at an early age, he tended to put mothers on a pedestal and frequently invited my mother when we went out to dinner, the theater, or the movies. And, until she was well into her nineties, whenever we rented a house in the country for the summer, my mother would spend a week with us.

Our first few years together were years of tremendous social upheaval. In the spring of 1968 student frustrations exploded with a force new to American college campuses. I witnessed daily the increasing frequency and deepening intensity of student actions taking place across the street at Columbia. Talking to student activists and reading student newspapers and flyers, I could see that these students took their actions very seriously. I watched as many—including a fair number of Barnard women—risked their academic careers and more to voice their strong disapproval of Columbia University's role in permitting military recruitment on campus as well as in sponsoring research beneficial to the Pentagon. They held meetings, demonstrations, and teach-ins. They sat in and took over campus buildings, almost closing down the university. I saw something else that was disturbing: many students were beginning to question the quality and the content of their own education. Suddenly, to many, most of what they were learning seemed irrelevant.

Jay and I participated in many public actions. Two very different marches left an indelible imprint on me. The first was an antiwar protest held in Washington in November of 1969. We went to register our indignation and to show that concern extended across generations. We arrived Friday evening and joined thousands making preparation for what the young organizers called the March Against Death. It was a cold, damp night and we stood in the mud shivering for several hours, waiting to begin a symbolic four-mile march. Starting after midnight at the Arlington Cemetery Bridge, we marched single file through the streets of Washington to the White House. There, each marcher, carrying a lit candle and a placard, called out the name and state of one dead soldier, then continued down to the Capitol where each placard was put into one of four open coffins. The march was policed by a remarkable band of young volunteer marshals, who maintained an air of good humor and gentle discipline despite the bitter cold. We sensed a special appreciation extended toward us as older adults and were embarrassed as many of the marshals greeted us by saying, "Thank you for coming."

Despite the bitter cold the following day, we were joined by tens of thousands of people. It was a long day of marching and standing and trying to keep warm while listening to impassioned speeches. As we left, we noticed that many government buildings were guarded by soldiers stationed inside the buildings. Even the White House was cordoned off by empty public buses. We couldn't help reflecting on the irony of Nixon's administration, which was so clearly fearful of its children. It was a grim weekend, peppered with tear gas and an absence of support from any government officials. I was chilled to the bone, physically and emotionally.

How different was the Nationwide Strike for Women's Equality, in New York City in August 1970. We marched down Fifth Avenue on a fine summer afternoon with thousands of women, many with children, and a few men, some of whom were marching for the first time in their lives, to commemorate the fiftieth anniversary of the Nineteenth Amendment, which gave women the right to vote. We walked with pride, determination, and optimism to express our unity for three major demands: equal opportunity in employment and education, free abortions on demand, and twenty-four-hour childcare centers. Although we knew we were not yet representative of all women since almost all of the marchers were white, similar marches were taking place in cities and towns all over the country, making this the largest demonstration for women's equality in United States history. It was a strong beginning. I saw many women I knew on the march, including some I would not have expected to be there, and I felt proud to be a woman marching with my sisters and proud that Jay was there as well.

Closer to home, at Barnard, people were increasingly vocalizing their support for the women's movement. The boldest voice was that of Kate Millett, a young instructor in the English department who later, for a brief period, served as the director of the Experimental College, a Barnard program established in 1969 in response to student discontent and pressure for more relevant education. I had first met her when she picketed my office, and we had become friends and allies. I watched her develop into a major feminist force on and off campus, speaking out at public meetings and leading demonstrations. During the late 1960s, she was also writing her dissertation at Columbia, which was to be published in 1970 as *Sexual Politics*. When I read the manuscript for her first chapter, I was awed. Here was a young scholar examining the system of patriarchy through literature, making the claim that men used sex, often with violence, to exert power.

■

Despite her acknowledged brilliance, Millett's academic career was short lived. Although a popular teacher, with a first book that became an immediate best-seller and a classic, Barnard let her go long before she might have been considered for tenure. Clearly, both the English department and the Barnard administration couldn't tolerate a faculty member so outspoken and radical.

The magnitude of the social revolution that was developing outside the ivory tower was much larger than I had ever imagined. In the fall of 1970 I joined a small group of faculty members, administrators, students, and alumnae who began meeting informally to explore what Barnard could—and should—do to formally acknowledge the challenges of the women's movement. After a few months the group was much smaller due to attrition. We settled in to work on what turned out to be a year-long effort. President Peterson designated us as an official college task force and charged us with drawing up a plan for action.

We were a varied group, with different backgrounds, interests, and commitments, but we shared the conviction that it was time for Barnard to do more than provide a superior education for women. We believed that "this superior education for women" should offer more than admission to a still discriminatory, white-male tradition. After months of arguing, pleading, suggesting, agreeing, and disagreeing, we voiced our hopes in a persuasive report that became the basis for the establishment of the Barnard Women's Center.

Knowing the reluctance of traditional institutions to change and to innovate and recalling the hostility shown in response to the antiwar movement, I honestly didn't expect anything concrete to emerge from these discussions. I knew that the final decision would be made by the president of the college, a woman who had made her way up the academic ladder through discretion, not innovation. My own experience at Barnard had suggested that she would not be a strong ally.

But these were extraordinary times, and we were an extraordinary group. Although all the students had dropped out—most of them mistrustful of a college-run project—seven of us had stayed to become the task force and the founders of the Women's Center: three faculty members—Annette Baxter, Patricia Graham, and Catharine Stimpson; two alumnae trustees—Eleanor Elliott and Iola Haverstick; and two administrators—Barbara Hertz and myself.

Catharine Stimpson, a young, charismatic English professor, chaired the task force, providing strong leadership, unflagging enthusiasm, and good humor. Her understanding of the importance of feminism and its place within the academy was undoubtedly the most important factor in the creation of the Women's Center and of some of the early women's studies course offerings. She kept us together, moving forward, insisting that we focus on realistic goals. The two alumnae trustees used their influence with other trustees and with the president and managed to secure the necessary funding. Both women were steadfast in their commitment and scarcely missed a meeting. Iola Haverstick, after raising a family, was enrolled in the Ph.D. program in English at Columbia and was full of ideas for a women's library. When this didn't happen, she made a large personal contribution to augment the Overbury Collection, a small special collection by and about women, already housed in the Barnard library. Eleanor Elliott was a remarkable woman who had devoted her energies to taking leadership in organizations that she believed in, the most important of which was her own alma mater. I soon discovered that, whenever she took an interest, things happened. From what I knew of her, I wouldn't have expected her to care so deeply about Barnard's commitment to the women's movement. But she did, and no matter how radical the suggestions or the plan, she always ended a meeting by saying, "What do we need to do next?"

About this time, Barnard received a large bequest from Helen Rogers Reid, class of 1901, a feminist in her time. Eleanor Elliott went to the Reid family and obtained their permission to use the income from the bequest to start the Women's Center. This support was crucial.

Although there were many questions and reservations about the need for a separate women's institution in a women's college, the Women's Center opened in the fall of 1971. It was housed in a prominent spot on campus in a tiny, dingy room with a crumbling ceiling. Catharine Stimpson was given released time from one third of her teaching obligations to direct the center for one year, while we looked for a permanent director. Although it was underfinanced, understaffed, and unfocused, the establishment of the Women's Center felt like a major victory. We also knew we were not yet a permanent part of the college community. In the minds of many, we were simply an administrative gesture.

Our first public program was a spirited panel discussion entitled "Is There Male Chauvinism at Columbia?" It turned out to be an evening of high comedy: a packed audience listened to a panel of eight Columbia male professors, including such reputable figures as George Fraenkel, Eli Ginzberg, Loren Graham, Seymour Melman, and President William McGill, as they pontificated on an issue that most of them, obviously, were considering for the first time in their lives and, for the most part, without much understanding or conviction. The one exception was Loren Graham from the Graduate School of Arts and Sciences, who acknowledged the deep-seated chauvinism at Columbia and made several constructive suggestions for change, such as hiring husbands and wives with children on a part-time basis and, if they so desired, granting maternity and paternity leave.

Anne Sutherland Harris and Elaine Showalter skillfully moderated the panel. They controlled the question-and-answer period, maintaining a light touch, avoiding confrontation, and soft-pedaling the unspoken rage that some of the women in the audience must have felt as they listened to men baldly revealing deep-seated prejudices that they assumed were quite acceptable.

Having gained some public recognition for the center, we turned our attention to finding a permanent director; to defining the mission, goals, and governance procedures for the center; and to seeing that the center became a part of the regular college budget. Following normal academic and administrative protocol, this meant endless meetings. President Peterson set up a search committee for a director, followed by a charter committee and an executive committee. All the members of these committees were appointed by the president; most of the appointees were faculty members, although almost all of the original task force continued to serve on these committees.

Finding a director took almost two years and proved to be a difficult task. The process highlighted the fragility of our project. We advertised nationally for applicants with Ph.D.'s or doctoral equivalents and with research interests in and publications on women's issues. We looked at scores of résumés and interviewed numerous candidates. We found that the most suitable applicants wanted tenure in a department, which was not an option, since no academic department was ready to accept a feminist scholar as a colleague. Some candidates wanted a clearer picture of our focus and goals; some had a vision that we weren't ready to consider. At the very least, all wanted more security than we could offer at that time.

In the end I was appointed acting director in 1972 and permanent director in 1973. Having served on the search committee and participated in deciding on the qualifications for the executive director, it never occurred to me that I might be a candidate. I assumed that my lack of academic credentials—specifically a Ph.D.—would make me ineligible. So complete had been my acceptance of the wide chasm between faculty and administrators that I had never even permitted myself to fantasize about being the director. I was surprised when President Peterson invited me in August of 1972 to serve as acting director of the Women's Center for the coming year, while maintaining my job as director of career planning. I was fortunate that I could turn over many responsibilities to Lynn Stephens, my enormously capable and compatible associate director, who would take over as the director when I left the career planning office the following year. During this year, I spent half my working hours and most of my waking hours either at the Women's Center or thinking about it: mulling over which issues should be part of its agenda, how to organize projects with limited resources, and how to cement the connections between the college and the larger community to ensure our future.

It is hard to convey the excitement and exhilaration I felt when the search committee decided that I was their choice for permanent director. I knew the time was ripe for creating a women's center and I welcomed the challenge. I loved the familiar feeling of pioneering. As in the 1950s, when I had helped married women with children return to work, I had no models. The mandate was very broad: to build a nonhierarchical structure that would become a permanent part of Barnard, while assuring the Women's Center a fair degree of autonomy. I began to see that my understanding of the politics and dynamics of Barnard College and my experience as an administrator were valuable qualifications for my new job. I understood the importance of creating links with other segments of the college, identifying issues to work on, working with groups of women within and outside the college, and—wherever possible—reaching out to the ever-growing feminist community.

One of the first things I did was talk with the comptroller about my budget. Close to retirement, he had become a fixture at Barnard, intent on maintaining the status quo and quick to dampen the prospect of any new venture. He treated women administrators almost as children. In a kindly manner, he told me that he thought I was taking a large and foolish risk to accept this job. He likened it to jumping off a diving board when you didn't know how to swim. We were expecting a new president the following year, and he was quite sure that the Women's Center was simply a one-year whim. He pointed out that I could expect to be unemployed since I was giving up my career services job. I thanked him for his advice and asked him whether he didn't think that the Women's Center's future would be decided by the president of the college. He backed off and explained again that he was concerned only about my future. This concern, however, did not carry over to a significant increase in salary commensurate with the responsibilities of the new job. I had to bring up the question, and, when he asked what I thought I should get, I responded with a much-too-modest amount. I suspect that he was so surprised at my audacity in even raising the issue of salary, that, had I asked for more, he might have approved a considerably higher figure. Although a full-time position was economically and personally essential for me, I wanted the job so badly that I didn't hesitate for one moment. I didn't permit myself to think that I was taking a risk, even though I was. When I received the same yearly letter of appointment that I had received as an administrator of career services, I knew that the Women's Center was still marginal—not part of the regular College budget—and could be dissolved at the end of any year.

How did it happen? What made a traditional women's college acknowledge the force of the women's movement in such an innovative way, at the very beginning of the 1970s, when few other colleges and certainly no other women's college had shown such interest? And how were we going to build, shape, and maintain this structure? These important questions consumed me during the next few years.

There is no easy explanation. The strong commitment of a few women was essential, along with their willingness to heed academic protocol so that the Women's Center could be rooted firmly within the institutional fabric of the college. The charter was a great help (see appendix A for the complete text). The charter committee worked for a whole year and through nine drafts to satisfy the committee and to receive college approval. Its mission was inclusive: "to assure that women can live and work in dignity, autonomy, and equality. . . . [to address] the broad needs and aspirations of women. . . . [to serve as] a physical and psychological meeting ground for women [both within and outside the academy.]" The charter stressed "the open sharing of knowledge and experience" by encouraging "ties among diverse groups of women." It encouraged the creation of both academic and nonacademic programs and projects that "complement or coincide with Barnard's distinctive academic strengths in women's studies." All of this took place at a time when we still didn't have a formal women's studies program—just a handful of course offerings.

The charter was a remarkable document, both expansive and specific. It spelled out a wide range of academic projects the Women's Center might undertake, including a research library, departmental and interdepartmental courses, conferences, lectures, and publications. A framework was laid for a variety of nonacademic programs ranging from providing information on activities and organizations of special interest to women, to establishing noncredit courses on feminism, projects in the arts, vocational counseling for college women in the metropolitan area, to creating a clearinghouse for women's professional and educational projects.

Governance was a major issue for the charter committee. The executive committee was to be the policymaking body of the Women's Center. The committee, composed of twelve members, would represent the four major constituencies of the Women's Center: three students, three faculty members, three alumnae, and three administrators. After much discussion, the executive committee rejected the strong plea from the one student member of the committee, Janet Axelrod, to include members from the larger community. Although the first executive committee was appointed by the president of the college, procedures were spelled out in the charter for future openings. Student members were to be elected by the undergraduate association; all other members were to be nominated by the Women's Center Executive Committee, in consultation with appropriate officers of the college, and to be appointed by the president for a two-year term. Members would be permitted to serve two consecutive two-year terms and could be reappointed after a two-year lapse. The director of the Women's Center was defined as an administrative officer, appointed by and reporting to the president. She would serve ex officio on the executive committee, voting only when needed to break a tie. President Peterson served ex officio on the first Women's Center Executive Committee, although this was not spelled out in the charter.

There was no mention of men in any of the early drafts of the charter, but the dean of faculty, the one man serving on the charter committee, refused to give his approval until a sentence was added saying that "the Center welcomes the cooperation of all—men and women—who are in sympathy with its aims." Although I doubt that I would have noticed this omission at the time, I am glad this sentence was included. I see it as a testament not only to the committee's progressiveness but also to the broad goals of feminism.

When I became director, I inherited an executive committee appointed by President Peterson. In addition to the four founders with whom I had worked closely to establish the center, there were several other remarkable women: Suzanne Wemple and Danielle Haase-Dubosc, Barnard faculty; Pat Ballou, Barnard librarian; Susan Rennie, Barnard alumna and Columbia administrator; and Janet Axelrod, Barnard student. It took another year to develop procedures for the election of student members and to set into place procedures for replacing members who had completed their terms or had to drop out for personal or professional reasons.

After a year, we were given additional space, a large, sunny seminar room, adjoining our small office. We had two full-time staff members and several students working part time. From the beginning, I did a good deal of listening, mostly to discussions by the young women who visited the center and spent hours talking about issues that were stirring them up. They were consumed with anger about what they called "the weight of patriarchy." I listened to their anger directed at men and the nuclear family. I heard them describe their resentment about bearing men's surnames, about being unable to secure a bank loan without the signature of a husband, about getting lesser jobs and less pay, about being excluded from certain fields and denied deserved promotions, and about deferring to men on many decisions affecting their lives. I heard their specifically intense fury focused on male professionals—doctors, lawyers, therapists, accountants—who treated women as children.

Listening to these diatribes forced me to reflect on my own experiences and brought back memories of a one-year experience in therapy, which ended abruptly when Bernie had his first heart attack. I stopped therapy when my therapist said, "Now you have a real problem to cope with." Years later I met the therapist at a dinner party and his only acknowledgment of our former relationship was to ask about my husband's health.

I realized that I had been a willing accomplice by not challenging the assumptions male "professionals" often made about women. I had prided myself on being a good patient and not asking questions. I often had felt uncomfortable in a doctor's office when the doctor—always a man—called me by my first name while expecting to be addressed as Doctor so-and-so. The first time I went to a male doctor whom I didn't know and responded to being called "Jane" by using, with some awkwardness, his first name, I was rewarded by seeing a slightly startled look on his face.

Some young women expressed their pent-up anger toward men by deliberately foregoing efforts to look "attractive." I noticed young women who stopped shaving their legs and arm pits, who refused to wear makeup, high heels, girdles, and bras. As part of a statement of who they were and an insistence on looking natural, many stopped using perfume and nail polish, plucking their eyebrows, having their hair styled, and, in general, looking "feminine." Extreme though it seemed at the time, such behavior focused attention on conforming to artificial standards of beauty, which were often absurd and confined women's bodies.

Seeing women discard restrictive clothes and customs angered some men and even some women. But like many extreme positions, many of us could see the liberating value of these acts. For example, I stopped wearing a girdle, which I had worn throughout my adult life, not because I was fat or bulging but because that's what "nice" women wore. I also stopped using nail polish and wearing high heels; I never missed them for one minute. In fact, I often wondered how I could have tolerated these practices for as long as I did. To this day, my feet are misshapen from being squeezed into stylish shoes that didn't fit to make my legs look long and sexy. But I continued to dress essentially as I always had, with an eye to current fashion when it suited me, and to wear makeup and style my hair in ways I thought made me look my best. And I'm not sure anymore whether I do these things for men, for other women, or just for myself.

Like many women of my generation, I had been brought up to defer to men on most issues. I took most gender differences for granted and it had never occurred to me to feel anger at men as a group. I had also been raised to believe that expressing anger—even feeling it—was unladylike and unacceptable. Observing these young women, I was forced to acknowledge to myself that, in the 1950s and 1960s, when I had helped women who wanted to do more than just be wives and mothers, I had never fundamentally challenged the existing family framework or any of the basic assumptions about how women lived. Although at the time I had thought of myself as some sort of pioneer, I came to realize that we never really confronted our anger at men—that we were simply trying to open further possibilities for women while maintaining traditional family lifestyles.

In the early 1970s, the Women's Center's very existence tapped a great reservoir of feminist energy, which—in turn—helped to shape our identity. It was like opening a floodgate. At times I felt as if I were part of an ongoing consciousness-raising group. So many new issues were debated daily that I often left the office with my head spinning. Legal abortion, women-centered healthcare, sexual orientation, the new scholarship on women, and other issues that oppressed women joined those issues that we had been struggling with for the past decade—primarily discrimination in education and employment. We were faced with an embarrassment of riches: ideas, proposals, and offers of assistance for a wide range of projects and services, all designed to fill unmet and emerging needs.

We were also overwhelmed with inquiries: telephone calls, letters, and visitors inquiring about women's groups, services for women, women's events, women's studies courses, current research, and publications. What seemed to be needed most in the early 1970s was information about what was available. We started collecting this new material, which was emerging so rapidly that we could hardly keep up with it. We took on two major projects that helped us become a national resource center and a clearinghouse for information about women. Both projects were started and initially carried out by volunteers, a working precedent that was to become an integral part of the center's fabric and success. From the beginning, committed and capable women sought us out, wanting to participate in the burgeoning women's movement. Some gave time and assumed major responsibility for a project, others gave money, and a few gave both.

Kirsten Grimstad, a Barnard alumna and a Columbia graduate student, took on the responsibility of compiling the first national, interdisciplinary bibliography of scholarly research on women. Nothing like it existed at the time. With the help of Dorothy Marks, a graduate student in library sciences at Columbia, and the Women's Center's staff, 900 questionnaires were mailed to individuals teaching women's studies courses and to professional groups and academic organizations throughout the country. In addition, volunteers and staff conducted an extensive bibliographical search of standard sources. Our first publication, entitled *Women's Work and Women's Studies 1971,* was a 162-page volume with 1,495 listings of research publications, both published and in progress, as well as information on women's activist groups, organizations, and projects. About 1,000 copies were sold. An unexpected bonus was that women often included copies of their work when responding to our questionnaire. Two subsequent volumes reflected the dramatic expansion in research and in the number of women's studies courses and forced us to rethink how we could continue this enormous task, by now too large for volunteers alone. Using gift money from individuals—mostly Barnard alumnae—we hired a librarian and undergraduates to work on a freelance basis. We also placed an ad in a librarians' newsletter and were pleased that twenty librarians in different parts of the country volunteered to help comb literature in a number of different disciplines.

Our last bibliography, published and distributed by The Feminist Press in 1974, contained 4,000 listings. By that time a number of groups—professional associations, task forces, and women's caucuses within disciplines—were compiling and publishing this information more efficiently and more completely than we could. We learned an important lesson: that we could often serve the community best by temporarily filling an unmet need until other groups took over and were in a position to do the job themselves.

Other examples of projects we initiated and then relinquished in the early 1970s included a resource pamphlet entitled *Help* and several noncredit courses. In 1971, in cooperation with the Barnard Alumnae Advisory Vocational Committee, the Women's Center prepared and published a listing of national and local sources of information and services for women in the areas of continuing education, vocational guidance, family planning, daycare, volunteer activities, women's rights, and legal services. We included a bibliography on the women's movement and suggestions for action projects, ranging from working with community groups, to setting up abortion counseling clinics, to designing courses to teach women such skills as plumbing, electrical work, house painting, woodworking, and money management. We expected that alumnae groups throughout the country would be able to adapt this information to their own community needs. A second edition was published in 1973.

The most notable of our noncredit courses was one on women's creative writing, "Our Voices, Ourselves," taught by writer Louise Bernikow, Barnard alumna and one of our early, staunch supporters. I went to the public reading at the final session of the first series of the workshop in the spring of 1974. Listening to the participants, most of whom had never written before, read their own work with confidence, in this atmosphere of trust and support, was an experience I will never forget. It reaffirmed for me the value of what we were trying to accomplish at the Women's Center.

Our second major undertaking began unexpectedly and inauspiciously. One morning a woman, laden with a pile of reprints of articles on women, appeared on our doorstep. The woman was Myra Josephs, Barnard alumna of the class of 1928. She had just read about the opening of the Women's Center in an alumnae letter, and it seemed to be the answer to her prayer. She packed up the literature she had been collecting and took the next Broadway bus to the Women's Center.

For the past ten years Myra Josephs had been working as a part-time volunteer for Dr. Albert Ellis's Institute of Rational Living, combing over 200 journals in the behavioral and social sciences for articles of interest to the institute. During the late 1960s she had begun to notice an increase in articles on women, and she had started to make copies of these articles. She had kept them all together, noting how quickly the pile was growing and wondering where she could find a repository for them. When she heard about the opening of the Barnard Women's Center, she couldn't wait to come and talk to us. Her dream, she told me, was to have the Women's Center accept them as a beginning of a collection, which she hoped would eventually be cataloged and kept in the Barnard library. She was prepared to continue her clipping service and to supplement the collection with financial support. It was a splendid, well-conceived idea, and I was touched by her generosity and the depth of her commitment. After several meetings we decided it was the perfect way to set up a special library on women's issues, something we had wanted from the very beginning.

Myra Josephs was an amazing woman. Her mother, Birdie Goldsmith Ast, had been an active suffragist, a colleague of Carrie Chapman Catt's, and a founder of the League of Women Voters. She had encouraged her daughter Myra to aim high and to prepare for a profession. Myra Josephs majored in chemistry at Barnard and earned a Ph.D. in chemistry at Columbia, at a time when there were very few women chemists, and even fewer with Ph.D.'s. She had wanted to work in industry. She recounted how recruiters came to Columbia but never offered her a job. She received rejection letters, informing her that she was turned down because she was a woman. After several unsatisfying jobs, Myra married, and, for the next fifteen years, she told me, "succumbed to the prevalent climate" and lived as a full-time wife and mother. She never used her chemistry training again, although, during the period when she was at home raising a family, she gave a great deal of thought to the inequities that she and other women like her faced. In 1962 she started her volunteer job at the Ellis Institute, a job she kept for many years.

I went to talk with the director of the Barnard library, a youngish man whom I scarcely knew. I told him about Myra Josephs's proposal for a special library collection on women's issues, to be sponsored and partially financed by the Women's Center with ongoing help from Myra Josephs. I pointed out that the library already had a small historical collection on and by women that we could expand. I underscored that Barnard would be pioneering by making a major scholarly contribution to the women's movement and that the Barnard library would be the first in the metropolitan area to acknowledge the value of separately cataloging this new material on women. His response was immediate and negative. Although he had a number of reasons, none of which seemed valid to me, it boiled down to the fact that he didn't understand and wasn't really interested in women's issues. He said there were plenty of books in the library about and by women, and he couldn't see the value of isolating these works. He was very emphatic in his view that his job was to ensure the excellence of the Barnard library and not to respond to every new "fad" that came along.

Perhaps it was just as well. His response didn't stop us; it spurred us into action. We turned to a few good women librarians for help, the most important of whom was Barnard staff librarian Pat Ballou. Pat had been appointed by President Peterson to the first Women's Center Executive Committee, an appointment, she told me, which changed her life. She described herself as a traditional person with many years of training and experience as a librarian. But, on the committee, she found herself gradually changing many of the lifelong attitudes that she had held about women. And, as she began to think as a feminist, she was able to envision a truly nontraditional collection. Later she told me that she credited Martha Peterson with inadvertently making her a feminist.

We had shelving built to line the walls of our one large seminar room, and in 1973 we started The Birdie Goldsmith Ast Collection, named in honor of Myra Josephs's mother. Over the next decade, Myra made this project an important part of her life, coming in every few months with stacks of research articles, as well as making regular financial contributions to maintain and expand the collection. She even gave additional sums of money to Barnard to invest so that we could count on income after she died.

Using Myra Josephs's material as a nucleus, we added other articles, reports, pamphlets, clippings, papers, directories, bibliographies, books, and special issues of journals, as well as subscriptions to newsletters and periodicals covering a wide range of subject areas. Our holdings grew to the size of a small special library collection, with over 6,000 items and subscriptions to some seventy newsletters and periodicals. By the late 1970s we were regularly included in the two-day meeting of all of the Columbia University special libraries, a recognition of the value of our collection.

We were cautioned not to call our collection a library since we weren't professional librarians. We didn't follow library protocol in cataloging, and we included materials that libraries would regard as "ephemeral." From the start, we cataloged material according to women's issues rather than the Dewey Decimal system. We decided to limit the collection to current issues; not to include historical, biographical, or creative works; and to focus, wherever possible, while still including many significant mainstream books, on material that might not easily find its way into traditional library collections. In this way we were able to collect most of the classic feminist writings, much of which was either unpublished or published by small presses. Most important, our collection was open to the public twelve months of the year with no restrictions on its use.

The heart of the collection was the vertical-file material, easily accessible, in large green boxes. We encouraged students and researchers using the collection to give us a copy of their completed work. Initially, the subject headings were straightforward and concise, ranging from Education, Employment, and Legal Status to Sex Roles and Sex Differences. To accommodate the depth and range of the proliferating research and writing on women's issues, new categories were added, and other categories were subdivided. For instance, Abortion, Birth Control, Health, and Sexuality became Health with subheadings for Abortion, Birth Control, Drug Abuse and Alcoholism, Menstruation and Menopause, Pregnancy and Childbirth, Sterilization Abuse, and the Women's Health Movement. The largest category was Sex Roles and Sex Differences, which in time had fourteen subheadings, including Sexuality.

The changes in and rapid growth of the collection mirrored the development of the women's movement. We never had the staff to give the collection the attention it needed, but we all loved working on it whenever we could. On many late afternoons and early evenings when the day's activities had ceased and the Women's Center had emptied, I sat quietly at a table, sifting through new material and deciding where it should go. One part of me would have liked to work on the collection full time. It was exhilarating and sometimes overwhelming to see the new material that was delivered to the Women's Center each day.

Often I stopped to read an article or pulled one from the pile to take home to read. I remember the first piece I came across on women of my generation. Entitled "Women in the Middle" by Florence Rush, it appeared in *Notes from the Third Year*, the last of three annual collections of early, classic feminist writing, all of which became collectors' items. Rush describes the expectations of women as family caretakers, living their lives as wives, mothers, and finally as daughters caring for their elderly parents, with the responsibilities for others' lives always taking precedence over independent steps for their own growth and development. She relates how she started social work school when her children were of school age, only to be called to her children's school and told that one of them had a behavior problem. The school counselor attributed this problem directly to Rush's relinquishing her role as full-time mother and, hence, not tending enough to her child. She movingly recounts how she, as the middle-aged daughter, later had to take on the care of an aging father while her brother was excused on the grounds that he had important work to do. I had never seen anything like this in print, and I was surprised to find myself in tears. I recognized my own life: while I had felt lucky to have made a place for myself professionally, starting when my children were little, I also took care of my family and, later, of my mother when she was old and fragile.

The number of students, researchers, journalists, and activists who used our collection continued to grow, since we had research material that could not be found in any other place in the metropolitan area. People constantly thanked us for keeping and cataloging what so many libraries couldn't accommodate. One woman, sent by her publisher to research an introductory chapter on the origins of the women's movement for a book, came in one day, looked around, and said, "What a small collection; I thought it would be more substantial." I caught her comment as I left for a meeting, feeling chagrined by the rapid dismissal. I returned several hours later to find the woman still there. She exclaimed when I came in, "I'm so glad you came back so I can tell you it's a wonderful collection, concentrated and beautifully organized: just what I need." At the other extreme was the Columbia College junior who came in to find one book or one article for a term paper he was writing that referred to women. When he saw what we had, he was overwhelmed at the magnitude of the collection. He had no intention, he said, of spending more than fifteen minutes here, and he wanted someone to tell him exactly which article or book to look at.

Occasionally, we first learned of an emerging women's issue from someone using our collection, as in the case of two British women who were starting a center for battered women. Visiting United States women's projects, they spent several days going through our collection. They left us all the printed material they had about their project, and, within a few months, we had set up a subheading on Battered Women, soon to be accompanied by Incest and Child Abuse, Pornography and Media, Prostitution, Rape, and, finally, Sexual Harassment, all subcategories under the category Violence and Sexual Exploitation.

■ 12
BUILDING A WOMEN'S CENTER

For one who had worked with women and had thought about their lives and expectations for so many years, it was surprising how many assumptions I had left unquestioned. The first time I heard the phrase "the personal is political," I just didn't get it. I later learned that it came out of consciousness-raising groups and was shorthand for the realization that the commonalities of women's personal lives reflected the political and social constructs of the larger society.

Several books—all published between 1970 and 1973—deepened my understanding of emerging feminist issues. Four were anthologies: *Sisterhood Is Powerful: An Anthology of Writings from the Women's Liberation Movement*, edited by Robin Morgan; *Woman in Sexist Society: Studies in Power and Powerlessness*, edited by Vivian Gornick and Barbara K. Moran; *Black Women in White America: A Documentary History*, edited by Gerda Lerner; and *The Black Woman: An Anthology*, edited by Toni Cade Bambara. All four documented the universal oppression of women and the awakening of a feminist consciousness. The other, *Tomorrow's Tomorrow: The Black Woman* by Joyce Ladner, explored the ways in which society shapes Black girls' concept of womanhood and their goals and expectations.

There was another book that I found provocative but also troubling at that time, *The Dialectic of Sex: The Case for Feminist Revolution* by Shulamith Firestone. I was surprised to see how important it was to many young feminists in the early 1970s. Firestone made a strong case for the dissolution of the institution of the family as the only possible way to free women and children from the constraints of biology and patriarchy. Her rage at men and the privileged position they held was boundless and led her to solutions that still seem to me to be quite removed from reality: replacing the patriarchal family with what she called a "household" of people—a collective of adults and children of all ages, living together for a designated time, perhaps ten years, long enough to give children a measure of security. She never resolved the biological hurdle of childbearing, although she predicted a time when artificial insemination would be widely used.

She spoke in a voice that many women could relate to, a voice that provoked their anger at patriarchy. Even though I had serious questions about Shulamith Firestone's thesis, *The Dialectic of Sex* impressed upon me the depth of women's rage and the various ways in which women were controlled by patriarchy.

Many of the issues that women were beginning to talk about came into sharp focus at a conference the Women's Center held in the winter of 1973 called "Women Learn from Women." The conference was the joint effort of a small group of women from eight colleges in the metropolitan area. Among the planners were Barbara Buonocristo, Phyllis Chesler, Florence Howe, Gerda Lerner, Wendy Martin, and Catharine Stimpson. Most, but not all, of the planners were faculty members from either public or private, four-year or community, colleges. We started meeting in 1971 to talk about how to integrate some of the emerging feminist issues into the women's studies courses they were teaching. Out of these discussions came a plan for a conference. Initially conceived of as an academic conference, sometime during the planning process, a tightly knit group of faculty, administrators, and adult students from the School of General Studies at Columbia University insisted that the scope of the conference be broadened to include activists' concerns.

It took almost two years to plan this conference. The final product was quite extraordinary. Each college group organized and presented at least one of the twelve workshops, each covering one of the important current feminist issues the group had identified. I list all the workshop titles and descriptions, as they appeared on the program, because they illuminate so clearly the range and the flavor of the conference:

- After Consciousness-Raising, What?—strategies for change: violence, socialization, political action

- Androgyny—The Range of Human Sexual Expression—heterosexuality, homosexuality, lesbianism, bisexuality, pansexuality

- Controlling Our Bodies—contraception, legal abortion, new attitudes towards health care for women

- Do Women Have a Separate Experience of Education? Should They?—as students, as teachers; what women's studies courses are telling us

- Emancipated Lifestyles—can women combine life, work, and love without marriage? the experience of women who have done so

- How Far Will Legal Solutions Take Us?—how laws such as those on rape and abortion manipulate and limit women

- Lesbian Experience in Education—what is it? what lesbian women are doing to change it

- The Strength of Sisterhood: A Case History—administrators, faculty, staff, and maids working together to end sex discrimination in employment

- What *Do* Women Learn from Women?—power structures and access to information; feminism, and new pathways to knowledge

- Who Will Take Care of the Children?—new patterns for new lifestyles: mothers alone, parents who share, day care centers, communes

- Women in Search of Autonomy—fear of risk-taking, fear of failure and success, taking oneself seriously, finding options, acting in one's own self-interest

- Women over Thirty—Fears, Expectations, and Reality—ageism, the media and self-image, economic needs, and fulfillment

Except for one workshop, which dealt with the plight of women working as maids at Columbia University, we did not address the issues of race and class as feminist issues at this conference. And, with the exception of the panelists from this one workshop, none of the other panelists, speakers, or conference participants were women of color. Many of the workshop panelists are still active leaders in the women's movement of the 1990s: Phyllis Chesler, Blanche Wiesen Cook, Barbara Ehrenreich, Hester Eisenstein, Kate Ellis, Kris Glen, Carol Groneman, Florence Howe, Wendy Martin, Elizabeth Minnich, Florence Rush, Sue Riemer Sacks, Amy Swerdlow, and June Zeitlin.

We didn't preregister participants; we had no keynote speakers, only workshops and a final wrap-up session chaired by Catharine Stimpson. We charged a token entry fee—I think it was a dollar—and we included in our announcements the promise that we would provide childcare. As the coordinator, I faced a real challenge. With practically no funds and with no idea how many people would attend, I had to provide space with appropriate seating and other facilities, to set up a childcare center for women who might bring their children, and to arrange for publicity. While following new feminist dicta, which insisted on informal, nonhierarchical ways of doing things, I nevertheless had to be sure that a Barnard College event was run smoothly.

Each group assumed responsibility for bringing fifty women from their own institution and for publicizing the event as widely as possible. We projected a conference attendance of no more than 400. I was in a state of panic at the thought of coordinating a conference over which I had so little control and so little advance information about attendance. I was amused when Florence Howe told me that on the bus coming in from Old Westbury, one of her students asked how this conference would work. She responded by saying not to worry, "Jane Gould has run loads of conferences and will know how to do it." In truth, it was my first conference.

The conference clearly touched a nerve. On a bleak February day in 1973, close to 1,000 women streamed through the Barnard gates and spent the day considering issues, many of which they had never dared to talk about or even to think about before. Participants were mostly over twenty-five, white, and college educated. We ran our first childcare center for which thirty children turned up. At the end of the day, some children were not ready to leave. There were too many participants for the sessions to be called workshops, but it didn't matter. Women spoke up, listened to the panelists and to each other, and stayed for the wrap-up session late in the day. There were no firm answers, only new questions and insightful comments.

Just how far-reaching and experimental some of the workshops were was best illustrated by "Women in Search of Autonomy," a workshop organized by Hester Eisenstein and Sue Riemer Sacks, young Barnard faculty members who were to become two of my most loyal supporters during the next decade. The seventy-five women who attended the workshop divided themselves into small groups and were asked to draw depictions of their "life spaces" at the present moment. Using these drawings, each group named and discussed the conflicts women encounter when they try to become autonomous: the fear of failure, the fear of not being taken seriously, of having no creativity, of being dependent on others, and of not using one's energy efficiently. The stereotypes of being "daddy's little girl" and being swallowed up by husbands and lovers were recognized as major impediments in the struggle for autonomy.

At the other end of the spectrum was an activist workshop entitled "The Strength of Sisterhood: A Case History." Some of the major participants in the first labor struggle of its kind at Columbia University told their stories in such a way so that conference participants might glimpse the power that women could wield when they were organized and working together. During the unexpected recession of 1972, Columbia University had cut back on its service staff, firing a number of maids at the bottom of the wage ladder. Although these women were union members, initially, the union did nothing to protect them. A two-year-old group of Columbia-affiliated women, Columbia Women's Liberation, was outraged and decided to take action. Funds were raised to hire Jan Goodman, a feminist lawyer, and a suit was brought against Columbia and the union. After settling with the union, the suit was continued against the university. Blatant sexism was found not only on the part of the university but within the union itself. Clearest evidence of this was that two separate employment lists were kept, one for female maids and the other for male janitors. This way, seniority was never an issue between women and men. Moreover, although both groups did essentially the same work, the maids were paid less than janitors.

Much to the embarrassment of the union, which capitulated before the Columbia administration did, this young feminist group kept fighting until they forced the university to combine the lists into one, to rehire some of the maids, and to negotiate their wages so that they were comparable to the janitors'. One of the panelists described the dramatic gasp in court when the white-haired judge looked at the group of plaintiffs—all women of color—and said he thought too much was being made of this case, since they could all go on welfare.

For many conference participants, this conference was their introduction to the women's movement. The workshops were so charged with energy that it was difficult to bring them to a close. Throughout the day, women kept coming up to me and thanking me for holding the conference. No one complained about the crowded rooms or that they had to sit on the floor. I only heard two complaints. The first complaint was that participants wanted to attend all the workshops, and each woman could attend only two: one in the morning and one in the afternoon.

The other complaint was my own doing. I had encouraged Jay to attend, thinking of course that there would be a few other men. But he was the only man at the conference. As I made my rounds, visiting workshops, I pulled him out of one workshop and suggested that he visit a particularly volatile one, "After Consciousness-Raising, What?" A number of participants in the workshop were uncomfortable the moment Jay sat down. Several women said they couldn't tolerate a man in their midst, and, after a few moments, he was asked to leave. As he left the conference, I had a moment of guilt, then thought to myself how many times women have been made to feel unwelcome. I was sorry that it had to be Jay. But, to his credit, he took this rejection philosophically and relished telling what happened to him at "Jane's first conference."

The afterglow of the conference was such that, whenever I went to a meeting or event over the next several months, I heard people talking about "the pioneer Barnard conference." Its success and the explosion of challenging ideas underscored the force of the women's movement, which was beginning to ask hard questions about every aspect of women's lives while fostering meaningful connections among women. I was excited and proud. On the front cover of our first brochure, I used the phrase "a women's college responds to the challenge of the women's movement." I thought this was a bold statement— one that I could not have amplified very much at that time, but it proved to be prophetic and accurate.

From the perspective of the economy and of other social indicators in the 1970s, the women's movement was an anomaly. While this was a period of strong optimism for women, on the other hand, in many ways, this decade signaled the end of the American dream. Using real wages as a measure, the economy reached an all-time historical high in 1970, but, within a few years, there were indications that the nation was in serious trouble. Falling wages, a recession in 1972, the oil embargo in 1973, the horrors of the Nixon years, Watergate, and the dragging out of the Vietnam War until 1975 were harbingers of a changing society. The cold war continued. The United States was losing its dominant position in such basic industries as steel, electronics, and automobiles, with severe economic consequences. At the same time United States foreign policy was obstructing the achievement of basic human rights in Latin America and developing countries in Africa. Nevertheless, the momentum of the women's movement continued to grow with remarkable strength throughout the decade.

Personally, the 1970s were wonderful years for me. At home I shared the daily excitement of the women's movement with an unusual man who was always interested and supportive. Our lives together were both intermeshed and separate. We assumed that each of us would continue with all the obligations and interests we had before we met. Jay was building a new business, had a weekly men's tennis and poker game, and continued his regular choral singing. I had my graduate studies and my ongoing women's meetings and events, which occupied many evenings and weekends. There was much that we shared, but, freed from the responsibilities of young children, we also gave each other lots of space. There were weeks when we went our own separate ways most waking hours, managing to catch up with each other whenever we could find the time.

We were committed to building an equal partnership in which household chores would be divided fifty-fifty, but I could see that, if I insisted on a rigid definition of equality, it would never work out. I had learned from other women, as well as in my own marriage, how hard it was for women filled with high hopes of equality to start a relationship with a man. More than once I heard a woman say, "The list of chores, and whose turn it is, is posted on the refrigerator, and, if he doesn't make the bed this time, I'm not going home." At my stage in life, I would have been hard pressed to make such demands. I wanted the beds *made,* not just the covers pulled up, so I made them. To this day, Jay hasn't been able to master all the details of doing the laundry. But he found a niche for himself in the kitchen: he learned to cook as another creative activity. He never takes short cuts, enjoying the planning, shopping, even chopping vegetables. He built a repertoire of interesting dishes and enjoyed improvising. Even today, he loves to add what he calls "secret ingredients" and delights in constantly coming up with new flavors for recipes he has tried before.

Although none of our children lived with us, they were very much a part of our lives. Nancy, as a Danforth fellow at Yale, completed a Ph.D. in political science and went on to a successful college teaching career at Wesleyan, marred by a completely unexpected disability. She started losing her hearing in her mid-twenties, and, although helped by hearing aids, she was to face most of her adult life with a serious hearing problem, one which she handles with exceptional courage, determination, and aplomb.

David moved to California after graduating from college, and we kept hoping he would find his niche and be able to use his intellectual potential. But within a few years and after several visits in California and in New York, we had to face the truth that he suffered a serious, disabling chemical imbalance. I came to the realization that our responsibility was to provide whatever support he needed and to see that he had access to good therapy.

Jay's youngest daughter, Emily, went to Barnard, and, although initially our relationship was awkward, by the time she had grown beyond adolescence, our relationship improved dramatically. In her senior year at college, she came to Women's Center events and showed a readiness to include her father and me in her life. Soon she was visiting us, and gradually I began to know this wonderfully spirited, talented young woman. Diana, too, finally felt comfortable with us, and I like to date the beginning of our growing closeness to a marvelous day we spent together in July 1978 on a bus headed for an ERA demonstration in Washington, D.C. Diana was an early feminist activist, a member of Red Stockings, who had participated in the memorable sit-in at the *Ladies Home Journal* in 1970 protesting the unequal status of women in the field of journalism and the stereotypical images of women portrayed in the magazine. She had already achieved distinction in her field. As a senior at the UCLA (University of California, Los Angeles) Film School, she had written a screenplay, *Jenny,* which had become a film starring Marlo Thomas and Alan Alda. During the 1970s she was establishing herself as a television writer in Hollywood, known as a writer who could thoughtfully and realistically depict women characters.

While I had brought to my job a firm commitment to equality and to civil rights, and an understanding of the critical importance of highlighting and cultivating the connection between feminism and social change, I knew the center had to broaden its middle-class scope to include the particular experiences and perspectives of women of different sexual orientations and women of different race, class, and ethnic backgrounds. But, first, I was forced to acknowledge that I wasn't at ease with all the issues I heard women raising. In truth, I didn't understand some of the concerns I heard discussed. Some seemed inconsequential and others threatened my whole being.

Initially, I couldn't see the ways in which language reinforced sexism. I had trouble taking seriously the charge that language was male centered and excluded women and found myself thinking—and sometimes saying—that "mankind," "brotherhood," and "chairman" were generic terms and should be accepted as including women. I was even amused by feminists who insisted that the term "girl" only be applied to females up to a certain age—perhaps the end of high school—and found it quite a mouthful to call a first-year Barnard student a young woman. At the same time, I winced every time my mother referred to the woman who cleaned her apartment as "my girl," particularly since the woman was a grandmother, and I felt this showed a lack of respect.

Language didn't seem to me be part of the struggle for equality, but I was wrong. It took time for this inequity to penetrate my consciousness, but, when it finally did, it was like a light going on. I was sitting at a meeting sponsored by the Women's International League for Peace and Freedom, listening to a fine speech given by a good man, a leader in the anti–cold war movement. I heard him use all those charged words—"mankind," "brotherhood," "man,"—and I looked around at all the women, and, suddenly, I felt uncomfortable, excluded. It was evident that he wasn't addressing me or the other women. Afterward, two or three of us went up to the speaker and explained how angered and ignored we felt by his insensitive use of male terms. He was surprised and apologized profusely. He insisted that he used those terms generically and inclusively. I left the meeting knowing that I would never again accept the use of words with male roots as including me and other women. I came to realize that any civilization that could put a person on the moon could find a way to change its language so that it included those who had been left out.

When I was first introduced to the self-help part of the women's health movement, I thought it bordered on the ridiculous. But, in the spirit of the movement, I permitted a group of young women to use our space evenings, and, with the blinds pulled down, they learned how to use a speculum and see their vaginas for the first time. They took this very seriously and found it self-affirming to see that their vaginas were pink and rosy, not unsavory black holes as many had been led to believe. Again, as I watched the strong position the newly formed women's health movement took and read their classic, *Our Bodies, Ourselves* by the Boston Women's Health Book Collective, I began to understand how necessary it was for women to know their bodies in order to more fully control their lives.

I didn't understand lesbianism, but I knew it shouldn't be a Women's Center issue. On some unconscious level, I must have been homophobic, although, if so charged, I would have insisted that this wasn't true. To this day, I can't describe precisely how I felt. Until I came to the Women's Center, I had never known a woman who had said she was a lesbian. Although I knew there were women who related only to women, I was more comfortable not talking about it, since I assumed that all "normal" people were heterosexual.

As more women who preferred relationships with women to men came out of the closet and publicly talked about their sexual orientation, they insisted that their presence be accepted and their demands be included in the women's movement. The response to this by a number of women's organizations and by many individual women was deeply homophobic. There was a reluctance to identify with lesbians and, as late as 1977 at the Women's Conference in Houston, there were heated discussions about whether including lesbian issues would impede the passage of the Equal Rights Amendment, one of the priorities of the conference. In the end, recognition of lesbians won out.

I worried about the tensions among women about this issue, the baiting and other tactics used to discredit and divide women, and I could see that, even within the women's movement, lesbianism was to remain a thorny issue for some. This tension, however, heightened my resolve to ensure that lesbians felt comfortable in the Women's Center and to include the lesbian community and their concerns in all of our programs. I sensed that this was potentially a powerful, divisive issue, one on which we could rise or fall.

Perhaps it was my strong gut reaction that we must provide a supportive, inclusive atmosphere for all women that encouraged me to learn from and to empathize with women whose sexual orientation was different from mine. As I came to know and to work with the small lesbian community both within and outside the Women's Center, I realized that any discomfort I might have felt stemmed from fear of the unknown. I realized that I didn't have to understand everyone's sexual orientation and how it evolved. I simply had to accept all women as they defined themselves. I was rewarded for this by the trust and by the enriching contributions of lesbians to our center and our programs. I was particularly touched by a Barnard senior, editor of the undergraduate newspaper, who came to ask me for help in finding a therapist. And, she said, "Please find me one who won't treat my lesbianism as a problem. That's who I am and I don't want to change."

What we came to call the new scholarship on women, however, was the issue that touched me most deeply and in the most complicated ways. I began to hear objections about traditional scholarship, not only that it omitted serious mention of women but that it was skewed and even incorrect. I had often wondered why there was not more information about women throughout history and why there hadn't been more women leaders in all fields. My graduate school experience had opened my eyes to the omission of women and women's concerns in research studies on career development and to the ways in which patriarchal society excluded women's experience. For the first time in my life, I questioned the methodology of "objective" scholarship and its inherent values. The more I heard young scholars address questions of scholarship, the more radical and complex the issue appeared to be.

Over and over during the next decade, I observed with wonder and excitement as feminist scholars uncovered layers and layers of misconceptions about women's lives, asking new questions about a history that had been written by men and had focused on wars, explorations, and inventions— rendering invisible and voiceless the lives of half of the human population. During this decade I witnessed the development of a whole new body of knowledge, one which was to change our understanding about women and their place in history.

The most revolutionary discovery for me was that there is no such thing as value-free knowledge. It was as if all the parameters I had always known and never questioned were fading away. The deep-ranging implications of this new feminist scholarship was put in perspective by my brilliant young friend and colleague, Elizabeth Minnich. At a conference we held for vocational counselors of girls and women on the implications of the new scholarship on women, she described this major social revolution as similar to that which occurred when, after a millennium of accepting that the earth was flat, we learned that the earth was round. We couldn't add this new knowledge on to the old. Everything had to be rethought to fit the new paradigm.

There were two other important components of the women's movement that had a great impact on me in the early 1970s. The first was a sense of sisterhood, a keen enjoyment in being with women and in helping each other in a way that I had never known. Sharing insights, experiences, and commonalities created powerful bonds and a new sense of entitlement. The pleasure of being with other women and, thereby, giving and receiving support was a new experience that was to enrich the rest of my life. The second was the questioning of hierarchy and finding new, more egalitarian ways of getting things done, an outgrowth of the civil rights movement of the 1960s. Working in a highly traditional institution, there were limits to where we could take this new concept. One of the first things I did was to redesign the job of my assistant from a support-staff position to a professional administrative job. This took months of rewriting job descriptions and negotiating with the personnel office, but, in the end, I won, with a sizable salary increase for her. My reward was a young woman who could take pride in her job, stay for a few years, gain valuable experience, and be a colleague rather than a secretary.

The first time I heard my young assistant director answer the phone and say, "Jane Gould doesn't have a secretary," I smiled. It was important for students to come to an office that didn't have a traditional hierarchy. In this way, I was able to have an assistant who could share much of my work, who—because she was younger—could relate more directly to students than I, and from whom I could learn about some of the issues that only her generation could fully experience. It meant that we all did more clerical and receptionist work, but, even as we expanded, I was always careful that all our staff—including part-time student workers—had the chance to participate in as many activities as they could and, wherever possible, share in decision-making.

I tried to extend this nonhierarchical way of working to other activities and found that it usually worked well. I formed committees wherever thoughtful planning was needed, calling on women from within and from outside of Barnard, of different ages and of different backgrounds, to meet over lunch or late in the day or in the early evening to discuss an issue fully or to plan a conference or some other project.

I learned that process was as important as content. It meant more meetings, more people participating in the planning, more points of view, and more willingness to listen and to change—all resulting in a more inclusive, open-ended event than most of us were accustomed to. We made most of our decisions by consensus. I felt comfortable with the process; it not only proved to be effective but it also introduced new people to the Women's Center.

Occasionally, there were problems, either in reaching consensus in time for a deadline or in a committee veering off in a completely different direction than seemed appropriate. When this happened, I had either to point out that it was my responsibility to meet the deadline, which often involved printing schedules and invitations to speakers, or to explain that the Women's Center was a part of the college and that this imposed some limits on what the center could do.

Meeting the challenges that these issues presented propelled us and gave us our identity. Word of our existence spread so quickly that we were overwhelmed with requests from scholars, artists, filmmakers, writers, activists, and women's groups to hold public forums and creative programs on a whole range of emerging issues. Although we couldn't accommodate all these requests, in one way or another, most of the movers and shakers of the women's movement did participate actively in at least one Women's Center program during the tumultuous 1970s. This included visits from European feminist leaders, among them Hélène Cixous, Juliet Mitchell, and Sheila Rowbotham, and delegations of women from the Soviet Union and from China. Without any paid publicity or special media attention, I found I could depend on the feminist community to publicize an event and to ensure a good attendance. Within a few years, we became a strong feminist presence in the New York metropolitan area, living up to one of the principles stated in our charter, "to become a physical and psychological meeting place for women." So urgent was the need for public exploration of perspectives that were directly related to the new thinking about women and to the particular experience of women from different races, class backgrounds, and sexual orientations, that, once started, many of our programs—the Scholar and the Feminist conferences, a film and video festival, a series of monthly women's issues luncheons, and the Reid Lectureship—quickly became a permanent part of our calendar.

As we became known, the number of events multiplied and on any month our calendar might include such programs as a lecture entitled "A View of Women As Seen Through the Eyes of Christine de Pizan," a fifteenth-century woman of letters; a film entitled *Women of Wounded Knee;* a discussion of grass-roots organizing for battered women; a workshop on "Lesbianism and the Social Function of Taboo"; a women's art exhibition; an analysis of the theological question "Is There a Feminist Understanding of Sin?"; a discussion on "Perceptions of

Black Women Writers"; or a talk by a Salvadorean woman describing how women in El Salvador were oppressed both by the *junta* and by the machismo of the men with whom they lived. In addition, it was not unusual for the Women's Center to cosponsor a program with an outside group, an easy way to make connections with the feminist community and to provide space and support for programs that we might otherwise not be able to offer.

So great was the demand for space that our small office was constantly in use, either for our own meetings, which often spilled over into evenings and weekends, or by one of the many newly formed women's groups. A consciousness-raising group met regularly once a week for six years and, for a period of years, a women's caucus in sociology held their quarterly weekend meetings at the Women's Center. Walking down Broadway on almost any night and seeing the lights still burning in the Women's Center was confirmation for me of the vibrancy of the women's movement.

In 1975 we received additional money from the final disposition of the Helen Rogers Reid Estate to be used for "visible" programs that would publicly acknowledge the Reid family support. We took full advantage of this unexpected windfall and created the Women's Center Reid Lectureship. We designed a program that would annually bring to the Barnard campus women who had distinguished themselves in their field and had shown a strong commitment to other women. We wanted to select women who might not be heard at Barnard under normal circumstances and, whenever possible, who came from backgrounds that were traditionally underrepresented. Since I worried about the paucity of role models for minority students at Barnard and I knew that we all needed to hear more from women of diverse backgrounds, we included as one of the stipulations that at least half of these lecturers be women of color. I saw the program as an annual opportunity to broaden and deepen our understanding of women's experiences.

The lectureship started in the fall of 1975 and included such women as June Jordan and Alice Walker, Helen Rodriguez-Trias, Rhonda Copelon and Nancy Stearns, Ntozake Shange, Bella Abzug, Mirra Komarovsky, and Bernice Reagon. I asked these women to share their personal perceptions and experiences as women, as well as their professional experiences as feminists, both at a public lecture and informally with small groups of students, alumnae, faculty, staff, and community people over a period of a day and a half. The Reid Lectureship became an outstanding annual event. June Jordan described the pain of being Black at Barnard in the late 1950s and how she dropped out because the college had not answered her needs. She pointed out that no one had introduced her to a single Black author, poet, historian, or idea; nor was she ever assigned a single woman to study as a thinker, writer, poet, or life force. And, even worse, she learned nothing at Barnard that "might try to alter the political and economic realities underlying our Black condition in white America." Alice Walker spoke about the critical need for models in the artist's life and what it meant to her to discover Zora Neale Hurston, a Barnard alumna none of us had heard of at the time. Helen Rodriguez-Trias publicly defined, for the first time, the issue of sterilization abuse, especially as it affects the lives of poor women. Rhonda Copelon and Nancy Stearns of the Center for Constitutional Rights described their groundbreaking legal work that led to the Supreme Court's historic *Roe v. Wade* decision that legalized abortion. All the Reid lecturers added to our understanding of the commonalities and of the differences in women's lives.

In the early years of the center, we kept a log detailing visitors and callers along with their requests. The increase in the number and kinds of inquiries that came into the center was remarkable and underscored both the new interests women were developing and the lack of referral services in the metropolitan area. It was one thing to collect and to post information on new research on women, women's studies programs and courses throughout the country, foundations and fellowships for women, conferences, women's centers, women's professional groups and activist groups, and special events for women; but it was quite another thing to try to respond to the growing cry for personal referrals, which always had a sense of urgency. I was troubled by the many women who called or came in with questions about where to turn for information and for referrals on health, abortion, employment, sexuality, therapy, as well as legal and social services. I quickly learned that, as women's consciousness was being raised, no women's center could neglect to meet the constant demand for these referrals. A woman who needs legal help to collect child custody payments or who needs literature on affordable abortion clinics needs this information right away. I knew we lacked the staff to provide this essential service, but we certainly couldn't ignore the steady increase in such requests.

In those early years we turned these inquiries over to a small group of women who had formed a loose collective called the Women's Counseling Project. Started by a few faculty women from our neighbor, the Union Theological Seminary, when the New York State abortion law was liberalized in 1971, the Women's Counseling Project had been created to do abortion counseling and referrals. It operated out of a small basement room in Earl Hall, the religious center of Columbia University, a room shared with the campus Christian Scientists. The project received minimal funding from church groups and charged no fee for its services.

The staff was small, numbering eight in the beginning, all volunteers, except for two students who were on Work-Study. The volunteers were drawn from faculty, undergraduate, and graduate students at Barnard, Columbia, Union Theological Seminary, and other colleges in the metropolitan community. While some natural attrition occurred from year to year, the volunteers always included several women who were taking time off before starting a career. Some remarkable women made the Women's Counseling Project unique. One was Emily Heilbrun, who, for the four years she was a student at Barnard and the year after graduation before she went to law school, devoted all her free time and energy to the project. Another was Dr. Eleanor Schuker, a psychiatrist at the Columbia Health Service, who sought out the project and arranged her schedule so that she could serve as a consultant to the staff. She regularly attended their weekly staff meetings, providing general professional supervision, staff training, and guidance on problems that the staff encountered with women who called or came in for short-term peer counseling.

When I joined the Women's Counseling Project Advisory Board in 1973, the project had expanded its services to include referrals in all areas of healthcare, as well as therapy, sexuality, employment, and legal services. The staff routinely checked all referrals before using them, made on-site visits whenever possible, and were careful that information about location, fees, and services was up-to-date. Nothing is more discouraging to a woman in desperate need of help than to be given referrals about fees and locations that are no longer correct. It is even worse to be given a referral to services that are no longer in existence.

Few women in the metropolitan area knew that the counseling project existed; there were no funds to publicize this service, and the staff was unable to keep the office open full time. Messages were left with the Earl Hall switchboard, where they were kept until a member of the project picked them up. The Women's Counseling Project was often closed when the Christian Scientists were using their offices, as well as during vacations and right before exams. It was hardly a professional way to run such a service, but it was the best these dedicated women could do. And when they had started, no other group in New York City was even attempting to help women find services for abortion counseling and other emerging personal needs.

There was no doubt about the urgent need for an expanded project. Listening to discussions about problems of staff, space, and money at board meetings, I started to think about bringing the Women's Counseling Project to Barnard.

When I suggested this possibility to the project staff, they agreed to tell me under what circumstances they thought it might be possible. It didn't take them long to inform me that, if we had suitable space and could ensure the continuation of their autonomy, they would welcome the move.

I was fortunate in taking this proposal to our new president, Jacquelyn Mattfeld, who understood very clearly how important it was for Barnard to recognize the women's movement and the need to reach out to the larger community of women. She told me that all I needed was the approval of all deans and directors of departments whose activities the project might impinge on, as well as clearance from the college lawyer. This turned out to be a major undertaking, which was to take over a year.

None of the deans or directors liked the idea; the dean of studies found the notion that the project staff need not report to anyone—not even the director of the Women's Center—unacceptable. The college doctor thought students would confuse the project with the health services office; the admissions director worried that we would have "public riffraff" coming to Barnard, which would damage our image. All the heads of student departments had their reasons for not approving. The college law firm spent hours preparing a contract which was so rigid that, as I told President Mattfeld, if the Women's Center had had to abide by these rules, we never would have come into existence. By politicking and with sheer perseverance in convincing the president that she had to instruct the law firm that she wanted the project to come to Barnard, I finally won out.

The Women's Counseling Project moved to Barnard in 1978, to a pleasant spacious room a few doors away from the Women's Center. I helped it achieve nonprofit status, as a 501(c)(3) institution, and to build a board of directors. Initially, we dipped into our limited gift money to give the project financial support, while helping with proposals, which brought in several small foundation grants. Two paid part-time coordinators and several additional volunteers were added to the staff, which made it possible for the counseling project to remain open almost full time. The project maintained its autonomy while developing close ties with the Women's Center. We kept an extension of their phone in our office and took their calls when necessary; we attended and reported at each other's regular staff meetings, and we often worked on issues together, cosponsoring programs, such as a series of dialogues entitled "Women, Violence, and Violation" and a conference on feminism and therapy.

I watched with pride as the project became a valued public service, providing quality referrals and peer counseling to some 3,000 women annually in the New York metropolitan area. It was the best solution: to strengthen a service we could not possibly provide ourselves and to work out an affiliation that proved to be an innovative feminist model of expansion. This experience made me realize that feminism was producing a new breed of women: strong, young, independent, committed, and willing to challenge the establishment when necessary, and most possessed a degree of maturity that I hadn't seen before.

THE WOMEN'S CENTER AS CATALYST AND ADVOCATE

From the beginning the Women's Center occupied a somewhat paradoxical position within the institutional framework of the college. On the one hand, Barnard as an institution had pioneered in setting up the Women's Center as early as 1971 and in providing an operating budget that increased each year. I knew of no other women's college that had done this. On the other hand, Barnard, like other institutions with "special provisions" for women, regarded the Women's Center as marginal. The college's ongoing concern with presenting a smooth public image and its long-standing homophobia—so characteristic of women's colleges—created tensions between the center and the college. In addition, the college demonstrated a distaste for emphasizing its commitment to women—except as students in a highly traditional curriculum—in any way that might offend certain constituencies, particularly current and potential donors.

Like its sister colleges, Barnard often seemed locked into its history—a history that had its origins in establishing a college for women at a time when women were refused admission to most colleges, including Columbia University. The deep-seated fears of being "lesser" than or "different" from a male college or being labeled a "lesbian school" were part of this heritage. Although Barnard had taken the lead in offering one of the first women's studies courses in the country—Annette Baxter's "History of Women in America," given for the first time in 1966—in setting up the Women's Center, and, a few years later, in creating one of the first women's studies programs, we were constantly confronting the fear of difference and inferiority.

As late as 1979 at a Women's Center invitational conference, Special Programs for Women in Higher Education, for seventy directors of women's programs in the Northeast, I could see the remnants of these fears among representatives from women's colleges. The proliferation of women's centers and women's studies courses and programs was much greater at coeducational colleges and universities than at women's colleges. Although some of the women's colleges had fine special programs for women—research institutes, libraries, continuing education programs, and graduate studies—there was a reluctance among the women's colleges to take on issues of feminism. Lingering homophobia made it difficult for some to support a resolution acknowledging the needs, interests, and rights of lesbians. After some discussion the resolution was passed, supported by all.

In 1976, in the midst of negotiations with Columbia University on the question of merging Barnard with Columbia College, President Mattfeld asked each department head to write a short statement making a case for a women's college, including specific references to Barnard's offerings. At a time when most colleges and universities were becoming coeducational, the challenge for women's colleges was no longer to simply provide access to higher education but to provide access to meaningful participation in all segments of the larger society.

The research studies of Elizabeth Tidball, professor of physiology at the George Washington University Medical Center, made it clear that women fared better in the atmosphere of a women's college than in coeducational institutions. Her studies, which documented that a higher percentage of graduates from women's colleges receive Ph.D.'s and also that the greater the ratio between women faculty and students, the greater the number of women graduates who subsequently achieved, made a strong case for a women's college. Barnard had all the desirable components for helping women achieve their optimum potential. It had a woman as its administrative head and more than half of its faculty and administration were women. It offered small classes and a faculty committed to teaching in general and to teaching women in particular. The curriculum was supplemented with a variety of programs—preprofessional counseling, alumnae vocational counseling and placement, internships, and a range of programs on professional concerns—all of which created a supportive atmosphere with role models and an opportunity for young women to learn to be independent and to assume leadership positions.

But the contradictions between public posture and internal practice created an ambivalence that permeated the college community. The college regularly made use of the Women's Center whenever the occasion arose to demonstrate its commitment, open-mindedness, and good faith. For example, when delegations of women from the Soviet Union, China, and other countries expressed a desire to visit a women's college and talk about women's issues—visits arranged by the State Department, the American Association of University Women, or the Columbia University Visitors' Service—the college proudly turned to the Women's Center to host the group and to plan an appropriate program. In addition, the college frequently directed visitors from the United States and abroad to the center. It was not unusual to see a woman from Pakistan, Germany, or Iowa using our collection, spending days, even weeks, doing research at the center.

Initially, few Barnard faculty, administrators, or students showed an interest in the Women's Center. Some expressed feelings of unease at what they saw as a lesbian presence at Barnard. I had trouble understanding the grounds for this assumption until I realized that, from the very beginning, we had adopted a policy of extending our hospitality to all feminist groups, including the newly formed student lesbian group on campus. Knowing that name-calling and baiting have been used throughout history to discredit, frighten, and divide women, we made a conscious and determined effort to create a supportive, tolerant atmosphere. We insisted on being inclusive and we knew that attacks on us laid bare a deep-seated fear of lesbianism. Many members of the college community feared stigmatization through association. And, despite regular articles and reports on our varied activities and programs in the undergraduate and alumnae publications, the questions, "Why a women's center in a women's college?" or, "Why does a women's center need its own voice?" regularly recurred.

Recognizing Barnard's ambivalence and learning how to work with it presented both a dilemma and a challenge. My administrative experience at the college served me well. I had learned how the bureaucracy worked, how necessary it was to go through the right channels, and how valuable it was to involve as many people as possible from different constituencies in our activities. I had learned when and how I could bend the rules somewhat, and I had learned that our ability to raise about one third of our budget ourselves—through gifts and grants—gave us a significant degree of independence that other administrative departments didn't have.

By no means did I do this all alone. The executive committee provided crucial support and gave us license to take positions and to organize programs that we might not have been able to do otherwise. We met regularly once a month over lunch in the center, and I made sure that these meetings were substantive and lively. The agenda was posted outside our door on the day of each meeting, and, since our meetings were open, we often had visitors. Decisions were made by consensus. We didn't always share the same point of view on everything, but, when there were differences, I sensed that some members were swept along by the will of the majority, approving decisions they might not have agreed with individually. And it was heartening to see student members have a chance to get to know a few strong adult women on an almost equal footing.

In those early years, I found we spent considerable time reacting to criticism from the administration. This forced us to think through each issue carefully and to develop strong policies earlier than we otherwise might have. For example, the director of the admissions office asked us to carefully screen the announcements we put on our bulletin boards, since these boards occupied a prominent place in the main building of the college. She feared that notices announcing such events as counseling groups for recent rape victims or dances for "women only" might deter parents of prospective students from sending their daughters to Barnard. After a full discussion, we decided to continue our policy of posting notices of all events for women and not censor those that might not please everyone. We felt it was important to send a message to the feminist community that we would publicize all women-related events and not attempt to judge which activities were "appropriate." Establishing trust with the larger community was crucial. At the same time, we decided that to be truly inclusive the Women's Center would no longer hold events exclusively for women, except in the area of women and health.

Our relationship with the college administration was always prickly. I learned to live with constant pressure to conform to college protocol. The president wanted to see men on the executive committee, even going so far as to submit a few names of male professors who had never shown any interest in women's issues. The college doctor was unhappy about the demands for reforms in the health services, which she felt originated at the Women's Center. Several administrators were uncomfortable with the growing visibility of an increasingly strong and vocal lesbian community at Barnard and, again, laid the blame on the center.

We considered each complaint and each challenge carefully. We informed the president that we would welcome men on the committee when there were openings and when we found men who were interested in and supportive of our work. After filling several committee slots that were allocated for faculty with women, we added John Chambers, an American peace historian, who was genuinely committed to feminism. He was an exemplary member, always making it clear that his opinion was his own; he wouldn't and couldn't speak for *all* men. I invited the college doctor to give a series of lectures on women's health in the center, which she did in a halfhearted way, simply confirming the discontent among students over the health services provided by the college. And, of course, we stood behind the newly formed Lesbian Activists at Barnard and insisted that the college recognize them as one of many student special-interest groups that were entitled to funding from the undergraduate association.

Although, at first, we found ourselves primarily responding to requests to cosponsor programs with groups outside the college, I soon realized how important it was to gain college support by cosponsoring programs inside Barnard. We organized a program on math anxiety with the mathematics department, a panel on feminism with the political science department, a talk by psychologist Carol Nagy Jacklin with the psychology department, and a documentary Italian film on rape with the Italian department. We cooperated with the physical education department in an annual day-long program on women in sports and cosponsored, with the Barnard library, an annual film and video festival and an exhibition of "Five Centuries of Feminism." Although the number of these joint programs and events increased over the years, they always remained somewhat peripheral to the Women's Center's central concerns and activities.

I was always mindful of the need to present the Women's Center to the college in the best possible light. It was in this spirit that I sent out the minutes of the executive committee meetings to a wide circle, including Barnard trustees, viewing the minutes as one effective way of letting people in the college community know who we were and what we did. One member of the executive committee told me she didn't mind missing a meeting because the minutes captured the essence of the proceedings so well that she almost felt as if she had been there. In the same spirit I made sure that all of our printed materials—flyers, announcements, posters, memos, reports—looked professional. At a time when most young, struggling women's groups sent out mailings done on what looked like home mimeograph machines, I had all the center's materials professionally printed. I felt it gave us credibility that we sorely needed, and I was amused when the college public relations director asked us for the names of our designer and printer.

I learned all the details of all the college facilities, their seating capacities, their costs, and the availability of and procedures for the use of classrooms, conference rooms, auditoriums, theater, the gymnasium, and special meeting rooms. I made it a point to get to know the people who controlled and managed events—people in housekeeping, building and grounds, security, and food services. Most of these administrators were used to receiving requisition forms and were not accustomed to being approached personally. But it made a difference. Afterward, most took great pains to see that our events went smoothly. A few even developed an interest in our work. I watched one housekeeper become the first woman security guard at Barnard, and we always asked for her when we needed security for an event. I noticed that she stepped in to listen whenever she could. I worked with food services to develop creative vegetarian menus for all our luncheon meetings, which elicited praise and remarks that the food was tastier than the usual college fare. I even persuaded food services to include a recipe of mine for a minestrone soup and to stop using iceberg lettuce in support of the Farm Workers Boycott.

Our strongest college support came from alumnae. Although the number was never large and most were recent graduates, we received expressions of interest and approval from a wide range of Barnard graduates of all ages, interests, and accomplishments. Five of the seven original founders of the Women's Center were alumnae who continued to devote critical time, energy, and money to its support. We could not have survived those early, shaky years without their extraordinary commitment. Others wrote, called, or came in to tell us how proud they were that Barnard had a women's center, to suggest projects they wanted to work on, and to give money. We received class gifts from several recent alumnae classes, and I was particularly touched by the support expressed in individual gifts from alumnae from early classes, going back as far as 1913 and including several gifts from the 1920s and early 1930s. Jane Teller, a sculptor from the class of 1933, felt so deeply that she dropped into the Women's Center one day, unannounced, to tell me how pleased she was to learn that we existed. After hearing about our activities, our hopes, and our dreams, she told me she had never given money to Barnard before, but now she was eager to show her support. She started turning over stock to the Women's Center, a generous act that she continued for the rest of her life. In addition, she worked with us in arranging an exhibition of New Jersey Women Artists held at Barnard.

We had a regular column in the *Barnard Alumnae Magazine,* and I frequently spoke to alumnae groups in New York and in other parts of the country. We worked closely with the alumnae office and the career planning office, locating successful professional alumnae who would be available to talk with Barnard students and alumnae about opportunities in their fields. I continued to press for the development of an old girls network.

From time to time in those early years, I was reminded that the majority of college women, even Barnard women, were not ready for some of the stong feminist issues. In the fall of 1973 two members of the class of 1949 came in to ask me to speak at their twenty-fifth reunion the following June. In preparation they were sending out a questionnaire to their classmates and thought I would be able to use the responses in my talk. Neither they nor I were prepared for the responses; an overwhelming number replied that they felt only disdain for the women's movement. They were content with their lives as wives and mothers; only a few had returned to work, mostly part time. I was a little shaken by this and suggested to the committee that perhaps they should choose another speaker. No, they said, they wanted the class to hear me. This was a class that had graduated in the beginning of the immediate postwar period of "togetherness," when women were urged to stay at home. After thinking it over, I decided to describe my own life and how I had arrived at the place I was now. It went well and there was lots of good discussion, although I doubt that I changed any minds.

From the day the Women's Center opened its doors, a small number of Barnard students were eager to make the center an important part of their college life. These few students and those who worked at the center or at the Women's Counseling Project became a strong, articulate group. Though their number was small, these unusually independent young women made up in passion and commitment what they lacked in numbers.

I was initially disappointed that, on the whole, few Barnard students showed an interest in the Women's Center. But I should have known better. I had only to remember my own experience counseling undergraduates just a few years earlier. As the 1970s progressed, however, young college women began to think differently about their futures. Many now had clear professional goals. They were applying to medical, law, and business schools in large numbers, and, in smaller numbers, to engineering and architectural schools, as well as to Ph.D. programs in mathematics, physics, and chemistry. There was a surge of women planning to enter what we used to regard as traditional male professions, and I could see that this represented an important shift in women's aspirations.

The meetings we cosponsored with the alumnae and the career planning office where successful professional women described their lives and their work were always well attended. Students came with very specific questions and an eagerness to learn how these women had achieved their success. At these meetings I could see how single-minded students were about their professional goals and how careful some were not to show support for issues or causes that might hinder their acceptance into professional school or, later, into their chosen profession. I realized also that they took their cues from their teachers and their advisors—some of whom were hostile to or fearful of the women's movement. In addition to thinking about future careers, I realized that many—for the first time in their lives—were grappling with more immediate and often more basic concerns: being away from home and family for the first time, acknowledging and exploring their sexuality, and learning how to set priorities at a college with high academic standards. Their quest for independence and autonomy was an important first step to understanding and to accepting feminism.

As I saw more and more students tentatively coming in to use our collection for research for term papers on women for a wide variety of courses, I realized that the most important component in raising feminist consciousness for students at Barnard was a women's studies program. Barnard had taken the lead in offering some of the first women's studies courses; ten courses, offered between 1971–72, were listed in the first Women's Center brochure, and, over the next few years, this number would grow. But, even with the success of these early courses, gaining acceptance of a program with a full-fledged major proved to be incredibly difficult. It took an inordinate amount of time and commitment on the part of a very small and devoted, but also very overextended, group of faculty. Again, there were only a few with the degree of dedication willing to take on this extra work. Over a period of four years—under the leadership of Domna Stanton, a faculty member of our executive committee—a program was developed that, by 1977, was approved by the Barnard faculty. It took until 1981 to gain approval for a full-time tenured faculty member to head the program. I was pleased that Nancy Miller, a Barnard alumna and a former executive committee member who had been teaching at Columbia, was selected for the job.

Throughout the process the Women's Center served as catalyst. Before the program was approved and had a budget of its own, the center provided administrative, secretarial, and research help: preparing lists of women's studies courses given at Barnard and Columbia, distributing these lists widely, seeing to it that faculty advisors had this information at the beginning of each semester. We also collected information about other women's studies programs, held open houses for students and faculty, publicized the program, and even funded the first independent junior reading course with one of our gift funds, which was to be divided among the four faculty members teaching the course. In addition, the women's studies program was enriched by the annual Women's Center the Scholar and the Feminist conference. After the women's studies program was established, the Women's Center continued working closely with the program, sharing speakers and special programs and also sitting on each other's committees. Each was stronger for the existence of the other.

Initially, I was so preoccupied with the details of building the center's place within the college that I neglected to acquaint myself with and earn the trust of the small group of student supporters who spent time in the Women's Center. This was a serious mistake. I didn't realize that they regarded me as an administrative plant, appointed to give lip service to the women's movement, which the administration regarded with some ambivalence. However, I began to notice that students often stopped talking when I joined them as they sat around the tables discussing an issue.

I was puzzled and decided I needed to hear what they were thinking about the center and about me. During several informal discussions, they told me directly that they didn't trust me since my job as a loyal department head was to make the Women's Center a showplace for the college without any real commitment to feminism. They had no faith that the Women's Center would represent their concerns, which were, as it turned out, the same as mine. With the help of student executive committee members and students who worked at the center, we talked about the center's origins, charter, and goals. I insisted that we shared common goals, and we couldn't achieve these with out their support, ideas, and active participation.

I learned a great deal from students whose experiences, backgrounds, and perspectives were very different from my own. They or their sisters, mothers, or best friends had suffered abuses and indignities that were being talked about publicly for the first time. I listened carefully to these young women who were clamoring for serious attention to be given to rape, battery, sexual harassment, and discrimination on the basis of sexual orientation. Their insistence on finding solutions through public action made me rethink the role of the Women's Center.

I had to be careful. As an administrative office depending on financial support from the college, I knew that we could not take activist positions. We did not lobby, picket, or demonstrate as a group, although as individuals we were free to do what we felt was necessary. There was one notable exception, made with the full approval of President Mattfeld: we chartered a bus in order to participate in the large ERA demonstration in Washington in the summer of 1978.

We also began to respond to pressure from women on campus that we take advocacy positions. We supported student activist groups such as the Barnard chapter of CARASA (Committee for Abortion Rights and Against Sterilization Abuse), provided background information on different advocacy and activist groups, invited speakers, and offered and reserved space for different groups and discussions, as well as planned and cosponsored programs with a wide range of groups addressing critical women's issues.

It wasn't always easy. When planning a program on Women and the Arms Race with the Columbia Catholic Women's Group, the Catholic women announced they intended to include a session on "personal violence," meaning abortion. This caused me several sleepless nights as I wrestled with the question of free speech and presenting different points of view. Finally, we decided that it would be inappropriate for the Women's Center to sponsor a session that challenged women's abortion rights, a basic tenet of the women's movement, at a conference on women and the arms race. I explained our position and suggested that there seemed to be sufficient interest in the arms race to support two separate programs—one at Barnard and one at Columbia. Ultimately, the group decided to forego the issue of "personal violence," and we did the program together as originally planned.

When students came to us needing money for abortions, we set up a Women's Center Emergency Medical and Legal Loan Fund, which we maintained, unlike other college loan funds, independent of connections with the registrar or bursar's office. No pressure other than a call from the Women's Center was put on students to return the money, and, in general, the repayment record was good, although not always as fast as we would have liked. We built up the fund with generous gifts from executive committee member Elizabeth Janeway, who frequently donated her honoraria from speaking engagements, and from our own fundraising efforts, the most successful of which was an annual auction held in the spring for several years. This auction brought in money and lots of laughs, as we auctioned off such items as a Bella Abzug hat and a visit to a *Ms.* magazine editorial meeting.

Some issues were difficult to address because of the reluctance of the administration and even students to talk about them. When a student came in to tell us she had been raped in broad daylight in Morningside Park, a dividing stretch of land between Columbia University and a section of Harlem, I knew it was time to take action. She told us that, when she went to a dean to report the incident, she was told she should have known better than to set foot in this park, regularly frequented by alcoholics and other undesirables. She was frustrated because the administration seemed more concerned about the bad publicity the college might receive than addressing the horrendous act itself and its impact on the victim. This and several other reports of rapes in the area prompted us to work with the Women's Counseling Project and several other groups on the Barnard and Columbia campuses to create one of the first rape crisis centers in New York City. A committee of Barnard and Columbia students, faculty, administrators, and staff met for months and then worked with Ronnie Eldridge, an alumna member of our executive committee, who set up a meeting with important representatives from the community, city government, and officials of St. Luke's Hospital. The program opened in the summer of 1977. With the full cooperation of the medical and nursing staff of the emergency room of St. Luke's Hospital, a special hotline was established, providing a rotating list of patient advocates—practically all students—who, after going through an intensive training program, volunteered to be on call one night a month to respond to calls for help, accompany rape victims to the hospital and to the police, help them find counseling services, and keep in touch with them for a few days after the incident.

Although most of the issues that were identified in the 1970s had always been with us, it took the women's movement to permit us to acknowledge them publicly. I feel abashed as I think of how I did nothing when, as director of the career planning office, I watched one of my staff members come to work from time to time with a black eye. In the beginning, when I asked her how it happened, she would say she tripped on the steps or bumped into a kitchen cupboard. Even then, I knew she wasn't telling the truth; I knew her husband had hit her, but I never said so. Eventually, she left her husband, but she never spoke about the battering she had endured. Before domestic violence was publicly acknowledged, we all knew some woman who had been battered, yet, for the most part, we looked the other way.

Sexual harassment was first brought to my attention as a public issue in 1977 by Karen Sauvigne and Susan Meyer, two young women who came to the Women's Center to describe their efforts to define and publicize this issue. They had found free space in the basement of a church and had established the Working Women's Institute, which became so successful in bringing the issue to public attention that it was gradually taken over by other, more established groups.

Shortly after I had met with Karen Sauvigne and Susan Meyer, a student came to the center, irate and frustrated over an encounter she had as a volunteer reporter at the Columbia radio station. She had been harassed verbally and later physically by a male student producer. She had taken her grievance to the Columbia dean who supervised the radio station and received no satisfaction. In fact, he laughed at her. We decided it was time to take action so that this kind of assault could not happen without penalty.

Once we started talking about sexual harassment, other students came forward. One of the most startling revelations concerned an extremely popular teacher at Columbia. At the start of every semester, he asked for volunteers to work on one of his research projects. They would be paid for their work, which would be done at his apartment after hours. Though the class was mostly male, he always chose women, the youngest and the prettiest. Several students reported to us that he made sexual advances when they went to his apartment. They didn't want to drop his course and were fearful that, if they complained, they would be punished with a low mark.

Clearly, the time had come to set up grievance and discipline procedures for sexual harassment. I sent out a call and a committee was established; composed of students, faculty, and administrators, the committee was coordinated by the Women's Center. After several months, a clear, strong document was completed, one which defined sexual harassment, outlined grievance procedures, and set up appropriate disciplinary measures. One of the first sexual harassment policies within academe, the document sat on the college lawyer's desk for almost two years before it was finally approved and put into action.

In like manner, we responded to complaints by two young faculty members about the lack of any policy for parental leave, either during pregnancy or for time taken off after a baby is born for childcare. At the time, should a woman faculty member become pregnant, she could only use disability leave and then negotiate with the head of her department. Again, we set up a committee called the Ad Hoc Faculty Committee on Pregnancy and Childcare, which met diligently until it crafted a policy, one which also took several years to gain approval and to be put into motion.

In the beginning, none of us had a clear vision of what we wanted the Women's Center to be. It was exhilarating simply to see the center exist with a broad charter and official college support. The Women's Center was a bold idea, built on strong faith that it could flourish and make a difference for women at Barnard and in the larger community. As we responded to requests to do programs, events and projects—often cooperating with other groups—we began to have an identity. After two or three years, I developed a vision. Like most visions, it never fully materialized; it remained somewhat amorphous, evolving over time and in response to specific, changing needs.

I saw the Women's Center as an initial response to the challenge of the women's movement, to be followed by other components: a women's studies program, a research institute, an oral history program, an adult education program for women, a women's library and archive, a women's film program, and a counseling center that offered personal, educational, and vocational counseling and referrals for women in the metropolitan area. I believed that Barnard could become a leader in the education of women, incorporating all the important feminist issues and the new scholarship on women into its institutional fabric. My vision claimed

Barnard as the jewel in Columbia's crown: the first stop for scholars, journalists, activists, and artists from the world over seeking resources on women's issues.

We didn't achieve all the goals encompassed in my broad vision. Yet, in some modest way, the dream became reality: In addition to the Women's Center, we did establish a women's studies program, a women's counseling project, and some adult education for alumnae. We became a strong feminist presence in New York City, looked to for help and support by a wide range of women's groups. And we created an annual conference, the Scholar and the Feminist, which each year provided leadership on the changing debates and progress in feminist thought and action.

■ 14
THE SCHOLAR
AND THE FEMINIST
CONFERENCES

My single most important accomplishment as director of the Women's Center was to bring into being and to nurture the celebrated annual Scholar and the Feminist conference. The first ten conferences (1974–1983) addressed many of the questions women scholars were beginning to ask and provided the opportunity for scholars and activists to present their work and their experiences—often for the first time—in a supportive atmosphere. The conferences led to the publication of a number of books and articles and became an integral part of the Women's Center; to this day the conference is an important date on the center's calendar.

With a small grant from the Helena Rubinstein Foundation, which increased steadily over the years, we created an exciting annual spring happening, anticipated eagerly by women—and a sprinkling of men—not only from the metropolitan area but, as the word spread, from other parts of the country and, on occasion, from abroad. Initially, we limited attendance to 250, the capacity of our auditorium, but it soon became very clear that we were excluding many who wanted to come. After the first three conferences, we sacrificed comfort and moved the morning plenary session to the college gymnasium, an uninviting space with poor ventilation and dreadful acoustics. Once again conference participants were willing to sit on uncomfortable folding chairs and on benches for almost three hours, straining to hear, until—several years later—the college finally installed a proper sound system. Although we tried to maintain a manageable conference size so that workshops could truly be workshops and participants could interact with each other, in some years, we had as many as 700 participants, and at one conference, 800.

Each year I selected an academic coordinator, either an assistant professor or, on occasion, a graduate student. I was always able to find women passionately committed to the new scholarship on women who were eager to work on this conference. Next, I sent out a call to the Barnard and Columbia community and formed a planning committee. Initially the committee was very small, but realizing the need for more diversity, after the first three conferences, I broadened the invitation to include others. I was delighted by the positive response from scholars, activists, journalists, writers, and artists from different institutions and diverse communities. In time, as the conferences became known and as we demonstrated our determination to enlarge our perspectives to include issues of sexual orientation and race and ethnicity, we successfully recruited lesbians and women of color. In later years the committee represented a truly broad feminist community.

Once again, we were inspired by the feminist tenet that process was as important as the conference itself. When choosing conference themes, workshops, and speakers, the committee carefully considered a broad range of emerging issues and pressing questions about women's lives, their work, and their place in history—questions that were on the cutting edge of the new scholarship on women. Decisions were reached by consensus.

In the early fall the committee would begin to meet regularly in our large, pleasant office. We sat at long tables arranged in a square, facing each other, surrounded by our growing collection of books, articles, and journals. Meetings were held in the late afternoon, with the sun streaming in and with the bustle of students and faculty outside our windows, and often continued until long after dark. Most of us stayed till the end of the meeting, without seeming to notice the long hours or the missed dinners. So many meetings on so many innovative projects were held in this space over the next decade that, in my mind, the room became a symbol of successful collective creativity. I was touched by the dedication of the number of women who spent time on projects, which, they suspected, would rarely be appreciated or recognized by their own institutions.

Discussions were so lively and open-ended that it was easy to forget that we had a job to do. We often felt more like a study group. We shared readings and new ideas, and we identified scholars and activists working on themes that we were considering. In addition to inviting women who were well known in new areas of inquiry, we also included others—less well known—who may have been working in isolation. We adhered to a policy of allowing speakers and workshop leaders to speak at only one conference, enabling us to bring in new people each year. This policy significantly enlarged the network that women were beginning to build.

Looking back, it is clear that the conference themes paralleled the growth, development, and tensions inherent in the new scholarship on women with notable accuracy. Almost unwittingly, we achieved a continuum that mirrored the issues that dominated feminist scholarship and the women's movement during a most significant decade. Reflecting the explosive expression of the women's movement in its universal reaction against patriarchal traditions, the first five conferences stressed the connections and ties among *all* women and the search for the commonalities of women's experience.

At the first conference, a one-day program of panels and workshops held in the spring of 1974 and focused on the general theme of conflict, compromise, and creativity, we asked scholars from different disciplines to talk about the personal impact of feminism on their scholarship, their disciplines, their identities as scholars, and their understanding of women. The second conference, subtitled "Toward New Criteria of Relevance," moved from the personal to a broader, theoretical perspective, examining the impact of feminism on the research process in general, and addressed how criteria of relevance in traditional scholarship are challenged and redefined by a feminist perspective. A high point of this conference was the late Joan Kelly's classic paper, "History and the Social Relations of the Sexes," which offered a new perspective on the standard forms of "periodization." Kelly postulated that nodal periods in history, such as the Renaissance, had been so defined because they were moments of flowering for men, not for women. She theorized a radically different kind of historical scholarship based on the social relations of the sexes. This conference also marked the development of a format that we would use for all succeeding conferences: a plenary morning session with two or three speakers followed by a wide spectrum of concurrent afternoon workshops, including several that introduced activist issues related to the conference theme.

The third conference, "The Search for Origins," went a step further, asking: What does the present unsatisfactory position of women stem from? and focusing on the search for the historical, cultural, and psychological origins of women's oppression. Especially noteworthy was Elaine Pagels's brilliant case study of early Gnosticism's acceptance of both male and female images of gods, replaced, during the establishment of the early Christian church, by a solely male image and the ideological and political exclusion of women. The fourth conference, "Connecting Theory, Practice, and Values," identified and illuminated some of the major contradictions between the conceptions of reality developed by feminist scholars and those accepted in traditional scholarship. This was the conference which boldly asked the question, "Is traditional scholarship value free?" In 1978, the fifth conference, "Creating Feminist Works," focused on *how* feminist works are created and how individual feminists can break away from internalized sexism. In a morning panel, an artist, a writer, and a scholar talked together about how they attempt to free themselves from biased scholarship and values to create a new vision, theory, or concept—in short, how they do their work.

As the women's movement and feminist scholarship matured and became more diverse, some basic concepts shifted focus, adding new dimensions. Women's differences from men, originally seen chiefly as sources of oppression, began to be viewed also as sources of strength. Scholars also began to acknowledge and to examine "differences" among women, especially with regard to class, race, and sexual orientation. The second group of five conferences reflected these developments as well as the strong social reaction to the women's movement, most notably the emergence of the New Right and the backlash against women.

Drawing heavily on contemporary French feminist theories and psychoanalytical, political, and linguistic perspectives, the sixth conference, "The Future of Difference," explored those structures that organize and determine concepts of sexual identity, differences among women, and differences between women and men. The conference considered such questions as: What do we mean by difference as a theoretical construct? What are the logics and politics of difference? Is there an accepted notion among feminists of difference?

Early in the fall of 1979, the academic coordinator for that year, Amy Swerdlow, and I attended a celebratory conference on Simone de Beauvoir at New York University. We were stunned by the number of African American women who lined up at the open mike to voice their anger at being invited to a feminist conference for which none of them had been included as planners. We considered this a valid and serious criticism and successfully recruited women representing racial minorities as well as lesbian activists for our own conference. By 1980, therefore, we had a truly diverse committee of twenty-four planning the seventh conference, "Class, Race and Sex—Exploring Contradictions, Affirming Connections." Scholars and activists analyzed how economic, political, and cultural institutions divide women along the lines of class, race, and sexual orientation, emphasizing the power and the limits of sisterhood as an idea and as a social force. Continuing this dialogue, the eighth conference, "The Dynamics of Control," examined the numerous and complex ways in which women's autonomy is regulated and their activities and energies directed into socially defined channels: how laws, public policy, institutions, and ideology combine to control women differently depending on their class, race, and sexual orientation.

The ninth conference, "Towards a Politics of Sexuality," was undoubtedly the most controversial conference of all. It addressed women's right to sexual pleasure and sexual autonomy, "acknowledging," as stated in Carole Vance's conference statement (see appendix C), "that sexuality is simultaneously a domain of restriction, repression, and danger as well as a domain of exploration, pleasure, and agency." The tenth conference, "The Question of Technology," focused on the impact of technology on women's lives and expectations, raising questions about the relationship between technology and gender in the workplace and in the household and considering how these questions might affect women of different race and class backgrounds.

Throughout all ten conferences, the themes presented in the morning plenary sessions were clearly in the vanguard of the new scholarship on women. These conferences, however, were also distinguished by the unique ways in which their themes were fleshed out in twelve to eighteen concurrent afternoon workshops. These workshops were conceived and led by remarkable women, all engaged in pioneer work specifically relevant to aspects of the conference theme. Workshops took on scholarly, activist, and creative concerns, ranging from the politics of housework and wagelessness, to the evolution of the Black woman artist, to linkages between racism and sexism, to lesbian history, and to the need for feminist literary theory. The roster of morning plenary sessions and afternoon workshops with speakers and workshop leaders appears in appendix B.

To maintain the delicate balance among the center, the college, the Helena Rubinstein Foundation, and the larger community required all my skills and experience. Anticipating problems, and being ready to prod, cajole, placate, improvise, and run interference whenever necessary became part of my daily life for months before each conference. I quickly learned how to combine the collective process with responsible leadership to make substantive decisions, meet necessary deadlines, stay within our budget, and ensure that all the logistic details were in place.

As an administrative officer of the college, I had the final responsibility for seeing that the conference was a success and also that it maintained Barnard's commitment to excellence. I looked forward to the challenge, year after year, though this was often my most difficult professional task. I knew that I needed the trust of the feminist community to ensure the success of the conferences; hence, I had to make it clear that I would not control the conference. This was tricky; in one sense the conference came to belong as much to the feminist community as to Barnard and to the Women's Center, a fact that created good feelings among the planners and the participants. Yet I knew that the college held me totally responsible for everything at the center. Should any conference or program evoke criticism from any important college constituency or be portrayed in the media in a way that did not meet the approval of the college, I would be held accountable. And this, in fact, did happen from time to time.

The Scholar and the Feminist was always a one-day conference, held each year on a Saturday in the spring. After a few years, we added a Friday night reception since speakers and workshop leaders were eager to meet each other and to talk with members of the planning committee. These proved to be happy occasions, generating pleasant feelings of anticipation and excitement for everyone.

The morning of each conference I was in my office by 7:30 A.M. The phone was ringing, and women started to arrive at 8:00 for a program which would begin at 10 A.M. Although all participants were supposed to preregister by mail, we always had eager women arriving on the morning of the conference who hadn't made the mail deadline and others who, after picking up their registration packet, wanted to change their workshop assignment, which was made on the basis of their top three choices. For the first hour or so it was often pandemonium, but we were prepared. I made it a policy to honor people's requests to change workshops and to permit all latecomers to register. I learned how to build these last-minute changes into our estimated attendance, and, though it sometimes upset the balance of participants we had carefully assigned to some of the workshops, this flexibility created such good will that it was worth the inconvenience.

By 9:00 A.M. the lobby of Barnard Hall was crowded with women, some of whom came year after year, others of whom had just heard about the conference and were coming for the first time. Women came early to see other women; it was a way to start networking. I was invariably stopped by women I didn't know who thanked me for holding these conferences and told me how these conferences broke the isolation they were experiencing at their institutions.

In all ten years, no plenary speaker or workshop leader ever canceled. And it never rained on our conference day. Although there was often still a nip in the air, it was always warm enough to sit outdoors between sessions or during the lunch break, and, since we used several buildings, participants could fan out all over our small campus. Our childcare center was a big success since children could romp outdoors with their student caretakers.

Unlike many other conferences, participants didn't wander off during the program in order to network. They stayed at the conference, attending sessions the whole long day, even the final wrap-up, which we added because we felt we needed to recap the formal proceedings. We later turned this final session into a creative hour for poetic and dramatic readings, a welcome change from the intensity of the day-long program.

We made sure that there was ample opportunity for informal conversation.

The program spilled over into the coffee and lunch breaks and the final cocktail reception, which were as well attended as the conference sessions. It was clear that conference participants were hungry for opportunities like this, for they stayed to talk and to talk some more. It was hard to end the conference. At 6:30 P.M. we finally had to say good night over a microphone.

The day of the conference was always the high point in my work year. It was like stepping into a magical world for one whole day—seeing the plans of a year unfold and fall into place, just as I had hoped they would. And then, since we couldn't wind down, it became a yearly custom to take all the speakers, workshop leaders, and members of the planning committee back to my house for dinner. How we did it, I often wonder. But Jay came through with the kind of help that made it possible. He attended the morning plenary session and then went home to complete arrangements for dinner for some forty weary, overstimulated women.

We never did an analysis of who actually came to the conferences, but there were clearly more scholars than activists, although many were both. Most, but not all, of the scholars were young and passionately involved in reexamining their work and asking new questions about women in their disciplines. They looked to these conferences for support and stimulation. Activists who attended represented every age, ethnicity, and work background and included a small number of older women who had spent their lives waiting for the women's movement to resurface or who were ready to make the connection between activism and feminism. The number of Barnard participants was always very small, never more than fifty students and a handful of faculty, administrators, and support staff. And despite our success in creating a racially diverse planning committee, very few women of color ever came.

I believed that we were holding a major intellectual conference, one that would put Barnard, a women's college, in the forefront of the rigorous exploration of all aspects of the impact of feminism on scholarship. And it did. I was enormously proud that we could put together a conference that was hailed by feminist scholars all over the country as a major contribution. Of all the center's projects, I expected that the Scholar and the Feminist would be the one viewed as the most appropriate for the college and the one which would have its full support. But I was naive. These conferences, our most ambitious and groundbreaking undertaking, planned with the same high standards of excellence that the college insisted on in all its academic endeavors, were met with surprising resistance—regarded by many on campus as frivolously unacademic and even dangerous. Judging from the small number of women faculty who attended and from comments made to me, to members of the Women's Center's Executive Committee, or to our few other faculty supporters, most of the faculty regarded the conferences as highly charged, intellectually flawed, and political in the worst sense. It was painful for me to observe that, although the president almost always opened the conference with welcoming remarks, Barnard's major administrators, for the most part, showed little interest in the conference and some years viewed it with distaste.

Nowhere were the tensions between feminism and the academy more evident than in these conferences. For they challenged traditional scholarship, and most faculty—not only Barnard faculty—were not ready for such a challenge. They viewed it as an attack on their work. They contended that including activists and advocacy issues in an "academic" conference clouded the "purity" of the scholarship under question. Many Barnard faculty seemed to feel that this new scholarship on women was unobjective, trivial, radical, and in bad taste.

We seldom had the cooperation of the public relations department in getting media attention. No doubt the college administration was nervous about how the media would portray the event and whether one of these controversial conferences would affect the amount of money individual donors, foundations, and corporations gave to the college. During the conferences, members of the administration popped in and out, perhaps checking for any unusual behavior. I also sensed a great feeling of relief on the part of the administration when the day passed and the world, the college, and all of us were, in effect, unharmed, none the worse for raising critical, polemical questions. I am quite sure that the resistance to and ambivalence surrounding the new scholarship on women were not peculiar to Barnard, that they were endemic to traditional institutions of higher education with outspoken women faculty and developing women's studies programs.

In the summer of 1981 when I approached Carole Vance, a medical anthropologist at Columbia, about serving as the academic coordinator of our ninth conference, she was interested, particularly if the conference would have as its theme sexuality. I hesitated. I was committed to having the theme emerge from the free-flowing discussions of the planning committee. Further, I realized this was a highly charged topic and wondered how the planning committee would react to it. I struck a bargain with Carole. We would send out our usual call to the feminist community for women to serve on the planning committee, including any names she might suggest, and introduce Carole Vance as our academic coordinator along with her proposed theme. If the planning committee was not satisfied with the theme or preferred to have the theme emerge from discussions and readings, as in former years, Carole said she would accept the group decision and work with us. To state her case strongly, Carole Vance followed my letter with an invitation of her own, outlining some of the issues she would like developed in a conference on women's sexuality.

I was impressed by the enthusiastic response to our initial invitations. We ended up with the largest planning committee we ever had, an interesting mix of twenty-five scholars, activists, artists, and journalists: heterosexuals, lesbians, and bisexuals, all eager to work on a conference on sexuality. Most of them had been thinking about issues of sexuality for some time and came from Carole Vance's list of potential candidates for the planning committee. Several were working on a book of essays on women's sexuality, *Powers of Desire: The Politics of Sexuality,* with a publication date in the offing. Others—including three artists, Hannah Alderfer, Beth Jaker, and Marybeth Nelson—had worked as part of a collective responsible for an entire issue on sexuality in *Heresies,* a young feminist journal, which—in those days—lived up to its name. The committee was a formidable group.

"Towards a Politics of Sexuality," held in April 1982, was, without a doubt, our most controversial and perhaps our most important conference. Addressing women's sexuality plunged us into new territory. From the first meeting in September 1981, it was clear that this topic stirred up strong feelings. Carole Vance introduced the theme, stressing its timeliness in light of the growing Women Against Pornography movement led by such feminists as Andrea Dworkin, Susan Brownmiller, and Robin Morgan. Committee members expressed strong distaste for this movement, and several women pointed out that the antipornography movement had dominated the issue of sexuality within the women's movement for almost a decade. Moreover, some said that as the antipornography movement grew in numbers and in strength, it leaned more and more to the right, almost forming an alliance with the "moral majority." Up until now, feminists had hesitated to speak out against it lest they appear unsisterly, but the opinions expressed over and over at these first meetings was that the time had come for another point of view to be presented.

I had never endorsed the antipornography movement and had never gone on one of its yearly Take Back the Night marches. In truth, I had actually drawn back from it, believing it to be an infringement of free expression. But when committee members refused the offer of an antipornography group to serve on the committee and to present a workshop at the conference, I felt uncomfortable and questioned this decision. It was the committee's consensus that, if permitted either a place on the planning committee or a workshop at the conference, Women Against Pornography would destroy the spirit of open inquiry.

I thought about this issue for weeks; I couldn't be certain that the planning committee's concerns were not valid. I liked to think we tolerated different points of view at our conferences, but, when I thought about it, I had to acknowledge that I would not have countenanced a workshop given by an antiabortion group such as Operation Rescue. Was this a similar situation? No one on this committee of strong, articulate women expressed disagreement with the decision to exclude the antipornography position, although I suspect at least a couple shared my unease. What I experienced in these early meetings brought to the foreground the deep split in the women's movement over sexuality, a split that many of us had been unaware of until then and that remains to this very day.

We met almost weekly for seven months with the intensity of a closely knit study group. Carole provided vision and strong leadership, and the committee responded with dedication, determination, and creativity. I trusted the process, but I found the topic stirred up more personal discomfort than I had experienced with any other issue. I felt awkward and sometimes uneasy because my socialization had kept me from ever talking about my own sexuality to other women. At sixty-two, I was at least twenty years older than anyone else on the committee. I could have told them volumes about my confusion: about my feelings of sexuality as I was growing up, and about how, like many women of my generation, I had accepted what was proper, even what we called the "double standard," how I had never talked about my own sexual needs and experiences. Throughout the planning process, I never volunteered a personal revelation. In fact, I seldom participated in the discussion of issues. I listened, I read, and I learned, grateful that the committee never turned the spotlight on me—though I wondered what they thought of me.

Discussions were so spirited that soon my initial fears and uneasiness faded, and I began to understand the need for a conference on women's sexuality with the dual focus on the tensions between pleasure and danger. Paraphrasing Carole Vance—whose brilliant conference statement lays out these tensions so well—to have spoken only of pleasure would have left out how patriarchy still governs women's lives, and to have spoken only of sexual violence and oppression would have overlooked pleasurable sexual experience, which women need to claim and acknowledge. I learned how the juxtaposition of these two extremes adds to the confusion and fear that many women silently endure.

As highlighted in Carole Vance's conference statement—and to further paraphrase from her account—we started off by recognizing the importance of the topic at a time when the antipornography movement and the increase of violence against women were polarizing feminists. We agreed that our aim was to move beyond debates about violence and pornography and to focus on sexuality apart from reproduction. Discussions and readings ranged from the feminist premise that sex is a social construct to how women get sexual pleasure in patriarchy and still feel sexually vulnerable. Looking at how men controlled women's sexuality under nineteenth- and twentieth-century patriarchy, we saw the extent to which women's sexuality was regulated by the "traditional bargain" that offered protection in exchange for being a "good woman"—a bargain which caused some women to choose "asexuality." We saw how this dynamic continues today to a lesser degree and still diminishes women's feelings about their right to sexual pleasure. We acknowledged that the sexual revolution and the second wave of feminism had transformed women's sexuality, affirming women's sexual desire, their right to pleasure, sexual autonomy, and choice, while also making women more visible and, hence, more vulnerable. We discussed how women still fear reprisal and punishment for their new sexual autonomy. Collectively, we explored issues of sexual safety, sexual styles, the meaning of pornography, taboos, the role of psychoanalysis, the place of fantasy, and what is and isn't considered "politically correct" (Carole Vance, appendix C). We explored the diversity and similarities of women's sexual experiences and recognized among ourselves the tensions, anxieties, and hesitancies in talking about sexual pleasure in a personal way. The process fostered honesty and, gradually, personal revelations and observations, which provided depth and an extra dimension to this groundbreaking conference.

Guiding this particular conference through birth pains to successful delivery was both a familiar and different experience for me. What was different this time was the way most people reacted to the theme. I presented the theme to the Women's Center's Executive Committee with sufficient detail so that they saw this conference as one more positive and innovative project. They gave their full support. But in my daily contact with Barnard faculty and administrators, I heard expressions of disapproval, not on the grounds that the scholarship was not rigorous, but rather objections to the topic itself. Some expressed fear that the conference was embarking on a course of sheer sensationalism, which would be bad for the college. I was frequently asked, "What are you women up to now?" Or being told, "We don't need a bunch of lesbians telling us about women's sexuality." One woman faculty member raised the question as to whether a conference on sexuality was appropriate for the college and went so far as to suggest that we omit "Scholar" from the title, calling it just "The Feminist." I also noticed that some of the Barnard faculty women who had come to the first couple of planning meetings had dropped out, leaving only three Barnard women on the committee, along with the Women's Center staff. When I asked several why they had stopped coming to meetings, they said they found that they didn't have the time this year. I suspect that this was not the whole answer. For some, like me, the topic was scary. Perhaps when they heard that we hoped to talk honestly and personally about our own feelings, they left.

None of this skepticism or disapproval dampened the enthusiasm of the hard-working planning committee. The energy level was high and the group process was going well. We were deep into deciding which issues should be addressed, and how, and by whom. The positive, eager responses we received from prospective speakers and workshop leaders suggested that we had selected a theme that was of serious interest to many scholars and activists.

It was hard to keep to our commitment to a one-day conference. There were many suggestions for extensions and add-ons, but I was firm that we follow our standard format. One recurring idea, which we finally accepted, was to publish a booklet containing some of the rich material from our planning committee meetings. We decided it would be our "diary," that it would include background information about the conference, the concept paper sent to all speakers and workshop leaders, excerpts from minutes of our meetings, descriptions of all the workshops, suggested readings by workshop leaders, and the bibliography used by the planning committee.

We named it *Diary of a Conference on Sexuality*. A few committee members assumed editorial responsibility, and we asked the three artists on the committee to design the publication and supervise its production. We asked them to put the material together in a creative, upbeat way, adding lively historical and contemporary graphics. We decided to further enliven the *Diary* by inviting speakers and workshop leaders to join committee members in writing personal notes about the conference, or about their experience on the committee, to be inserted throughout the *Diary*. Finally, we added a few blank pages here and there so that the booklet might serve as a diary for conference participants as well.

Since we hadn't budgeted for this expense, we cut corners on editorial and production costs. We didn't hire a professional editor; we used the cheapest newsprint; and we printed the entire publication in black and white—with just a touch of gold on the all-black cover. I took money from one of the Women's Center's gift funds to be repaid by the sale of the *Diary* as part of the registration fees for the conference.

Due to the pressures of time, I did not see the final copy with the graphics and layout before it went to the printer, but I had already relinquished control of the *Diary* when I, along with the committee, had given the three artists permission to choose the graphics, do the layout, and organize the artwork within the text. I had knowingly agreed to a somewhat less professional pamphlet than previous Women's Center publications, but I knew that the content of this seventy-two-page publication would be as rich and as innovative as the conference. I was convinced that sharing this material with conference participants would more than compensate for a slightly amateurish format.

The publication arrived just forty-eight hours before the conference. When I pulled one out of an open carton and saw the finished product for the first time, my heart sank. It wasn't quite what I had expected. The volume looked provocative: the stark black, somewhat shiny cover, the cheap paper, and the confrontational graphics. At first glance, the graphics dominated the booklet. Most of them were provocative and witty but some were sexually titillating, and a few were sexually explicit. The mixture of scholarly material, personal notes, and the bits of playfulness with bold sexual images interjected here and there all added up to a quirky publication—one that could only elicit strong reactions.

The first thing I did was to put one in a registration packet and send it over to the public relations office, as we routinely did before each conference. Then I stopped what I was doing—working with staff and others who had come in to help assemble the registration packets. I took the *Diary* and went to my office, closed the door, and spent a half hour alone going through it for the first time.

Reading the minutes, I found myself reliving some of those wonderful meetings, remembering how we made some of our decisions, and chuckling over Esther Newton's personal note, which read "explored the dream of my girls and found the girl of my dreams. Thanks to the planning committee." I was moved by some of the statements: the note by two of the morning speakers, Linda Gordon and Ellen Dubois, who expressed their gratitude to the conference for giving them the opportunity to collaborate, something they had wanted to do for a long time. In the personal notes, there were several admissions of how difficult it was at first to talk about one's own feelings of sexuality. One woman had written, "Talking about sex, if not false, is intimate. It turned me inside out at times." Another wrote, "When we talk about the possibilities for sexual pleasure under Patriarchy many of us, myself included, get nervous." Journalist Ellen Willis captured the very essence of what we were trying to do in her personal statement:

> For me, the planning committee meetings had a compelling,
> politically urgent quality I hadn't experienced in a long time—
> maybe not since the early years of the women's liberation move-
> ment. I believe that as the sexuality debate goes, so goes
> feminism. The tendency of some feminists to regard women pure-
> ly as sexual victims rather than sexual subjects, and to define
> the movement's goals as controlling male sexuality rather
> than demanding women's freedom to lead active sexual lives,
> reinforces women's oppression and plays into the hands of the
> New Right. It is a dead end, a politics of despair. Feminism is
> a vision of active freedom of fulfilled desires, or it is nothing.
> In these meetings we have been concerned with preserving and
> extending such a vision. Given the current social atmosphere,
> this is a radical act!

And Carole Vance wisely observed in her personal note, "We reaffirmed that the most important sexual organ in humans is located between the ears."

As I leafed through the *Diary*, noting the wide range of topics covered by the eighteen workshops, from Gayle Rubin's "Concepts for a Radical Politics of Sex" to Diane Harriford's "Sexual Purity: Maintaining Class and Race Boundaries" to Dale Bernstein and Elsa First's "Aggression, Selfhood and Female Sexuality: Rethinking Psychoanalysis," I felt the *Diary* would help conference participants understand what we had tried to do, even if it offended some, as the actual conference itself might very well do. I had taken strong positions before, and, although I admit I had some anxiety over how the administration would receive the *Diary* and now the conference, it never occurred to me that anything more than strong disapproval and distaste would be expressed, both of which I felt we could weather after a successful day.

As the phone rang, summoning me to the president's office, my confidence wavered. Perhaps, I thought, I should have dipped deeper into my discretionary fund and insisted that the publication be done more professionally. Maybe I should have anticipated official disapproval and vetoed the whole project. Even the conference itself may have been too much for a traditional college to handle. But to maintain credibility with the planning committee and the larger feminist community, these had not been realistic options.

As I left my office, I learned that the public relations director had sent for copies of the *Diary* for the president's review. As I walked across the campus to the president's office, I told myself that the worst that could happen would be strong remonstrations. One of the basic tenets of higher education was academic freedom, and I was sure that this would protect us from anything more than a verbal chastisement. Barnard's young new president, Ellen Futter, had only been in her job for a year. Her first administrative priority was to stabilize a working relationship with Columbia University, while maintaining Barnard's autonomy and access to Columbia's vast resources. She had important constituencies to consider. In the period she had been president, I had only the most brief, pro forma conversations with her. Also, as I was to later learn from her secretary, the president's office had been inundated with calls from Women Against Pornography attacking the conference, calling it pornography, and announcing their intention to picket on the day of the conference. One of the calls informed the president that the conference planning had been dominated by a California lesbian group called Samois, which supported sadomasochism.

When I entered, President Futter, the director of public relations, and the college lawyer were waiting for me, all with copies of the *Diary*. President Futter's expression said it all. She plunged right in, saying that she regarded the publication as a piece of pornography and that she was not going to tolerate its distribution to the conference participants and to the public. She asked me how I could have permitted this tasteless publication to be printed. I was shocked and struggled to find words. I tried to explain what the *Diary* was and that it represented the joint efforts of a large committee and that it was also integral to the conference. I acknowledged that its appearance did not measure up to other Women's Center publications and explained how this had happened. Her reply was unequivocal. She regarded it as my mistake, my responsibility, and she was unwavering in her decision not to permit the publication to be distributed publicly or even to exist. She insisted that it must be destroyed, shredded immediately. When I expressed dismay about the impact this would have on the conference, she brushed me aside. She was adamant that this "offensive" publication should not blemish Barnard's name. And she told me how far she was prepared to go. If I refused to remove the *Diary* from the registration packets, she would close down the conference. I pointed out that some 800 people were coming and that closing the conference would be a public relations disaster. Near the end of our interchange, during which the other two college administrators never said a word, President Futter asked how I could permit the printing of the *Diary* on "porno" paper, meaning, I learned later, newsprint.

During our meeting, she called the Helena Rubinstein Foundation—which had funded these conferences from their inception—to inform them of this publication and to lay out what steps she was taking to protect Barnard and the foundation. I said little through most of this. I realized that I should never have come to this meeting alone and that I couldn't simply capitulate. I left her office shaken but determined that the conference must take place. It was then that I learned from her secretary of the interference from Women Against Pornography, which partially explained some of President Futter's alarm. Had I known, I would have understood her decision more clearly, but I doubt that anything I might have said would have made a difference.

Walking back to my office, I felt a renewed obligation to all the women who had given their time and energy to our conference and to the Women's Center, which, by now, was recognized as a sounding board for feminist thought. I knew now, more than ever before, that it was time for our side of the debate to be heard.

When I reached my office, there were already several buildings and grounds workers with dollies, picking up the unopened cartons and retrieving loose diaries that were being stuffed into registration packets. I tried to save what I could, but I only managed to salvage about a dozen, all of which have since become collectors' items. What to do? How to restore trust destroyed in one hasty act.

I called an emergency meeting of the executive committee and another for the planning committee. The concerns and functions of the two committees were different, but we all shared a commitment to the *Diary* and to the conference. We formed a small subcommittee to talk with the administration and to make the most of our limited options. With the help of Elizabeth Janeway and Ronnie Eldridge, members of the Women's Center Executive Committee, and with two Barnard members from the planning committee, we were able to work out an arrangement whereby the administration agreed to republish the *Diary*—without substantive changes—deleting all references to Barnard College, the Women's Center, and the Helena Rubinstein Foundation. It was to be printed on better-quality paper, and the college agreed to assume all printing and mailing costs and to take the responsibility for sending it to all conference participants.

This was a small victory but an important one, although with time running out and with all the rumors swirling about, I was suddenly confronted with the much larger problem of how I was to run a successful conference. How could I maintain the trust of speakers and of workshop leaders, most of whom had now heard about the debacle and were angry with Barnard for withholding the *Diary*?

The Friday night reception for speakers, workshop leaders, and planning committee members, normally held at Barnard, was quickly moved to the neighborhood apartment of a member of the planning committee. As I walked in, conversation stopped and one of the workshop leaders came over to me and told me they had been discussing withdrawing their participation, even picketing the conference, to show their strong feelings about Barnard's imperious decision to confiscate the *Diary*. With the possibility of no conference and, even worse, of an action against Barnard and the Women's Center, I began to panic. Something had to happen before things got out of hand. I did the only thing I could think of that might make a difference. I told the group that I would guarantee that Barnard would do what the administration had promised. I would put my job on the line and resign publicly if the *Diary* was not republished and sent out to all conference registrants and others who had requested it within a reasonable amount of time. For a short while, I wasn't sure this would work. I held my breath. But in about fifteen minutes, the group agreed that the conference was more important than the Barnard administration's decision to shred the diaries. They would go ahead, as a sign of their trust in me and, even more important, in feminism and the conference itself.

I left the reception and went home with my head spinning. It was calming to have an interested, supportive husband, eager to hear all the details and give me encouragement as I talked about all the mishaps that I could expect the next day, but I certainly didn't sleep much that night. Conference day dawned with the sun shining brightly, which I took as a good omen, and I arrived at my office at dawn, with no idea of how the day would go.

People came early to register and there was no "*Diary* talk" until I was asked to step outside by a senior member of the Barnard administration. She wanted to speak to me on behalf of the president to make sure that there would be no public mention of the *Diary*. At first I didn't understand what she was asking. I assured her that I had not planned to make any announcement. No, she said, that wasn't what she meant. I was to inform all the speakers that they were not to mention the *Diary*. I was outraged and replied that I had no control over what anyone said, that I wouldn't dream of telling the conference coordinator or any of the speakers what they could or couldn't say. Further, I told her, either the president could fire me or I would resign on this very day and that, after the conference, I would hold a press conference to say why I was leaving Barnard. She shrank from my outburst and said no one wanted to see me leave, at least not now. She continued, however, by asking me where the conference coordinator was; she would talk to her herself. Although I maintained an amazingly calm composure, my fear turned to anger. I told her I had no idea where she was, that I had many details to take care of, and I left. I never heard whether that administrator ever found Carole Vance or any of the morning speakers, and, if so, whether she tried to get them not to mention the *Diary*.

But the *Diary* incident did not end there. The existence of the *Diary* was announced briefly throughout the conference but not in a way intended to provoke action or response. The emphasis was always on the fact that everyone would receive a *Diary* when it was reprinted. Without consciously articulating it, there seemed to be general agreement that our job was to put on a good conference and not to belabor the absence of the *Diary*. And that is what we did. Members of Women Against Pornography, wearing T-shirts with the words "For a Feminist Sexuality" on the front and "Against S/M" on the back, formed a small picket line and handed out leaflets and written protests, which added to the dynamics of the discussions. Some participants thought the conference outrageous and beyond the pale because we talked about the full range of women's experience, including erotic fantasies, butch/femme relationships, and sadomasochism. Most people stayed for the whole day and applauded loudly at the final session after Amber Hollibaugh colorfully summed up her thoughts on sexuality and Hattie Gossett, Cherríe Moraga, and Sharon Olds read selections from their own erotic poetry.

The debate didn't end with the conference. In the days immediately following the sexuality conference, there was conjecture both on and off campus as to whether the Helena Rubinstein Foundation would fund the next conference, even as to whether there would be another conference. A letter-writing campaign was organized by feminist scholars Marilyn Arthur and Rayna Rapp. Letters supporting the conference, stressing the importance of all the Scholar and the Feminist conferences poured into the president's office and the Helena Rubinstein Foundation. A petition prepared by Carole Vance and a few colleagues was circulated to the feminist, gay, and radical media, criticizing the actions of the group calling itself the Coalition for a Feminist Sexuality and Against Sadomasochism—a group organized by Women Against Pornography, Women Against Violence Against Women, and New York Radical Feminists—for its protest against the conference and its personal attacks on several of the speakers. The split in the women's movement over sexuality and specifically pornography heated up, and articles from both viewpoints appeared in a wide range of feminist publications.

The college did honor its commitment and, a few months after the conference, sent out a revised version of the *Diary* to all conference participants. The Helena Rubinstein Foundation withdrew its financial support, and Barnard took a new, hard look at the structure and place of the Women's Center. I found myself giving a good deal of thought to the deep split in the women's movement over sexuality and pornography. Perhaps, had I understood this initially, I would never have taken on such a conference. And, of course, I wondered whether anything would have been different had we permitted Women Against Pornography to join the planning committee and present a workshop at the conference. Other thoughts intruded as well. Would it have made a difference had I been a tenured academic? Would I then have been in a better position to gain support from other colleagues? And would this have ensured the freedom that I thought I had? There probably were trade-offs. Still, I clung to the belief that the Women's Center's marginal status granted it certain freedoms that it might not have enjoyed as an academic department.

The conference left its mark in a fine book, edited by Carole Vance, entitled *Pleasure and Danger: Exploring Female Sexuality,* a collection of essays based on conference material, revised and expanded. I view the book with pride, though unlike earlier ones, there is no mention of coeditorship with the Women's Center. Long before the conference, I asked Carole whether she was planning a book. When she said she was, I told her I had been giving the prospect of a book on sexuality a good deal of thought and had arrived at the conclusion that the Women's Center and Barnard should not be involved. This way, she would have complete freedom as editor and would not have to cope with any effort on the part of the college administration to question titles, graphics, or any portions of the text. I said I would put a letter in the files indicating that I suggested she publish the book on her own, absolving Barnard from all responsibility. Widely used in many women's studies courses, the book made a major contribution to understanding female sexuality. I was delighted when a Barnard women's studies professor told me recently that she uses the book, that her students enjoy it, and that they are proud that Barnard held this important conference.

With the conference over, I was eager to turn my attention to other matters. On June 3—six weeks after the conference—as Jay and I fastened our seat belts on British Airways for takeoff to Zimbabwe, I turned to Jay and said, "I don't want to think about the conference until we come home." The flight attendant passed out newspapers, and as I casually leafed through the current issue of the *Guardian,* I stumbled on an article called "Sex and the Egghead." There it was: a description of our sexuality conference by a British journalist, Elizabeth Wilson. She had attended and had found the conference full of contradictions, which she described by saying, "Who can imagine it happening here [in the United Kingdom]?" She alluded to the "mixture of academic formality and hard core—or if that's an unfortunate choice of words, `alternative politics'—feminism." She pointed to the reading of formal papers, to funding by the Helena Rubinstein Foundation, to the elegant salad lunch, and to the workshops where such far-out topics as sadomasochism, sexuality as pleasure, and the harassment and repression of "sexual deviants" were explored. "The mood," she wrote, "was one of academic primness bursting from its buttons." She summed up by saying, "Free sexuality may be a meaningless goal, but in a world in which such images are considered offensive, a little more speaking out must surely be no bad thing."

■ 15
MOVING ON

In 1983, a year after the sexuality conference, I resigned from my job at Barnard. I could have stayed longer, but I was sixty-five and ready to shed administrative work. I yearned for something I had never had before: a life with more flexibility, with time to explore new options.

I was sure I would continue to be engaged in some productive activity. Even after a long and satisfying career, I knew that a good part of my identity was rooted in working and helping women make changes in their lives. I had enough confidence to know that I would find useful things to do and that I would stay connected with the women's movement, which had been a major part of my life for so many years. Most important, as I took my leave of Barnard, I never thought of it as retirement but rather as a change in my life that I was making while still young enough to go on to other projects. Still, I approached retirement with mixed emotions. I knew it was time to leave, and I loved the feeling of freedom I would have—perhaps for the first time in my life. But, even though I had no hesitations in making this decision, I also had flashes of anxiety.

I had heard about the "problems" of retirement from several friends and had received plenty of gratuitous advice. One friend told me never to sleep late; another advised me always to know what I was going to do when I got up in the morning. I couldn't picture myself sleeping late, something I hadn't done since I was a teenager, and I couldn't imagine not knowing my direction every day.

Jay and I were both in good health, and my mother, by then in her nineties, was still managing alone. Two years later, when she broke her hip at the age of ninety-four, her life changed dramatically. She needed special care, and I was the appointed one since my brother didn't live in New York. She stayed in her own apartment for five years with round-the-clock nursing care, but, as her health deteriorated, she required more medical attention, and she finally had to be moved to a nursing home.

During the five years she was still in her own home, I saw more of her than I had in years. I engaged and supervised the women who cared for her, paid her bills, and handled all her affairs. Mixed with the resentment of these new responsibilities was a renewed admiration for the strength and gutsiness my mother had shown throughout many years of adversity. She was often cranky and complaining, due I'm sure to having to compromise her independence and depend almost completely on me. She clung, however, to whatever control she could have over her life, checking her bank statements as long as she could, even calling my attention to a ten-cent error that I might have made.

I was finally able to acknowledge that we did care for each other, and she was finally able to praise me occasionally. I tried to get her to talk about her own life, her marriage to my father, and my childhood. I also tried to get her to talk about how she managed and how she felt about the difficulties in her life. But she did what she had always done, offered sentimental platitudes devoid of honesty, and, once again, I felt the old anger toward her. I saw that part of her fierce independence depended on her clinging to what she called "her ideals." I felt guilty when I had to send her to a nursing home, thinking she would die quickly, and I would feel it was my fault. She lived for three more years and died peacefully in the summer of 1993 at the age of 102.

As I thought about what I would do next, I realized that what I had missed in my work at the Women's Center was the one-to-one vocational counseling I used to do for women, particularly mature women. Once again, I focused on my age group, just as I had in the 1950s. I looked around and saw a growing unmet need for women over sixty who were retiring or thinking about retiring, for women who had lost a partner or who were at loose ends after taking care of an ailing parent who had died. Once more I was thinking about middle-class women, those in good health, who, it seemed to me, could have up to twenty-five more productive years were they helped to find appropriate work, either paid or volunteer. I visited senior centers and talked with educators who coordinated programs for seniors, and with leaders in the field of gerontology in New York City.

After learning that no group was doing what I wanted to do, I designed a project which I called Options for Women over Sixty. I drafted a proposal that described the need for such a project and pointed out the benefits it could bring in physical and emotional health for a growing number of women. I proposed starting with a small program, using graduate students pursuing counseling degrees as interns. My plan was to offer individual and group counseling, which would help women to assess their needs, experience, and skills, and to provide information and referrals, which would direct them to jobs, either paid or volunteer.

I gave myself a year to get it started and took my proposal to every educational institution that had courses for seniors and to all the social agencies I could think of that served this group in New York City. As I talked to directors of programs, it became clear that my proposal was a "quality of life" project and didn't address any of the basic problems most older women faced—problems of poverty, housing, and healthcare. Although it was a project for a privileged population, many people encouraged me to pursue it, agreeing that it would not only provide an important service for women, which might very well ensure a sense of well being in what has come to be viewed as the "declining years," but would also fulfill a societal need in using otherwise wasted talent in a productive way.

Despite the validity of my proposal, I couldn't find an institutional base from which to operate in the time I had allotted to getting started. I was turned down even by educational institutions such as the New School for Social Research, which had an institute for seniors, and Marymount College, which offered a program of courses for this age group of women. The usual reason was lack of funds and that trying to raise money for a new project would compete with programs already in place. Only one group, the YWCA, gave it serious consideration, but their main building was about to undergo renovation and they couldn't take on any new projects for the foreseeable future. Perhaps I should have persevered longer, but, in this respect, I was age conscious and not eager to wait for what might be an indefinite length of time before finding the kind of support I needed. I still believe the time will come when such a project will be seen as a valuable contribution, but this won't happen until society commits itself to nurturing human potential.

As I put this project aside, others came my way. From the day I retired, I was never at a loss for useful activities. I participated in the Women's Encampment for a Future of Peace and Justice protest over the storage of nuclear weapons at the army depot at Seneca Falls in August 1983 and also in the United Nations NGO Conference on Women in Nairobi in 1985. I was a workshop leader at the spring 1992 Hunter College conference, "Women Tell the Truth: Parity, Power and Sexual Harassment," at which Anita Hill was the keynote speaker. I was the cochair of the Columbia University Seminar on Women and Society for two years. I wrote about my Women's Center experience in an article for *Women's Studies Quarterly* and in chapters for two anthologies on women in higher education.

I served on the board of CCR (Center for Constitutional Rights) for eight years, from 1984 to 1992. Born out of the Southern civil rights struggle in the mid-1960s, the center is a unique organization with a proud history of providing innovative legal assistance to individuals and social movements whose constitutional rights have been denied or infringed. CCR's litigation and educational campaigns focus on such issues as racial justice, government misconduct, criminal justice, economic and environmental justice, First Amendment rights, international human rights, women's rights, and lesbian and gay rights. I was attracted to CCR because it had a particularly strong record in women's rights, and, as in all its work, the center showed particular concern for those with the least power—often women of color. All my professional life I had worked with middle-class, white women, and I felt that it was time for me to work on projects that touched the lives of those who were most oppressed. For a few years I was so deeply involved with CCR that, in addition to serving on the board, I took a forty-five-minute subway ride twice a week and, as a volunteer, set up a speaker's bureau, wrote a history of women's rights at CCR and a proposal for a program called Empowering Women.

Jay retired a year after I did. He sold his computer database company in 1981, staying on to complete a three-year management contract. This unexpected sale gave us a measure of financial security and comfort I had not experienced since I was a child. It also enabled us to buy a summer house, which we would use as a weekend retreat all year round.

Our lives changed, but not always in predictable ways. I had assumed that we would both live at a more leisurely pace, that, interspersed with selected work projects, we would have time for travel and other pleasures that we had put aside because of the pressures of work. This did not happen.

Instead, Jay renewed his interest in environmental research, which began when he served on the Science Advisory Board of the EPA (Environmental Protection Agency) in 1977 during the Carter administration. Upon retirement he was drawn into a new career; using the research he had done for the EPA, Jay wrote a book on the health effects of toxic chemicals. He then went on to study the neglected problem of the health effects of ionizing radiation from bomb tests and nuclear reactors, which led to two more books, numerous articles, and dozens of requests for lectures and participation in conferences.

I watched him become so absorbed in his work that he scarcely had time for anything else. For the first time there were serious tensions between us. I was used to having a supportive, interested, sharing partner, and Jay was suddenly so deeply engrossed in his work that he often didn't hear me. I felt shut out of his world. He neglected his share of the housekeeping, which was modest to begin with, and even forgot to give me telephone messages. For a time I found his passion for his new work so overwhelming that there was little left for any kind of normal life. As I watched this man of broad interests narrow his focus, almost to the point of obsession, I found myself resenting his work and then feeling ashamed for having such feelings.

Although I could understand that part of the reason for this all-consuming involvement was that Jay felt himself to be a crusader for a cause that was neither accepted by the mainstream nor taken seriously by the progressive community, it made him hard to live with. But I knew I couldn't turn my back on what had been such a special relationship. I sought professional help, and, because Jay basically is an open, flexible person, he agreed to talk with a therapist. Within a short time we were both ready to make whatever compromises were necessary to resolve the tensions. Some of the remedies were simple, such as installing my own phone and answering machine. Others took bending a bit on the part of both of us. Today, Jay continues his work with single-minded devotion and, on occasion, will admit that he is virtually obsessed with the need to bring the dangers of low-level radiation to public attention. I know that his work is important, and I am proud of him. But I am equally pleased that he is able to step back from time to time to reaffirm our relationship.

I, too, have settled into a life centered around work at home. Whether in the city or in the country, we both have our own work rooms, our own computers, our own telephones, and our own writing schedules. We have fashioned a life together that does not include sharing all the mundane details of day-to-day living, but we both know that we are there for each other. I find I can give him more space than in earlier years, knowing that, whenever I need him to read a rough draft of a section of my manuscript and give me his comments or to fix the computer when I have pushed the wrong button, I can call on him. We both like working at home—knowing the other is there—and enjoy those occasions when our schedules mesh and we can meet in the kitchen at midday to prepare lunch.

My working pace is less frenetic than Jay's. Besides the burden of my share of the housekeeping, I take time for long walks through city streets or on the ocean or bay beach, time for visits with friends, and time for other relaxations. I savor the many pleasures we do share, but, for both of us, our work remains the central focus of our lives.

When I met Jay, I was surprised to learn that he could scarcely remember celebrating any holidays, and he was quite sure that even his own birthday had never been the focus of special attention. I loved family festivities and had always made a ritual out of birthdays and other happy holidays. From our first year together, I made sure that his birthday was properly observed. Since Jay's birthday is in August, on his sixty-fifth birthday, in 1980, I invited his children and Nancy to come to celebrate with us at our summer house in Connecticut. Diana came from California with her partner, my old friend Kirsten Grimstad. Kirsten had coordinated our early Women's Center bibliography and had met Diana in Los Angeles when Kirsten was editing the short-lived feminist magazine *Chrysalis*. Emily came with her husband, Tom Kavet, whom she had met when she was at Barnard and he at Columbia. They started married life in New York, moved to Massachusetts when Emily went to law school, and, after a few years, bought land and built a house in rural Vermont. Nancy came from nearby Middletown. It was too stressful for David, who was living in the Southwest, to come.

Through the years these birthday celebrations have expanded to become a family tradition. They all come to our house, now on Long Island: Nancy, Diana and Kirsten, and Emily and Tom and their two young children. For up to two weeks, our house is full to bursting. The grandchildren enliven the household, and, each year, we all vie for their attention, marveling at their distinctive personalities and their developing talents. This past summer it was Alexa's flute playing and two-and-a-half-year-old Aaron's insatiable curiosity and passion for doors, drawers, cupboards, anything he could open and close.

These yearly visits on Jay's birthday have become more than a celebration. I note the way Jay's two daughters—with eleven years' difference in age—use this time to cement the bonds between them. And I watch with pleasure as Diana, Emily, and my daughter Nancy delight in being together and make plans to visit each other throughout the year. Fortuitously, Tom comes from the Southwest and, on several occasions, has combined trips to his parents, with Emily and their children, with Nancy's visit to David. The most recent trip was to Sedona, Arizona, for a memorial service for Tom's grandmother, which Diana attended along with David and Nancy. So, gradually, in one way or another, everyone in the family has had a chance to get to know each other.

Nancy is now a full professor at Wesleyan; Diana a successful television writer; and Kirsten a faculty member of a nontraditional graduate degree program, which keeps her traveling a good deal. Emily and Tom both work and, from time to time, reverse roles as primary caretaker. Emily is a lawyer in the attorney general's office in Vermont, and Tom, an economic and business consultant, is the parent currently at home with the children.

David still struggles to make a life for himself. He has moved several times, from California to Mexico, to Hawaii, back to California, and most recently to Arizona. He takes courses and does beautiful landscape photography. I still hope that he will find a way to live more fully and contentedly, but I have had to accept that his life is something over which I have little direct control.

Learning to understand the powerlessness women feel as women, sharing experiences and perceptions and connecting with other women—both individually and collectively, both professionally and personally—not only changed the way I worked but also the way I related to other women. Besides the satisfaction of having worked in a field I believe in deeply, I think that I am a happier person today because I interact with other women more openly and honestly than I once did.

This was not always true. In the early 1970s my exhilaration over being part of a major social revolution was tempered by a feeling that some of my old friends disapproved of me. I was changing, becoming more outspoken, more confident, and more passionate in my convictions. As I learned about the emerging issues affecting women's lives, I was eager to share my enthusiasm and new insights with my old friends. It never occurred to me that they might not be interested. After all, these were women of my generation, who, in a number of ways, had lived lives similar to mine. We had raised our children together, many of us as wives of busy professional men.

Most of my friends had shown a genuine interest in my work helping women return to work and to school in the 1950s and 1960s, some to the point of coming to see me professionally when they were ready to think about their own career plans. But these same friends showed little interest in the women's movement in the 1970s. In fact, some expressed hostility. They knew only the clichés perpetuated by the mainstream media, which focused on the most sensational actions taken by a few extremists. I was constantly explaining that women hadn't burned bras in their protest of the Miss America beauty contest in 1968. It was frustrating to see intelligent women accept the myths that surrounded the attack on such a stereotypical American institution. Most of them didn't see feminism as a political issue; some made a point of insisting that they were quite happy with their personal lives.

By and large, these friends were strong, independent women, active in the struggle for civil rights and against the war in Vietnam. They accepted, for example, the "extremists" who had burned their draft cards or had gone to Canada as part of the antiwar movement. But their reactions to the allegedly extreme actions of the women's movement were quite different. They couldn't understand women who would stage sit-ins at male bars or protest at annual corporate stockholders meetings. They couldn't tolerate expressions of anger at men, and they said such outbursts made them feel ashamed of women. And further, they regarded feminism as strictly an indulgence, a white middle-class movement that wouldn't improve the chances for wide-reaching peace and social justice.

I was distressed by the way many of my old friends perceived me. One friend said that I was obsessed with "extreme" ideas and that I had lost my objectivity; another called me strident. I enticed a good friend to attend one of the all-day Scholar and the Feminist conferences, only to have her tell me later that she left early because she found it boring. Even the fact that Jay shared my views seemed to anger some. On several occasions I tried to discuss the new women's health movement with some of my old medical friends, but the few women doctors whom I had known for years felt attacked and vehemently defended their entrenched authoritarian positions.

I was puzzled. Even more, I had a sense of loss. But then, over the years, I watched as some of my old friends began to take an active interest in some of the issues women were insisting be a part of the public agenda, particularly reproductive freedom, domestic violence, and discrimination in all its obvious and subtle forms. Some of the truths of feminism gradually crept into their consciousness, changing the way they thought and how they related to each other. Most of them now applaud the new division of labor within young families, where both parents work and share household tasks and even childcare. And they now regard a whistle or catcall, in response to a woman passing by, as a form of sexual harassment, and not a compliment. And perhaps best of all, they increasingly enjoy being with other women socially, free from having to have a male partner for an evening out.

Although I had temporarily alienated a number of these friends by vehemently expounding feminist issues in the early 1970s—perhaps before they were ready to listen—most of those friendships have endured and deepened. Perhaps, I, too, no longer have the need to express my views in quite the same passionate manner.

Over the years I have also maintained close friendships with women younger than myself—a few of these friendships bridge a generation. I was unusual in that I was several decades older than the women I worked with. But because we worked together in a nonhierarchical, inclusive way, with passion, determination, and a shared vision, we created an ambiance of equality and closeness that laid the groundwork for some lifelong friendships.

One of these young women was Elizabeth Minnich. A graduate student completing her doctorate in philosophy under Hannah Arendt at the New School for Social Research, she was recruited in 1976 by the newly appointed Barnard president Jacquelyn Mattfeld. In the four years Elizabeth worked at the college, first as assistant to the president and then as associate dean of faculty, she made the Women's Center an important part of her activities, and we often worked closely together. She served on a number of Women's Center committees and was the coordinator one year, and the moderator of the morning panel another year, for the Scholar and the Feminist conference. In addition, she was the cocoordinator and speaker at an invitational Women's Center conference on Special Programs for Women in Higher Education in 1979, funded by the Rockefeller Foundation. She had a deep understanding of feminism and its relation to the academy and was a superb administrator. She was often instrumental in smoothing the way for us as we introduced new, frequently controversial programs. Even after she left Barnard, she returned to be a speaker at a conference we held in 1981 on "New Perspectives on Women and Work: Implications of Feminist Scholarship for Vocational Counselors," funded by the New York Council for the Humanities.

Elizabeth continues to be as important to me as when we worked together at Barnard. I treasure the visits we have either in New York, our home in the country, or—on occasion—at her home in Charlotte, North Carolina. We never tire of spending hours reviewing our lives, reflecting on the state of feminism and the world, and relighting the burning fires of those earlier years. She remains my touchstone for clear thinking on feminism.

Another is Fanette Pollack, whom I have known since she was a sophomore working at the Women's Center the first year it opened. I have watched her grow up, marry her high school sweetheart, go to law school, have two children, and become a labor lawyer. For the past several years, Fanette has made it an August ritual to rent a house near us, so that, with her husband and her children, she can be part of Jay's birthday celebration. She has become a member of our extended family, and, whenever we get together, we invariably slip into the same discussion we have had again and again, ever since she was a student: where the women's movement is today and how it does or doesn't relate to race and class.

Christina Greene is a young woman whom I have kept in touch with since she came to the Women's Center when she was a graduate student in the Sarah Lawrence Women's History Program to coordinate one of our conferences. When that ended, she stayed on in a full-time job for another two years, leaving to run a college women's center on her own, then to coordinate a women's research center at Duke University and to work on her Ph.D. in Women's History, to marry, and to have a child. When I first asked her to critique a draft of an article I had written, she hesitated and said, "Wow, you want me to criticize my boss?" But, after a few moments of hesitation, she agreed to do it; she knew exactly what was wrong and told me.

Through the years most of us have met each other's partners and children, shared meaningful occasions, and agonized over tribulations in our lives, both small and large. We have read and criticized each other's manuscripts and visited back and forth. A couple of friends have the keys to our New York apartment, which they use when they come, whether we are here or not. Despite our age differences, I like to think that these are essentially equal relationships.

For the past several years, I have been part of a women's group, not too unlike the early consciousness-raising groups. We meet fairly regularly and share concerns about some of the common problems we all are confronting as we grow older. As I reflect on the twenty-five years I was married to Bernie, I realize that I never shared my apprehension about his illness with any of my friends or my feelings of isolation as, near the end of his life, he retreated into solitary diversions. At the time I thought it would have been disloyal to show my vulnerability, to talk about him and my feelings. In like manner, I look back at some of the consuming guilt that I felt when I wanted more time to myself and that made me wonder if I was always a good wife and mother. Now, I see that these old feelings were not, as I thought then, simply my inadequacies but feelings shared by many women. Until the rebirth of feminism, these were feelings most of us didn't dare talk about.

The women's movement has made it easy for me to connect with women wherever I go. Since my life with Jay has included extensive travel—much of it to professional meetings and to conferences, rather than as sightseeing tourists—it has given me the opportunity to talk with women in other countries, even those with whom I couldn't converse directly because we spoke different languages. Wherever we went, I met with leaders of women's rights organizations who were as eager to talk with me as I was with them. Invariably, we started off with rhetoric, but it didn't take long to find true common ground.

The first time this happened was in 1974 when I accompanied Jay to Hungary on one of several professional trips he made as part of a delegation of business executives and economists to promote trade between Eastern and Western countries. The Hungarian delegation was an official government group, all of whom were men. There was one woman in the United States delegation, and I was one of several wives accompanying their husbands.

In addition to the professional discussions, I noticed that each host country was eager to show off its accomplishments. At an early session the Hungarians asked members of the United States delegation to select specific sites individuals would like to visit: a factory, a bank, or a special government office. They told us they had arranged a fashion show for the visiting women. Through an interpreter I expressed my desire to meet with women who were prepared to discuss the status of women in Hungary. There was a long silence. Finally, after some whispered conversation among the Hungarians, which of course I wasn't privy to, the interpreter seemed embarrassed and said that this would not be necessary because women had equality under Hungarian socialism. (I was to hear this again on a later trip to Bulgaria.) I said I understood this, but I pressed further, saying that I felt that we in the United States had much to learn from their experience. More whispering and more embarrassed vague replies: they would see what they could do. At the next session, I was told that an appointment had been made for me with the chair of the Hungarian women's rights group.

Sure enough, a car was sent to take me to a small office on the outskirts of Budapest where I met with the leader of the Hungarian Women's Rights Organization, a wonderful woman who spoke English. She received me graciously and acknowledged that in the new constitution women were treated equally, but she confided that this did not reflect the true condition of women in Hungary. More women were professionals than before the revolution, but, since there were very limited consumer services and since men had *not* changed, women still had to do everything, including queue up for groceries at the end of a full working day and then go home and cook dinner for their husbands and children. Further, she told me that, particularly in rural areas, customs remained as they had been for centuries. When a man comes home from work, he expects his wife to be there to pull his boots off, and, when the family goes out walking, the wife walks behind her husband, not next to him. She opened a drawer and pulled out Betty Friedan's book and told me how much she would like to read more books about women in the West. When I returned to New York, I sent her a package of books, and we kept in touch for several years.

At the final reception in Budapest, when thanks were being exchanged, I asked the chair of the United States delegation if I could add my appreciation for the visit I had with the head of the women's rights group. He felt this would embarrass the Hungarians. In his concluding remarks he voiced my thoughts awkwardly and added that my views did not represent the views of the American delegation.

I could tell similar stories about visits to other countries. I was particularly moved by my experiences in Zimbabwe, which Jay and I visited twice, first in 1982, one year after liberation, and again the following year. Jay was asked to plan and participate in a conference on business education and the use of computers. These visits provided me with an opportunity to learn about women. I was told that, since women had fought alongside men in the struggle for independence, the government had begrudgingly created a Ministry of Community Development and Women's Affairs and had appointed a twenty-five-year-old former freedom fighter as minister. She had studied in the United States and proved to be too strong a feminist for the government. She was quickly transferred to another ministry and replaced by a mature woman who had formerly been a nurse.

I learned that, although the liberation government leaders had made a public commitment to equality for all its citizens, at the same time, they were fearful of upsetting the tradition of Shona and Ndebele tribal customs, which provided the underpinnings of life for African families. The tribal customs were so deeply imbedded in African culture, that, even with modern legislation, women still were legal minors from birth until death. Before marriage a woman was under the guardianship of her father or other male relative. Upon marriage, a bridal price, the *lobola,* is paid by the husband to the bride's family. After marriage she belonged to her husband, and, in the event of divorce, separation, or death, she returned to the guardianship of her father or other male relative.

My link to understanding the strength of the tribal culture of Zimbabwe was Sheila Perry Nemapare, a Barnard graduate who had been a student member of the Women's Center Executive Committee. She put me in touch with several Zimbabwean women leaders who were happy to talk with me. Sheila, an American, represented the conflicts of this struggling society. While at graduate school in the United States, she met a native Zimbabwean, educated in Canada and the United States and living in exile. They married and, upon Zimbabwe's independence, returned there, he to head the national television station and she to edit a women's magazine. When we met them, they were living as part of a group of young professionals who were building this new independent state. But Sheila told me how difficult it was to be part of a family that adhered to old customs and how even her emancipated young husband tended to fall back into the old male-female roles.

Since 1986, when Jay's central focus shifted to environmental problems, we have traveled to conferences both in the United States and abroad on the dangers of low-level radiation emitted from nuclear power plants. Initially, I accompanied Jay with some reluctance, feeling that this was his work, and I drew back from learning more about such a frightening issue.

But the first thing I noticed at many of these conferences was that most of the leadership came from women. I found the energy that women focused on environmental issues exhilarating and irresistible, reminiscent of the same strong commitment women had for the women's movement at an earlier time. Our long-time feminist leader, Bella Abzug, and her lifelong associate, Mim Kelber, had set up an international organization called WEDO (Women's Environment and Development Organization), linking feminism with environmental concerns; thus sending a strong message that environment is a women's issue.

While I did not need to be convinced intellectually of the connections between feminism and the environment, one conference I attended with Jay had a great emotional impact on me. In April 1996 Jay was invited to testify in Vienna before the Permanent Peoples Tribunal, a group of judges established in 1978 in the tradition set by Bertrand Russell to render judgments on world catastrophes of the magnitude of Bhophal and Chernobyl. The conference was convened by the International Medical Commission of Chernobyl, headed by Dr. Rosalie Bertell, a distinguished epidemiologist, to commemorate the tenth anniversary of Chernobyl. A dozen Russian physicians and scientists—most of them women—testified to the shocking health conditions they were observing in the areas most heavily affected ten years after this catastrophic meltdown. In some districts, the proportion of live births that were hopelessly malformed had risen to the point that women in desperation were terminating all pregnancies. As I listened to this recital of the rising incidence of premature and malformed births, childhood and adult cancer, and shortened life expectancy, I realized that I could no longer close my eyes and simply say this was Jay's work. Low-level radiation affects the future viability of all human life and is especially devastating to women, who have the responsibility of bringing babies into an increasingly polluted world.

Age is a condition that I give little thought to. Both Jay and I continue to lead lives full of commitments and activity, always surprised when something happens that temporarily slows us down. We have each had our share of physical problems associated with aging, but we refuse to admit that we are old or that we need special treatment or any changes in our lives. I find no more peace in these "golden years" than in all the earlier turbulent years. The struggle continues for me as I try to feel comfortable in a world that I feel less able to understand.

I see the dissolution of order in a world engulfed in nationalistic conflicts and environmental abuses, all of which have the greatest impact on women who have the least power. I see the rights of women being threatened everywhere, but I cling to my basic conviction that the women's movement is a necessary component of our aspirations for an egalitarian, democratic, and more humane society. I think about my grandchildren and the kind of world they will grow up in, and I hope they will have the chance to experience what I think has so greatly enhanced the quality of my life: the privilege of working for something I passionately believe in.

I. PURPOSE

Since its founding in 1889, Barnard College has distinguished itself as a women's college within the challenging atmosphere of a large, urban, male-oriented university. To affirm its traditional commitment to educate women in the changing context of its closer relationship with Columbia, Barnard in 1971 established a Women's Center. The realization of a purpose long shared by many in the Barnard community, the Center's underlying aim is to assure that women can live and work in dignity, autonomy, and equality. Acknowledging that the broad needs and aspirations of women are often unrecognized or inadequately defined by the society at large, the Barnard Women's Center is dedicated to addressing those needs through the various groups it serves: students, faculty, administrators, alumnae, and women in the larger community. It endeavors to foster a heightened sense of woman's identity to the end that women may be free to cultivate their interests and talents and realize their potential as fully creative and contributing human beings. To encourage the open sharing of knowledge and experience, it seeks to increase ties among diverse groups of women. Its further aim is to create an atmosphere and develop programs which will invest women with confidence and a sense of purpose. The Center welcomes the cooperation of all—men and women—who are in sympathy with its aims.

II. ACTIVITIES

The Center is a physical and a psychological meeting ground for women. Because it is open to a diversity of cultural styles and endeavors, its projects reflect wide ranging points of view.

As a part of Barnard College, the Center draws upon the academic community whenever a member of the College can further, through teaching, research, or other personal endeavor, some aspect of its work. The Center concentrates on developing projects which complement or coincide with Barnard's distinctive academic strengths in women's studies. These projects include a research library, departmental and interdepartmental courses, conferences, lectures, and publications. The Center encourages members of the Barnard faculty to engage in research in women's studies and to participate in the ongoing intellectual dialogue on feminist scholarship in professional and interdisciplinary organizations.

In addition, the Center engages in a variety of non-academic programs. It regularly provides information on activities and organizations of special interest to women, initiates non-credit courses on feminism, and sponsors projects in the arts. It provides vocational counseling for college women in the metropolitan area, acts as a clearinghouse for women's professional and educational projects, and carries on research on the career development of women.

III. GOVERNANCE

Serving the College at large, the Women's Center is directly responsible to Barnard's President and Board of Trustees. It is governed by an Executive Committee which is its policy-making body. Representing the four major constituencies of the Center, the Committee is composed of three students, three faculty members, three alumnae, and three administrative staff members. The Director of the Center is an *ex officio* member of the Committee; she does not vote except to break a tie. The student members of the Committee are elected according to procedures determined by the Undergraduate Association in consultation with the Director. Other members of the Committee are nominated by the Executive Committee of the Center in consultation with appropriate officers of the College: in the case of alumnae members, the President of the Alumnae Association; in the case of faculty members, the Dean of the Faculty; in the case of administrative staff members, the President of Barnard College. Upon the nomination of the Executive Committee, the President appoints the members for two year terms. Members may serve two consecutive terms. A member who has served on the Committee for four consecutive years may be reappointed only after a lapse of two years. The meetings of the Committee are always open and the minutes are available to the public.

The President of Barnard College appoints the Director, subject to Trustee approval, upon the recommendation of a five-person Search Committee of which at least two are members currently serving on the Executive Committee. The President, in consultation with the Executive Committee, will invite members to serve on the Search Committee. The Director's general functions are to initiate programs and projects with the approval of the Executive Committee and to implement the decisions taken by that body. She personally maintains liaison with the Columbia community. She also contributes to good public relations with other institutions and organizations. She and the Executive Committee, jointly or separately, are empowered to form subcommittees which deal with matters of concern to any or all parts of the Center's constituency. These subcommittees report their findings and recommendations to the Director and Executive Committee. The Director is responsible for seeing that these subcommittees include as members representatives from groups whose interest is at stake. She has the responsibility and duty of preparing and administering budgets, implementing personnel policies, preparing reports, participating in meetings, and cooperating with other administrators in developing and carrying out programs for the good of the College.

Amendments to this charter require a two-thirds majority vote of the Executive Committee and the approval of the Faculty, President, and Trustees of Barnard College.

Reprinted by permission of the Barnard Center for Research on Women.

THE SCHOLAR AND THE FEMINIST   MAY 11, 1974

THE SCHOLAR AND THE FEMINIST

What is the impact of feminism on scholarship? What are the implications for the disciplines? for academic institutions? and for scholars in their own research and their understanding of women? These questions are the focus of today's conference and will be examined by three concurrent panels of scholars from different disciplines. The thirteen afternoon workshops are planned around the general theme, "Scholarship and Feminism: Conflict, Compromise, Creativity," and will address specific questions within this framework.

MORNING PANELISTS

Electa Arenal, Hispanic Literature, Richmond College; Carolyn Shaw Bell, Economics, Wellesley College; Constance Carroll, Classics, University of Maine—Portland-Gorham; Lee Ehrman, Biology, SUNY—Purchase; Kate Ellis, English, Livingston College; Gerda Lerner, History, Sarah Lawrence College; Linda Nochlin, Art History, Vassar College; Miriam Schneir, History; Victoria Schuck, Political Science, Mount Holyoke College; Janet Siskind, Anthropology, Rutgers University—Newark; Judith Jarvis Thomson, Philosophy, Massachusetts Institute of Technology; Naomi Weisstein, Psychology, SUNY—Buffalo

Panel Moderators from Barnard College: Annette K. Baxter, History; Catharine R. Stimpson, English; Suzanne F. Wemple, History

AFTERNOON WORKSHOPS—SCHOLARSHIP AND FEMINISM: CONFLICT, COMPROMISE, CREATIVITY

1. New Literary Sources for Feminists
    Louise Bernikow, Women's Studies, Jersey City State College
    Elizabeth Diggs, English, Jersey City State College
2. War and Peace: Four Generations of Feminists
    Hester Eisenstein, Experimental College, Barnard College
    Gladys Meyer, Sociology, Barnard College
3. Women in Social Science: New Questions, Old Data
    Patricia Albjerg Graham, Education and History, Barnard College and Columbia University Teachers' College
    Donna Shalala, Politics and Education, Columbia University Teachers' College
4. Multiple Roles of a Feminist Scholar
    Harriet B. Applewhite, Political Science, Southern Connecticut State College
    Darline Levy, History, Barnard College

5. What Befits a Woman?
  Sue Larson, Philosophy, Barnard College
  Mary Mothersill, Philosophy, Barnard College
6. Is Woman the "Deviant Case" in Social Science Research?
  Julia Makarushka, Sociology, Barnard College
  Astrid Merget, Political Science, Barnard College
7. Films and Literature: Sources for Transcultural Analysis
  Leah Davidson, Psychiatry, William Alanson White Institute
  Barbara Miller, Oriental Studies, Barnard College
8. Feminist Literary Criticism in the University
  Nancy Miller, French, Columbia University
  Domna Stanton, French, Barnard College
9. Research in the Humanities: What New Perspectives?
  Carol Christ, Literature and Religion, Columbia University
  Elaine Pagels, History of Religion, Barnard College
10. Feminist Scholarship in Action: A New Look at Classical Tragic Heroines and Their Modern Counterparts
  Carolyn Heilbrun, English, Columbia University
  Ann Sheffield, Greek and Latin, Barnard College
11. The Economics of Sex Differentials
  Cynthia Lloyd, Economics, Barnard College
  Beth Niemi, Economics, Rutgers University—Newark
12. Women and Science
  Joan Birman, Mathematics, Barnard College
  Sigalia Dostrovsky, Physics, Barnard College
13. Feminism: Catalyst for Creative Energy
  Victoria Barr, Painting, Barnard College
  Jane Kaufman, Painting, Queens College

Conference Coordinator
  Susan Riemer Sacks, Psychology and Education, Barnard College
Student Coordinator
  Batya Hyman, Barnard College
Director, Women's Center
  Jane S. Gould

THE SCHOLAR AND THE FEMINIST II: TOWARD NEW CRITERIA OF RELEVANCE   APRIL 12, 1975

PAPERS AND DISCUSSION

Welcoming Remarks
  Martha Peterson, President, Barnard College
History and the Social Relation of the Sexes
  Joan Kelly-Gadol, CUNY—City College
One Biologist's Perspective on Sex Differences
  Helen H. Lambert, Northeastern University

Moderator: *Annette K. Baxter, Barnard College*
Commentator: *Catharine R. Stimpson, Barnard College*

Seminars

1. A Neglected Theme in Euripides' Medea: Interpreting Classical Literature
   Helen Bacon, Barnard College
2. Sexual Mythologies in the Avant-Garde: Joyce and Robbe-Grillet
   Jane O. Grace, CUNY—Lehman
   Susan Suleiman, Columbia University
3. Critical Approaches to Art and Literature: Beyond "Objectivity"
   Carol Duncan, Ramapo State College
4. Women's Studies, Phase II: The New Issues
   Domna C. Stanton, Barnard College
5. Surviving Graduate School
   Jo Freeman, SUNY—Purchase
6. Research and Activism: Bridging the Gap
   Mary Jean Tully, NOW
7. Women and the French Revolution
   Gita May, Columbia University
8. Women or Their Absence in the American Novel Before World War I
   Myra Jehlen, SUNY—Purchase
9. The Spiritual Quest in Women's Writing: At the Juncture of Literature and Religion
   Carol Christ, Columbia University
10. Feminism and Psychological Autonomy: A Participative Workshop
    Hester Eisenstein, Barnard College
    Susan R. Sacks, Barnard College
11. Personality Theory and Women
    Maxine D. Bernstein, SUNY—Empire State
12. Anthropology of Women and Sexism
    Sherry B. Ortner, Sarah Lawrence College

Conference Coordinator
   Nancy K. Miller
Planning Committee
   Hester Eisenstein, Jane O. Grace, Susan R. Sacks
Director, Women's Center
   Jane S. Gould
Assistant Director, Women's Center
   Emily Kofron

THE SCHOLAR AND THE FEMINIST III:
THE SEARCH FOR ORIGINS   April 10, 1976

Morning Session

Welcoming Remarks
   Elizabeth Janeway, Trustee, Barnard College
Unraveling the Problem of Origins: An Anthropological Search for Feminist Theory
   Rayna R. Reiter, The New School for Social Research
When Did Man Make God in His Image? A Case-Study in Religion and Politics
   Elaine H. Pagels, Barnard College

Moderator: *Hester Eisenstein, Barnard College*

AFTERNOON SEMINARS

1. The Female Threat: Patriarchal Ideology in the Odyssey
    Mary R. Lefkowitz, Wellesley College
    Joan Peters, CUNY—City College
2. Jung After Feminism: A Perspective from the Psychology of Religion
    Naomi Goldenberg, Yale University
3. The Politics of Wagelessness: Women, Housework, and the Wages Due
    Silvia Federici, New York Wages for Housework Committee
4. Anger As Inspiration and Inhibition: American Women Writers, 1850 to the Present
    Ann Douglas, Columbia University
5. Origins of Women as Sex-Objects in the Visual Arts
    Nanette Salomon, CUNY—Queens College and Fordham University
6. The Development of Sex Differences as the Development of Power Differences
    Rhoda K. Unger, Montclair State College
7. The Origins of Modern Marriage
    Heidi Hartmann, The New School for Social Research
    Ellen Ross, Connecticut College
8. Beyond the Mother Tongue: Repression and Expression of Sensuous Experience in Women's
Poetic Language
    Barbara S. Miller, Barnard College
    Agueda Pizzaro, CUNY—Brooklyn College
9. "Biological" Origins: Avoiding the Mire of "Genetic Destiny"
    Ethel Tobach, American Museum of Natural History
10. The Medieval Church: What Happened to Women?
    Suzanne F. Wemple, Barnard College
11. The Physical Abuse of Women: The Force of Patriarchy
    Nadia Telsey, CUNY—York College
12. The Perspective of the Black Woman Writer in American Literature
    Joan Hazzard, CUNY—City College
13. Origins and Aims of Socialist Feminism
    Barbara Ehrenreich
    Elizabeth Ewen, SUNY—Old Westbury

Conference Coordinator
    Hester Eisenstein
Planning Committee
    Nancy K. Miller, Susan R. Sacks
Director, Women's Center
    Jane S. Gould
Assistant Director, Women's Center
    Emily Kofron

THE SCHOLAR AND THE FEMINIST IV:
CONNECTING THEORY, PRACTICE, AND VALUES   APRIL 23, 1977

MORNING SESSION

Welcoming Remarks
    Jacquelyn Anderson Mattfeld, President, Barnard College
Social Implications of the Scientific Study of Sex
    Diana Long Hall, Boston University and Radcliffe Institute

Is Traditional Scholarship Value Free? Toward a Critical Theory
Mary E. Payer, Columbia University

Discussant: *Elizabeth Minnich, Barnard College*
Moderator: *Mary Brown Parlee, Barnard College*

AFTERNOON WORKSHOPS

1. Patriarchy as Paradigm: The Challenge from Feminist Scholarship
   Judith Long Laws, Cornell University
2. Androcentrism in Biology
   Ruth Hubbard, Harvard University
3. Sexism and Social Policy Issues in Urban Planning and Architecture
   Jackie Leavitt, Columbia University, School of Architecture and Urban Planning
4. Surviving as a Feminist Scholar Outside the Academy
   Cynthia Secor, HERS, Mid-Atlantic and University of Pennsylvania
5. Women's Culture/Male Philosophy/Human Thought: What Is the Question?
   Sara Ruddick, New School for Social Research
6. The Problems in Demystifying Women's Healthcare
   Sally Guttmacher, Columbia University, School of Public Health
7. Making Feminist Scholarship More Accessible
   Nancy Henley, University of Lowell
8. Taking Our Lives Seriously: Everyday Experience as a Source of Feminist Social Theory
   Pamela Fishman, New York City
   Linda Marks, New York City
9. The Need for a Feminist Literary Theory
   Elaine Showalter, Douglass College, Rutgers University
10. Medical Ethics and Sterilization
    Helen Rodriguez-Trias, Lincoln Hospital
11. Alternate Structures and a Utopian Proposal for an Institute for Advanced Feminist Studies
    Gerda Lerner, Sarah Lawrence College
12. Transsexualism—The Ultimate Homage to Sex Role Power
    Janice Raymond, Five College Faculty—Amherst, Massachusetts
13. Practical Theory and Working with Feminist Presses
    Charlotte Bunch, Institute for Policy Studies and **Quest**
14. Sagaris and the Politics of Feminist Studies
    Joan Peters, Douglass College, Rutgers University
15. Linkages Between Racism and Sexism
    Jane Galvin Lewis, Social Change Advocates

Academic Coordinator
   Mary Brown Parlee
Planning Committee
   Hester Eisenstein, Emily Heilbrun, Linda Marks, Nancy Miller, Mary E. Payer, Joan Peters, Susan R. Sacks, Maria von Salisch
Conference Coordinators, Women's Center
   Jane S. Gould, Ellen McManus

APPENDIX B

THE SCHOLAR AND THE FEMINIST V:
CREATING FEMINIST WORKS

APRIL 15, 1978

MORNING SESSION

Welcoming Remarks
Jacquelyn Anderson Mattfeld, President, Barnard College
Creating Feminist Works: A Panel Discussion
Eve Merriam, poet and playwright
Nancy K. Miller, Mellon Fellow in the Humanities, Columbia University
Harmony Hammond, artist and member of the Heresies Collective

Moderator: *Elizabeth Minnich, Barnard College*

AFTERNOON SEMINARS

1. A Feminist Perspective on Art History
Ann Sutherland Harris, Metropolitan Museum of Art
2. The Evolution of a Black Woman Artist
Catti James, artist/designer
3. Teaching Women's Studies: How Creative? How Feminist?
Catharine R. Stimpson, Barnard College, **Signs**
4. Blank Page/Empty Canvas—A Moment Both Political and Personal
Honor Moore, poet and playwright, editor of **The New Women's Theatre**
5. The Process and Product of Developing a Theory of Gender
Suzanne Kessler, SUNY—Purchase
Wendy McKenna, Sarah Lawrence College
6. Crafts as Feminist Experience: Making Connections
Sandra M. Whisler, fiber craftswoman
7. The Literary Salon: An Alternate Space for Feminist Writing and Theory
Erika Duncan, Karen Malpede, Carol McCauley, Gloria Orenstein, The Woman's Salon
8. Using Feminism and Politics to Change the Health Care Structure
Diane Lacey, Sydenham Hospital
9. Comedy and Performance in Scholarly Inquiry
Naomi Weisstein, SUNY—Buffalo
10. Creating a Feminist Novel
Alix Kates Shulman, author of **Memoirs of An Ex-Prom Queen** *and* **Burning Questions**
11. An Anthropologist Looks at Women's Traditional Arts
Elizabeth Weatherford, School of Visual Arts, member of Heresies Collective
12. Feminism vs. Journalism
Margo Jefferson, Newsweek
13. Creating the Book/Creating Ourselves
Wilma Diskin, Paula Doress, The Boston Women's Health Book Collective, co-authors of **Our Bodies, Ourselves**
14. The Autobiographies of 17th Century Hispanic Nuns From the Perspective of a 20th Century Feminist Scholar
Electa Arenal, CUNY—College of Staten Island
15. A False Dichotomy for the Artist: Individualism vs. Collectivity
May Stevens, painter, School of Visual Arts, member of Heresies Collective

Academic Coordinator
Elizabeth Minnich

Planning Committee
  Louise Adler, Hester Eisenstein, Irene Finel-Honigman, Pamela Fishman, Linda Marks, Mary Parlee,
  Susan R. Sacks, Maria von Salisch, Sandra Whisler
Conference Coordinators, Women's Center
  Jane S. Gould, Ellen McManus

THE SCHOLAR AND THE FEMINIST VI:
THE FUTURE OF DIFFERENCE   APRIL 21, 1979

MORNING SESSION

Welcoming Remarks
  Jacquelyn Anderson Mattfeld, President, Barnard College
Difference, Relation and Gender in Psychoanalytic Perspective
  Nancy Chodorow, University of California—Santa Cruz
The Powers of Difference
  Josette Féral, University of Toronto
The Straight Mind
  Monique Wittig, writer: The Opoponax, Les Guérillères, The Lesbian Body

Moderator: *Alice Jardine, Columbia University*

PANEL DISCUSSION

Difference and Language
  Audre Lorde, poet, CUNY—John Jay College of Criminal Justice
  Christiane Makward, Pennsylvania State University
  Sally McConnell-Ginet, Cornell University

Moderator: *Domna Stanton, Rutgers University and* Signs

AFTERNOON WORKSHOPS

1. Mothers and Daughters
   Jane Flax, Howard University
2. The Dialectical Treatment of Difference
   Alice Kessler-Harris, Hofstra University
3. The Anxiety of Difference: Rereading *Mme Bovary*
   Naomi Schor, Brown University
4. Lesbianism and the Social Function of Taboo
   Pamella Farley, CUNY—Brooklyn College and Barnard College (spring '79)
5. Women and the Uses of Power
   Elizabeth Janeway, author of **Man's World, Women's Place** *and* Between Myth and Morning
6. Black Women and Feminism
   Barbara Omolade, Women's Action Alliance
7. Androgyny and the Psychology of Sex Differences
   Carolyn Heilbrun, Columbia University
8. Psychoanalysis and Feminism in France
   Carolyn G. Burke, University of California—Santa Cruz
   Jane Gallop, Miami University
9. Sexual Difference and Artistic Production: The Debate over a Female Aesthetic
   Rachel Blau Du Plessis, Temple University

10. Mothers/Daughters/Sisters: Separation and Survival
    Clare Coss, Sondra Segal, Roberta Sklar, The Women's Experimental Theatre
11. Women in Power and Politics
    Ruth W. Messinger, Council of the City of New York
12. Differences in Women's Thinking about Self and Morality
    Carol Gilligan, Harvard University Graduate School of Education and Wellesley Center for Research on Women
13. Visibility and Difference: Black Feminism in History and Literature
    Quandra Stadler, Barnard College
14. Domination and Difference: The Roots of Rational Violence
    Jessica Benjamin, The New York Institute for the Humanities, New York University
15. The Sociobiological Rationale for Women's Oppression
    Eleanor Leacock, CUNY—City College

Academic Coordinator
    Alice Jardine
Planning Committee
    Louise Adler, Roberta Bernstein, Mary Jane Ciccarello, Hester Eisenstein, Irene Finel-Honigman, Suzanne Hanchett, Nancy K. Miller, Elizabeth Minnich, Ellen Pollak, Susan R. Sacks, Philippa Strum, Kathryn B. Yatrakis
Conference Coordinators, Women's Center
    Jane S. Gould, Janie Kritzman

THE SCHOLAR AND THE FEMINIST VII:
CLASS, RACE AND SEX—EXPLORING CONTRADICTIONS,
AFFIRMING CONNECTIONS   APRIL 12, 1980

MORNING SESSION

Welcoming Remarks
    Jacquelyn Anderson Mattfeld, President, Barnard College
On the Hem of Life: Race, Class and the Prospects for Sisterhood
    Bonnie Thornton Dill, Memphis State University
Class Divisions in Women's Productive and Reproductive Lives
    Rosalind Petchesky, Ramapo College
Embracing Deviance and Redefining the Norm
    Betty Powell, CUNY—Brooklyn College

Moderator: *Amy Swerdlow, Rutgers University*

AFTERNOON WORKSHOPS

1. Difference, Domination and Community in the Women's Movement
    Nancy Hartsock, The Johns Hopkins University
2. Women in Prison: A Sociological and Political Perspective
    Regina Arnold, Sarah Lawrence College
    Frances Borden Hubbard, Sophie Davis School of Bio-Medical Education, CUNY—City College
3. Cycle: The Psychological, Physical and Social Experience of Menstruation
        [Performance and workshop funded by the Creative Artists Public Service Program (CAPS)]
    Blondell Cummings, Madeline Keller and several other members of the Cycle Arts Foundation

4. Class and Race Issues in Women's Studies
   Florence Howe, SUNY—Old Westbury; The Feminist Press
   Angela Jorge, SUNY—Old Westbury
5. Sexual Politics and Afro-American Feminism: A Critique of Michele Wallace's *Black Macho and the Myth of the Superwoman*
   Maxine Bailey, Jobs for Youth, Inc.
6. Confronting Age Barriers Among Women
   Beth B. Hess, County College of Morris
7. Female Sexual Empowerment: Defining the Erotic from Our Personal Experience
   Frances Doughty, National Gay Task Force
8. A Historical Perspective on Feminism and Class Conflict
   Renate Bridenthal, CUNY—Brooklyn College
9. Modernization or Accumulation: Boserup Revisited
   Lourdes Beneria, Livingston College, Rutgers University
   Gita Sen, The New School for Social Research
10. Making Connections: A Workshop in Movement and Improvisation
    Barbara Annsdater, Gail Bederman, Catherine Franke, Helene Marshall, Twila Thompson—Woman's Collage Theatre
11. Feminists' Movements Against Prostitution, Pornography and "Male Vice": A Historical Review
    Judith R. Walkowitz, Rutgers University
12. The Boiling Pot: Race/Class/Ethnic Conflict in Housework
    Bettina Berch, Barnard College
    Carolyn Reed, National Committee on Household Employment
13. Reclaiming Lesbian Herstory: A Slide Show and Discussion
    Members of the Lesbian Herstory Archives
14. Women and the Church: Two Studies
    Black and White Women in the Baptist Church, 1870–1900
    Evelyn Brooks Barnett, W.E.B. DuBois Institute, Harvard University
    Women Activists in Radical Sects in 17th Century England
    Phyllis Mack, Livingston College, Rutgers University
15. Perspectives on the Black and Hispanic Family
    Nancy Boyd, Montefiore Hospital, Albert Einstein College of Medicine
    Elaine Soto, Lincoln Community Mental Health Center
16. Feminism, the Family and the New Right
    Rhonda Copelon, Center for Constitutional Rights; Committee for Abortion Rights and Against Sterilization Abuse (CARASA)
    Jan Rosenberg, SUNY—Empire State

SUMMARY SESSION

Diane Harriford, SUNY—Stony Brook, Catharine R. Stimpson, Barnard College, and Conference Participants

Academic Coordinator
   Amy Swerdlow
Planning Committee
   Bettina Berch, Roberta Bernstein, Lila Braine, Julie Doron, Frances Doughty, Hester Eisenstein, Irene Finel-Honigman, Catherine Franke, Susanne Gordon, Diane Harriford, Elaine Hughes, Angela Jorge, Diane Levitt, Sherry Manasse, Cynthia Novack, Barbara Omolade, Ellen Pollak, Carolyn Reed, Susan R. Sacks, Ellen Silber, Maxine Silverman, Philippa Strum, Angela Wilson, Kathryn B. Yatrakis
Conference Coordinators, Women's Center
   Jane S. Gould, Christina Greene, Janie Kritzman

THE SCHOLAR AND THE FEMINIST VIII:
THE DYNAMICS OF CONTROL   APRIL 11, 1981

MORNING SESSION

Welcoming Remarks
Ellen V. Futter, Acting President, Barnard College
Anti-Feminism, the "New Right" and Reagan
Zillah Eisenstein, Ithaca College
From Slavery to Welfare: The Control of Black Women
Cheryl Townsend Gilkes, Boston University
Repression and Resistance: A Historical Perspective
Blanche Wiesen Cook, CUNY—John Jay College of Criminal Justice

Moderator: *Hanna Lessinger, Barnard College*

AFTERNOON WORKSHOPS

1. Laid Bare by the System: Work and Survival for Black and Hispanic Women
   Elizabeth Higginbotham, Columbia University
2. Defending and Combating Sexual Harassment: Problems in Regaining Control
   Nadine Taub, Women's Rights Litigation Clinic, Rutgers Law School—Newark
3. Women, Media and the Dialectics of Resistance
   Lillian Robinson, Center for Research on Women, Stanford University
4. The Social Enforcement of Heterosexuality and Lesbian Resistance in the 1920's
   Lisa Duggan, Lesbian and Gay History Project of New York; University of Pennsylvania
5. Women Health Care Workers: Organizing and Resisting
   Karen Sacks, Business and Professional Women's Foundation; Duke University
6. The Controversy Over Sterilization Among Puerto Rican Women in New York City
   Iris Lopez, Columbia University
7. Crisis, Reaction and Resistance: Women in Germany in the 1920's and 1930's
   Renate Bridenthal, CUNY—Brooklyn College
   Atina Grossmann, Rutgers University
   Marion Kaplan, Institute for Research in History, Deutsche Forschungsgemeinschaft
8. Same-Sex Networks, Compulsory Heterosexuality, and the Family
   Rayna Rapp, The New School for Social Research
   Ellen Ross, Ramapo College
9. To Tell Us Who We Are: Storytelling as Perpetuation and Creation
   Jeannine Laverty, storyteller
10. Lesbian Rights and the Struggle for Reproductive Freedom
    Sara Bennett, activist and writer
    Joan Gibbs, Black activist and writer
11. Textbooks, Socialization and Control
    Beryle Banfield, Jamila Gastón, Ruth S. Meyers—Council on Interracial Books for Children
12. Images of Women in Latin America's Literature of Protest
    Lourdes Rojas-Paiewonsky, Hamilton College
13. "Mean Mothers": Independent Women's Blues
    Rosetta Reitz, writer and music producer
14. Myths of the "Model Minority": The Rebellion of Asian-American Women, 1965–1980
    Ginger Chih, photographer and picture researcher, Asian Women United
    Diane Mei Lin Mark, writer
15. Pro-Family Politics, Sexism and Sexual Repression
    Ellen Willis, **The Village Voice**

16. Women on Welfare: Public Policy and Institutional Racism
    Bettylou Valentine, anthropologist and writer
17. Religion as an Instrument of Social Control
    Judith Plaskow, Francine Quaglio—Manhattan College
18. Who Controls Women's Health?
    Diana Scully, Virginia Commonwealth University

CLOSING SESSION

Excerpts of *And I Ain't Finished Yet* by Eve Merriam
Preview of a new theatre piece about the lives of seven Black women in American history
    Introduced by Eve Merriam
    Anna Deavere Smith, actress

[ON EXHIBIT]

Generations of Women: Private Lives
An exhibit of photographs from family albums of women's studies students and staff at Jersey City
State College
    Doris Friedensohn and Barbara Rubin, coordinators
    Harold Lemmerman, artistic director, Jersey City State College

Academic Coordinator
    Hanna Lessinger
Planning Committee
    Bettina Berch, Janet Corpus, Julie Doron, Joan Dulchin, Wendy Fairey, Atina Grossmann, Diane Harriford,
    Elizabeth Higginbotham, Jacqueline Leavitt, Sherry Manasse, Cynthia Novack, Susan R. Sacks, Mary
    Sheerin, Barbara Sicherman, Maxine Silverman, Quandra Stadler, Laura Whitman
Conference Coordinators, Women's Center
    Jane S. Gould, Christina Greene, Janie Kritzman

THE SCHOLAR AND THE FEMINIST IX:
TOWARDS A POLITICS OF SEXUALITY   APRIL 24, 1982

MORNING SESSION

Welcoming Remarks
    Ellen V. Futter, President, Barnard College
How Feminists Thought About Sex: Our Complex Legacy
    Ellen Carol DuBois, SUNY—Buffalo
    Linda Gordon, University of Massachusetts—Boston
Interstices: A Small Drama of Words
    Hortense Spillers, Haverford College
The Taming of the Id: Feminist Sexual Politics 1965–1981
    Alice Echols, University of Michigan

Moderator: *Carole S. Vance, Columbia University*

AFTERNOON WORKSHOPS

1. Power, Sexuality, and the Organization of Vision
    Mary Ann Doane, Brown University
    Barbara Kruger, artist
2. Lacan: Language and Desire
    Maire Kurrik, Barnard College

■   **233**

APPENDIX B

3. Political Organizing Around Sexual Issues
   Cheryl Adams, Lesbian Feminist Liberation
   Noreen Connell, NYC Planned Parenthood
   Brett Harvey, No More Nice Girls
4. Pornography and the Construction of a Female Subject
   Bette Gordon, Hofstra University
   Kaja Silverman, Simon Fraser University
5. Teen Romance: The Sexual Politics of Age Relations
   Camille Bristow, The Center for Public Advocacy Research
   Sharon Thompson, The Center for Open Education
6. Everything They Always Wanted You to Know: Popular Sex Literature
   Meryl Altman, Columbia University
7. Beyond the Gay/Straight Split: Do Sexual "Roles" (Butch/Femme) Transcend Sexual Preference?
   Esther Newton, SUNY—Purchase
   Shirley Walton, Djuna Books
8. Sexuality and Creativity—A Theatre Workshop
   Shirley Kaplan, Barnard College
9. Aggression, Selfhood and Female Sexuality: Rethinking Psychoanalysis
   Dale Bernstein, psychotherapist
   Elsa First, psychotherapist
10. Class, Cultural and Historical Influences on Sexual Identity in the Psychotherapeutic Relationship
    Oliva Espin, Boston University
    Pat Robinson, clinical social worker
11. Beyond Politics: Understanding the Sexuality of Infancy and Childhood
    Mary S. Calderone, M.D., Sex Information and Education Council of the U.S. (SIECUS)
    Kate Millett, writer
12. The Defense of Sexual Restriction by Anti-Abortion Activists
    Faye Ginsburg, CUNY—Graduate Center
    Susan Hill, National Women's Health Organization
13. Politically Correct, Politically Incorrect Sexuality
    Dorothy Allison, Conditions
    Muriel Dimen, CUNY—Lehman College
    Mirtha N. Quintanales, Ohio State University
    Joan Nestle, Lesbian Herstory Archives
14. The Myth of the Perfect Body: Age, Weight, and Disability
    Roberta Galler, Postgraduate Center for Mental Health
    Carol Munter, Council on Eating Problems
15. The Forbidden: Eroticism and Taboo
    Paula Webster, Institute for the Study of Sex in Society and History
16. Sexual Purity: Maintaining Class and Race Boundaries
    Diane Harriford, SUNY—Stony Brook
17. Concepts for a Radical Politics of Sex
    Gayle Rubin, University of Michigan
18. Sex and Money
    Arlene Carmen, Judson Memorial Church

CLOSING SESSION

Desire for the Future: Radical Hope in Passion and Pleasure
   Amber Hollibaugh, Socialist Review
Poetry readings by *Hattie Gossett, Cherríe Moraga and Sharon Olds*
   Introduced by *Janie L. Kritzman, Barnard Women's Center*

234

Academic Coordinator
Carole S. Vance
Planning Committee
Julie Abraham, Hannah Alderfer, Meryl Altman, Jan Boney, Frances Doughty, Ellen DuBois, Kate Ellis, Judith Friedlander, Julie German, Faye Ginsburg, Diane Harriford, Beth Jaker, Mary Clare Lennon, Sherry Manasse, Nancy K. Miller, Marybeth Nelson, Esther Newton, Claire Riley, Susan Riemer Sacks, Ann Snitow, Quandra Prettyman Stadler, Judith R. Walkowitz, Ellen Willis, Patsy Yaeger
Conference Coordinators, Women's Center
Jane S. Gould, Janie L. Kritzman, Maria La Sala

THE SCHOLAR AND THE FEMINIST X:
THE QUESTION OF TECHNOLOGY   APRIL 23, 1983

MORNING SESSION

Welcoming Remarks
Ellen V. Futter, President, Barnard College
Man, Machine and Myth: A Feminist Historical Perspective on Technology
Judith A. McGaw, University of Pennsylvania
Advanced Technology, International Development and Women's Employment
Maria Patricia Fernandez Kelly, San Diego State University
New Machines, New Bodies, New Communities: Political Dilemmas for a Cyborg Feminist
Donna Haraway, University of California—Santa Cruz

Moderator: *Bettina Berch, Barnard College*

AFTERNOON WORKSHOPS

1. From Scrub Boards to Microwaves: Housework History in Perspective
   Ruth S. Cowan, SUNY—Stony Brook
2. Feminist Utopian Fiction
   Lee Cullen Khanna, Montclair State College
3. Workplace Automation: Studying Technological Discrimination
   Eve Hochwald and Mary Murphree, Women and Work Research Group, Center for the Study of Women and Society, CUNY—Graduate Center
4. The Electronic Cottage: Can We Bring the Power Home?
   Jaime Horwitz, CUNY—Graduate Center
5. Can We Make Science More Feminist?
   Rita Arditti, The Graduate School of the Union of Experimenting Colleges
6. Women and Weapons Technology
   Shelah Leader, American University
7. The Power to Create, the Power to Resist: Ecological Feminism and Technology
   Ynestra King, New York City
8. The Engineering of Reproduction
   Marsha Hurst, Mount Sinai School of Medicine
9. Health Hazards at Work
   Jeanne Stellman, Women's Occupational Health Resource Center, Columbia University
10. Women's Trauma? Women's Friend? Personal and Political Implications of the Microcomputer
    Beva Eastman, The William Paterson College of New Jersey
11. The Definition and Redefinition of Skill
    Lourdes Beneria, Rutgers University

12. Organizing the New Workplace
    Judith Gregory, 9 to 5, National Association of Working Women
    Marsha Love, New York Committee on Occupational Safety and Health (NYCOSH)
13. Videotape: A Women's Development Tool
    Sherry Delamarter, Martha Stuart Communications
14. Minority Women in the Workforce and Technological Change
    Harriett Harper, Women's Bureau of the U.S. Department of Labor

CLOSING SESSION

Excerpts from *Stone, Paper, Knife* and other works
    Marge Piercy
    Introduced by Quandra Prettyman Stadler, Barnard College

Academic Coordinator
    Bettina Berch
Planning Committee
    Alice Amsden, Leslie Calman, Sally Chapman, Eva Eilenberg, Wendy Fairey, Ruth Handel, Diane Harriford, Eve Hochwald, Jaime Horwitz, Marsha Love, Julie Marsteller, Nancy K. Miller, Mary Murphree, Susan R. Sacks, Quandra Prettyman Stadler, Norma Stanton
Conference Coordinators, Women's Center
    Jane S. Gould, Janie L. Kritzman, Lee Coppernoll, Maria La Sala

All conference programs reprinted by permission of the Barnard Center for Research on Women.

The ninth The Scholar and the Feminist conference will address women's sexual pleasure, choice, and autonomy, acknowledging that sexuality is simultaneously a domain of restriction, repression, and danger as well as a domain of exploration, pleasure, and agency. This dual focus is important, we think, for to speak only of pleasure and gratification ignores the patriarchal structure in which women act, yet to talk only of sexual violence and oppression ignores women's experience with sexual agency and choice and unwittingly increases the sexual terror and despair in which women live.

This moment is a critical one for feminists to reconsider our understanding of sexuality and its political consequences. On the one hand, the feminist community has been engaged by intense discussion about sexuality. The debate has moved from women's right to have sexual pleasure detached from reproduction to sexual violence and victimization. Most recent issues include: the meaning and effect of pornography; sexual safety versus sexual adventure; the significance of sexual styles, for example, butch\femme; male and female sexual nature; and politically correct and incorrect sexual positions. On the other hand, the Right Wing attack on feminists' recent gains attempts to reinstate traditional sexual arrangements and the inexorable link between reproduction and sexuality. In doing so, the Right offers a comprehensive plan for sexual practice which resonates in part with women's apprehension about immorality and sexual danger. To respond convincingly, as feminists we cannot abandon our radical insights into sexual theory and practice but must deepen and expand them, so that more women are encouraged to identify and act in their sexual self-interest.

Behind feminist debates and the Right Wing's focus on sexuality, we think are social and political changes wrought by capitalist transformations and the women's movement during the 19th and 20th centuries, most notably the breakdown in the traditional bargain women made, and were forced to make, with men: if women were "good" (sexually circumspect), men would protect them; if they were "bad," men would violate and punish them. As parties to this system, "good" women had an interest in restraining male sexual impulse, a source of danger to women, as well as their own sexuality which might incite men to act. Nineteenth century feminists elaborated asexuality as an option for "good" women, using female passionlessness and male sexual restraint to challenge male sexual prerogatives and the characterization of women as intrinsically sexual. Recent gains in the second wave of feminism call for increased sexual autonomy for women and decreased male "protection," still within a patriarchal framework. Amid this flux, women feel more visible and sexually vulnerable. The old bargain, which opposed sexual safety and sexual freedom, is breaking down, but women's fear of reprisal and punishment for sexual activity has not abated. For this reason, the sexual problematic has commanded the attention of feminist theorists in both centuries.

Feminist work on sexuality starts from the premise that sex is a social construction which articulates at many points with the economic, social, and political structures of the material world. Sex is not simply a "natural" fact. Although we can name specific physical actions (heterosexual or homosexual intercourse, masturbation) which occurred at various times and places, it is clear that the social and personal meaning attached to these acts in terms of sexual identity and sexual community has varied historically. In light of a wealth of material, we restrict our analysis to 19th and 20th century America, while retaining the notion of historical and cultural construction of sexuality. Without denying the body, we note the body and its actions are understood according to prevailing codes of meaning. Believing that biological sex is conditionable, we return to the question "What do women want?"—a question we can entertain now that it is *we* who are asking it.

Sexuality poses a challenge to feminist scholarship, since it is an intersection of the political, social, economic, historical, personal, and experiential, linking behavior and thought, fantasy and action. For the individual, it is the intersection of past, current, and future experience in her own life. That these domains intersect does not mean they are identical, as the danger of developing a feminist sexual politics based on personal experience alone illustrates. We need sophisticated methodologies and analyses that permit the recognition of each discrete domain as well as their multiple intersections. Despite the many interrelationships of sexuality and gender, we do not believe that sexuality is a sub-part of gender, a residual category, nor are theories of gender fully adequate, at present, to account for sexuality.

Feminist work on sexuality confronts three problems: 1) multiple levels of analysis, 2) limited data about women's experience, 3) overdeveloped theory, in light of limited data.

1) We talk as if information about sexuality comes from a single source, but in fact it comes from many sources: for example, sexual behavior and acts; inner, psychological experience; the public presentation of our sexual selves; sexual style; images and representations available in the culture; the place of sexuality in the discourse of the political community to which we belong; sexual ideology. When we compare the sexual situation between and within groups of women, it is important to remember that no conclusions can be drawn by comparing only one layer of sexual information without considering the others.

Within feminism, we find it easier and more politically correct to talk about sexual differences between women than sexual similarities. This is understandable, given our wish to acknowledge real diversity of experience and to insist on our visibility through *difference* from dominant groups, the same difference causing our long invisibility. We think it is important to simultaneously discuss women's similarities and differences, questioning whether the acquisition of femininity and the conditions for its reproduction affect all women in a distinct way, cutting across sexual preference, sexual object, and specific behavior.

2) We base our theories on limited information about ourselves and, at best, a small number of other women. Given the complex grid of class, race, sexual preference, age, generation, and ethnicity, our personal experience can speak to but a small part of the sexual universe. Yet we wish to develop a framework inclusive of all women's experience. (Sexuality must not be a code word for heterosexuality, or women a code word for white women.) To do so we must make a renewed effort to talk with each other, agreeing to break the taboo that denies us access to information that lies beyond the boundaries of our lived sexual experience. Such is the only way to remedy our ignorance and avoid a sexual theory circumscribed by the boundaries of individual lives and idiosyncracies.

3) We find it easy to say publicly: "Women want . . .," "Women hate . . .," "Women are turned on by . . .," "Women are afraid of . . .," "Women like. . . ." However, we find it excruciating to say publicly: "I want . . .," "I hate . . .," "I am turned on by . . .," "I am afraid of . . .," "I like . . . ." Clearly, our hesitation to make the private and personal become public and potentially political has significant implications. Our theory, as it stands, is based on limited facts marshalled by overdeveloped preconceptions. It is also clear that any discussion of sexuality touches areas of unconscious conflict and fear. Feminists have been remiss in failing to address the power of unconscious sexual prohibitions and the appeal of primitive myths and metaphors about the Child, the Good Girl, the Man and the Family. Unarticulated, irrational reactions wreak havoc in our own movement and at the same time are cleverly used against us by the Right.

Sexuality is a bread and butter issue, not a luxury, not a frill. Women experience sexual pleasure and displeasure in their daily lives, even as women in different communities and different situations may articulate and organize around these experiences in different ways. Sexuality cannot wait until other, more "legitimate" issues are resolved. The division between socio-economic and sexual issues is false; we reaffirm their intimate connection in domesticity, reproductive politics, and the split between public and private, fantasy and action, male and female. We cannot postpone the consideration of sexual issues until after the "revolution." Such a tactic implies a belief in a natural, unfettered sexuality which will emerge after more basic issues of production and redistribution are resolved. Feminists who oppose the biologized woman or man cannot put their faith in a biologized sexuality.

We see the conference not as providing definitive answers, but as setting up a more useful framework within which feminist thought may proceed, an opportunity for participants to question some of their understandings and consider anew the complexity of the sexual situation. Our goal is to allow more information about the diversity of women's experiences to emerge. In morning papers and afternoon workshops, participants will consider the question: what is the status of sexual pleasure—in feminist theory and analysis and in the social world in which women live? and by so doing, inform and advance the current debate.

Much has been written about women giving and receiving pleasure; the conference is a step toward women taking pleasure and a contribution to envisioning a world which makes possible women's sexual autonomy and sexual choice.

Carole S. Vance
Academic Coordinator

January 1982

Bambara, Toni Cade, ed. *The Black Woman: An Anthology*. New York: New American Library, 1970.

Boston Women's Health Book Collective, Inc. *Our Bodies, Ourselves*. New York: Simon and Schuster, 1973.

Campbell, Jean W. "Women Drop Back In: Educational Innovation in the Sixties." In *Academic Women on the Move*, edited by Alice S. Rossi and Ann Calderwood, 93–124. New York: Russell Sage Foundation, 1973.

Eisenstein, Hester, and Alice Jardine, eds. *The Future of Difference*. Boston: G. K. Hall and Co., 1980.

Firestone, Shulamith. *The Dialectic of Sex: The Case for Feminist Revolution*. New York: William Morrow, 1970.

Friedan, Betty. *The Feminine Mystique*. New York: W. W. Norton, 1963.

Gornick, Vivian, and Barbara K. Moran, eds. *Woman in Sexist Society: Studies in Power and Powerlessness*. New York: Basic Books, 1971.

Gould, Jane S. "Personal Reflections on Building a Women's Center in a Women's College." *Women's Studies Quarterly* 12 (Spring 1984): 4–11

———. "Women's Centers." In *Women in Academe: Progress and Prospects*, edited by Mariam K. Chamberlain, chapter 5, 83–105. New York: Russell Sage Foundation, 1988.

———. "Women's Centers as Agents of Change." In *Educating the Majority: Women Challenge Tradition in Higher Education*, edited by Carol S. Pearson, Donna L. Shavlik, and Judith G. Touchton, chapter 16, 219–229. New York: American Council on Education and MacMillan Publishing Co., 1989.

Gould, Jane S., and Abby Pagano. "Sex Discrimination and Achievement." *Journal of the National Association of Women Deans and Counselors* (Winter 1972): 74–82.

Hole, Judith, and Ellen Levine. *Rebirth of Feminism*. New York: Quadrangle Books, 1971.

Komarovsky, Mirra. *Women in the Modern World: Their Education and Their Dilemmas*. Boston: Little Brown and Co., 1953.

Kumin, Maxine. "The Care Givers." In *The Writer on Her Work*, edited by Janet Sternburg. Vol. 2, 61–71. New York: Norton and Co., 1991.

Ladner, Joyce A. *Tomorrow's Tomorrow: The Black Woman*. Garden City, NY: Doubleday and Co., 1971.

Lerner, Gerda, ed. *Black Women in White America: A Documentary History*. New York: Pantheon Books, 1972.

Lindbergh, Anne Morrow. *Gift from the Sea*. New York: Pantheon, 1955.

Mattfeld, Jacquelyn, and Carol G. Van Aken, eds. *Women and the Scientific Professions: M. I. T. Symposium on American Women in Science and Engineering, 1964*. Cambridge: The Massachusetts Institute of Technology, 1965.

Millett, Kate. *Sexual Politics*. Garden City, NY: Doubleday and Co., 1969.

Morgan, Robin, comp. *Sisterhood Is Powerful: An Anthology of Writings from the Women's Liberation Movement.* New York: Random House, 1970.

Myrdal, Alva, and Viola Klein. *Women's Two Roles: Home and Work.* London: Routledge and Kegan Paul Ltd., 1956.

National Manpower Council. *Womanpower: A Statement by the National Manpower Council with Chapters by the Council Staff.* New York: Columbia University Press, 1957.

Newcomer, Mabel. *A Century of Higher Education for American Women.* New York: Harper and Brothers, 1959.

President's Commission on the Status of Women. *American Women: The Report of the President's Commission on the Status of Women.* Washington, DC: Department of Labor, 1963.

Rossi, Alice. "Sex Equality: The Beginning of Ideology." *The Humanist* (September/October 1969).

Rush, Florence. "Women in the Middle." In *Notes from the Third Year: Women's Liberation,* edited by the International Women's History Archive, 18–21. n.p., 1971.

Schwartz, Jane. "Medicine as a Vocational Choice Among Undergraduate Women." *Journal of the National Association of Women Deans and Counselors* 33 (Fall 1969): 7–12.

———. *Part-Time Employment: Employer Attitudes on Opportunities for the College-Trained Woman.* New York: Alumnae Advisory Center, 1964.

Snitow, Ann, Christine Stansell, and Sharon Thompson, eds. *Powers of Desire: The Politics of Sexuality.* New York: Monthly Review Press, 1983.

Swerdlow, Amy, and Hanna Lessinger, eds. *Class, Race, and Sex: The Dynamics of Control.* Boston: G. K. Hall and Co., 1983.

Vance, Carole S., ed. *Pleasure and Danger: Exploring Female Sexuality.* Boston: Routledge and Kegan Paul, 1984.

■

Stanton, Domna, 180

Stats, Daniel, 45, 46

Stearns, Nancy, 168, 169

Stein, Gertrude, 51

Stephens, Lynn, 144

Stimpson, Catharine, 112, 142–43, 157, 158

St. Luke's Hospital (New York City), 183

Sulzberger, Arthur Hays, 35–36

Sulzberger, Iphigene Ochs, 36

Swerdlow, Amy, 158, 189

Take Back the Night marches, 194

Teacher's College (NY), 26, 27; JSG in graduate school at, 111–12

Teller, Jane, 178

Terris, Fanny (mother-in-law), 40–41, 69, 70

Terris, Lou, 41

Tidball, Elizabeth, 174

Tomorrow's Tomorrow: The Black Woman (Ladner), 156

"Towards a Politics of Sexuality" (conference), 194–205, 233–35, 237–39

Travelers Aid, 42–43

Truax Field (WI), 42, 43

Union of American Hebrew Congregations, 8

United Nations NGO Conference on Women (1985), 208

University of California, Los Angeles (UCLA), 74, 163

University of Minnesota. *See* Minnesota Plan

University of Wisconsin, JSG's wartime job at, 43–44

Vance, Carole, 193–94, 203, 204; sexuality conference statement by, 189–90, 195–96, 237–39

Vietnam War, protests against, 96, 103, 128–29, 140–41

Walden, Doris Silbert, 28, 29

Walden, Walter, 28, 29

Walker, Alice, 168, 169

Waller, Willard, 37

Washington, DC, antiwar protest of 1969, 140–41

Wechsler, Miriam, 39

WEDO (Women's Environment and Development Organization), 218

Wellesley College, 59, 76

Wemple, Suzanne, 147

Westchester County (NY): JSG's education in, 14, 17–18, 20–21, 24; JSG's family history in, 7–8; Job Finding Workshops in, 58–59

Westervelt, Esther, 74

White, Stanford, 33

WHN (radio station), wartime job at, 43–44

Willis, Ellen, 198–99

Wilson, Elizabeth, 204–5

WITCH (Women's International Terrorist Conspiracy from Hell), 113

Womanpower, 63

Woman in Sexist Society: Studies in Power and Powerlessness (Gornick and Moran), 156

women: attitudes toward feminism, 120–21, 135–36, 175, 178–81, 196–97, 212–13; battered, 154–55, 183; changing roles for, 97, 112–13; dissemination of resources for, 149–50, 169–72; restrictions of marriage for, 39, 48, 88–93, 99–101, 156

women, working: discrimination against, 77, 115–19, 123, 133–36; economic necessity vs. choice, 47, 59–60; family responsibilities vs., 48, 51, 62–63, 88–90, 95, 120; labor market shortages and, 73, 76, 80, 84–85, 114; limited opportunities for, 49–53, 55–56, 101–2, 115–17; mature, 62–65, 87, 94–95, 207–8; mentoring for, 132, 178; part-time, 51, 64–65, 77, 82–88, 94; in professional fields, 85–86, 102, 117–18, 132; stereotypes about, 65, 86–87, 94–95, 99–102, 119–22

Women Against Pornography. *See* antipornography movement

women of color, 209; at Barnard College, 168–69; feminism and, 156, 158, 187, 189

"Women Learn from Women" (conference), 157–61

"Women in the Middle" (Rush), 154

Women in the Modern World: Their Education